JOHNNY HIRO

Johnny Hiro
by Fred Chao

Published by AdHouse Books

Content is © Copyright 2009 Fred Chao
AdHouse logo is © 2009 AdHouse Books

No part of this book (except small portions for
reviews) may be used without express written
consent from Fred Chao or AdHouse Books

ISBN 1-9352330-2-5
ISBN 978-1-9352330-2-2
10 9 8 7 6 5 4 3 2 1

Design: Chao + Pitzer

AdHouse Books
1224 Greycourt Avenue
Richmond, VA 23227-4042
www.adhousebooks.com

First Printing, June 2009
Printed in Canada

For Dylan,

whose grace and clumsy has inspired
so much within these pages

"A-Yo, this rap game got me in a figure four leglock
I lock and love but that lock is submissive
the ref holdin' my arm like I'm gonna pass out
but never ever in this world I gonna tap out.
And you can never put words or explain perseverance
or what it takes just to get this rap out.
And yeah left to get a degree
and a house, wife and kid ain't far fetched
but for now, yo, it's our sketch.
And my first foot forward is my best step
and I ain't trying to deny the fact: I'm trying to earn to live a better life
but it's a life hanging with its bread and butter knife.
Well you gotta perfect it just to get it right.
And man, once you get it right it leads to longer nights
and longer nights, man, just leads to make or break
'cause chasing a dream's a bitch when you wide awake."

—The Alias Brothers, *Gone Head*

"Perhaps one day I will be able to tell you what I have learned of the eye
and the romance it carries on, quietly and in a most halting manner,
with the veiled beauty of the world."

—Ethan Canin, *Carry Me Across The Water*

JOHNN

Y HIRO

{ Half Asian, All Hero }

Fred Chao

greytones Dylan Babb
letters & edits Jesse Post

AdHouse Books
Richmond, Virginia

裏庭にいる大なとかげは、

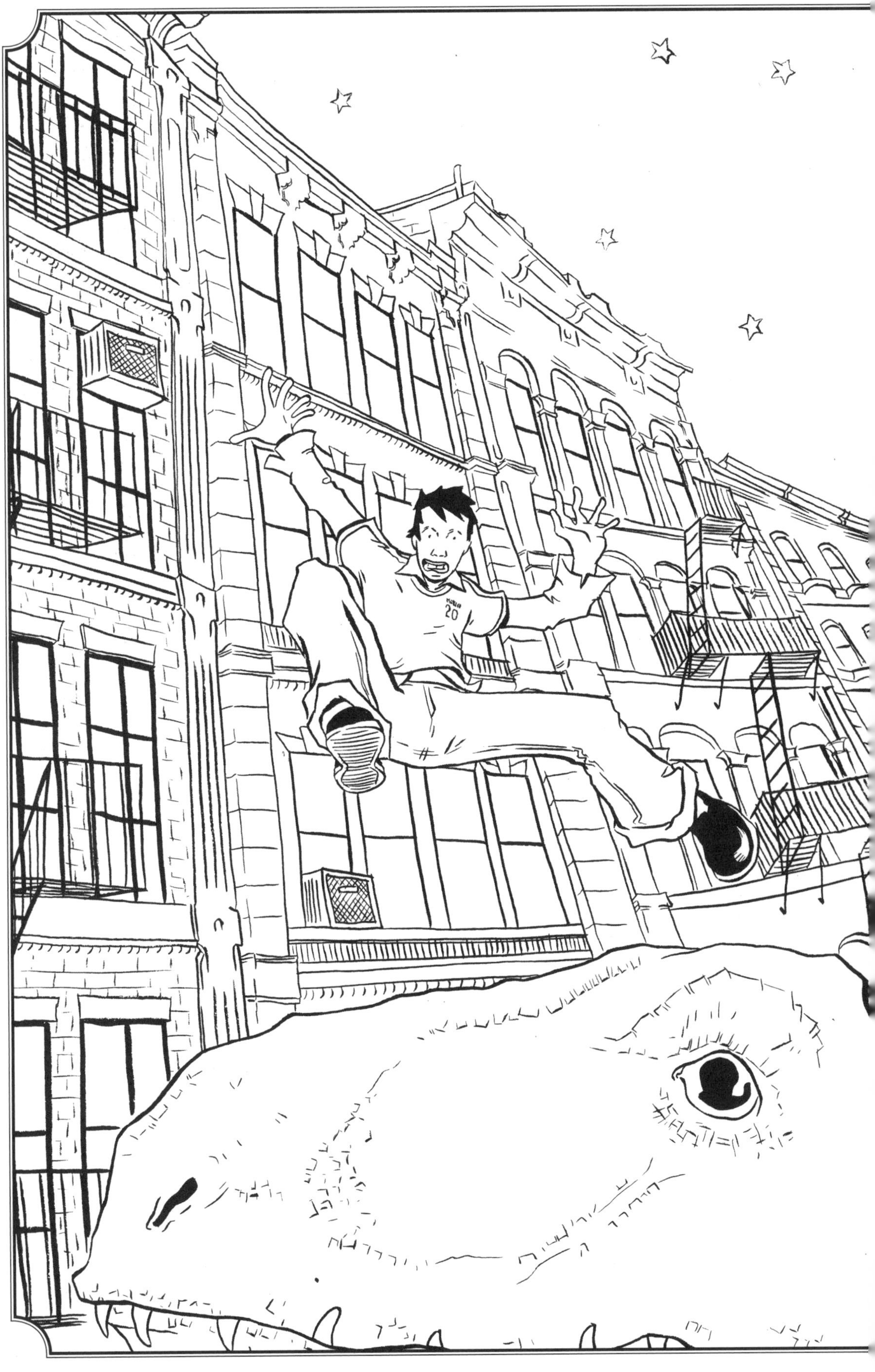
20

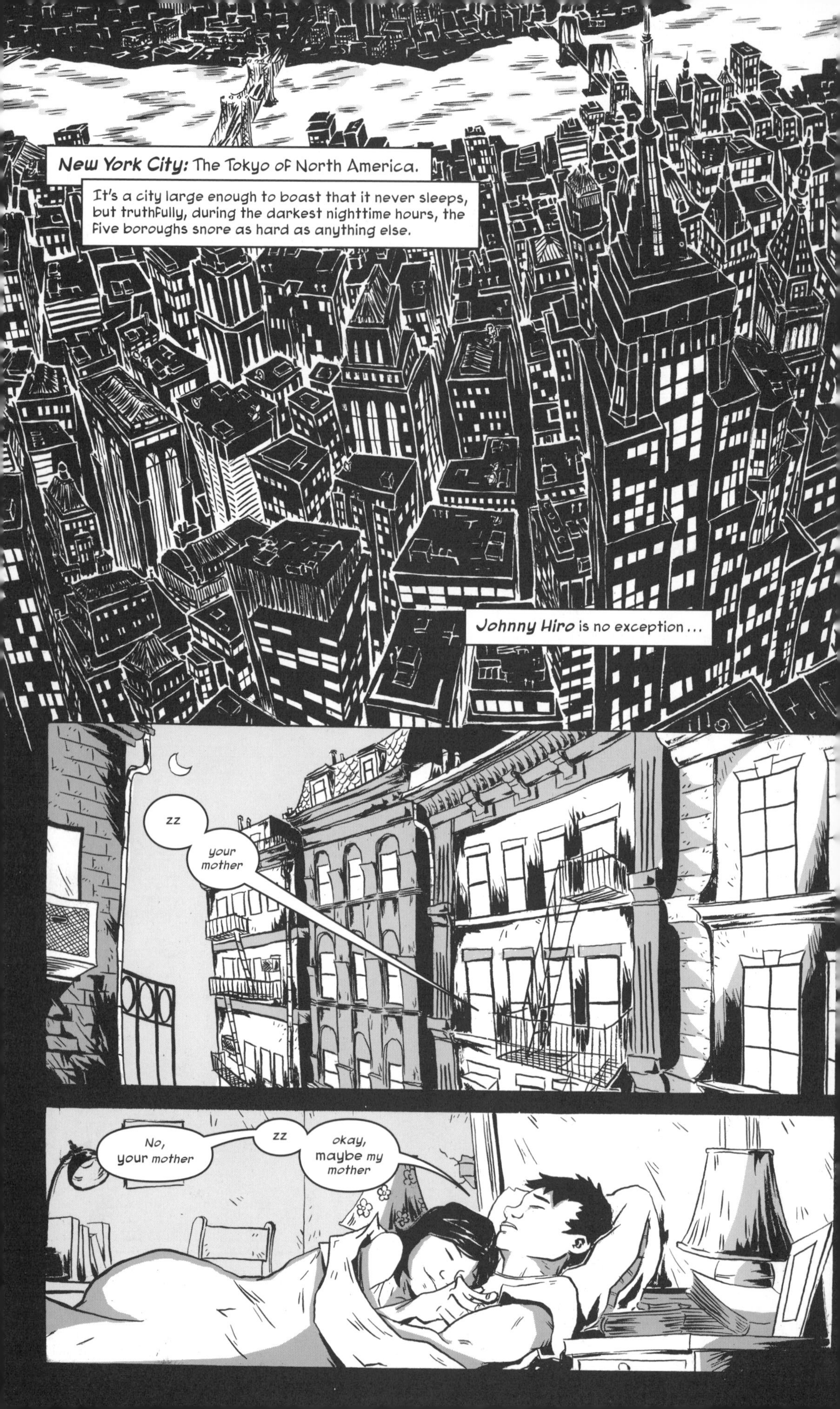

New York City: The Tokyo of North America.
It's a city large enough to boast that it never sleeps, but truthfully, during the darkest nighttime hours, the five boroughs snore as hard as anything else.
Johnny Hiro is no exception...
zz
your mother
No, your mother
zz
okay, maybe my mother

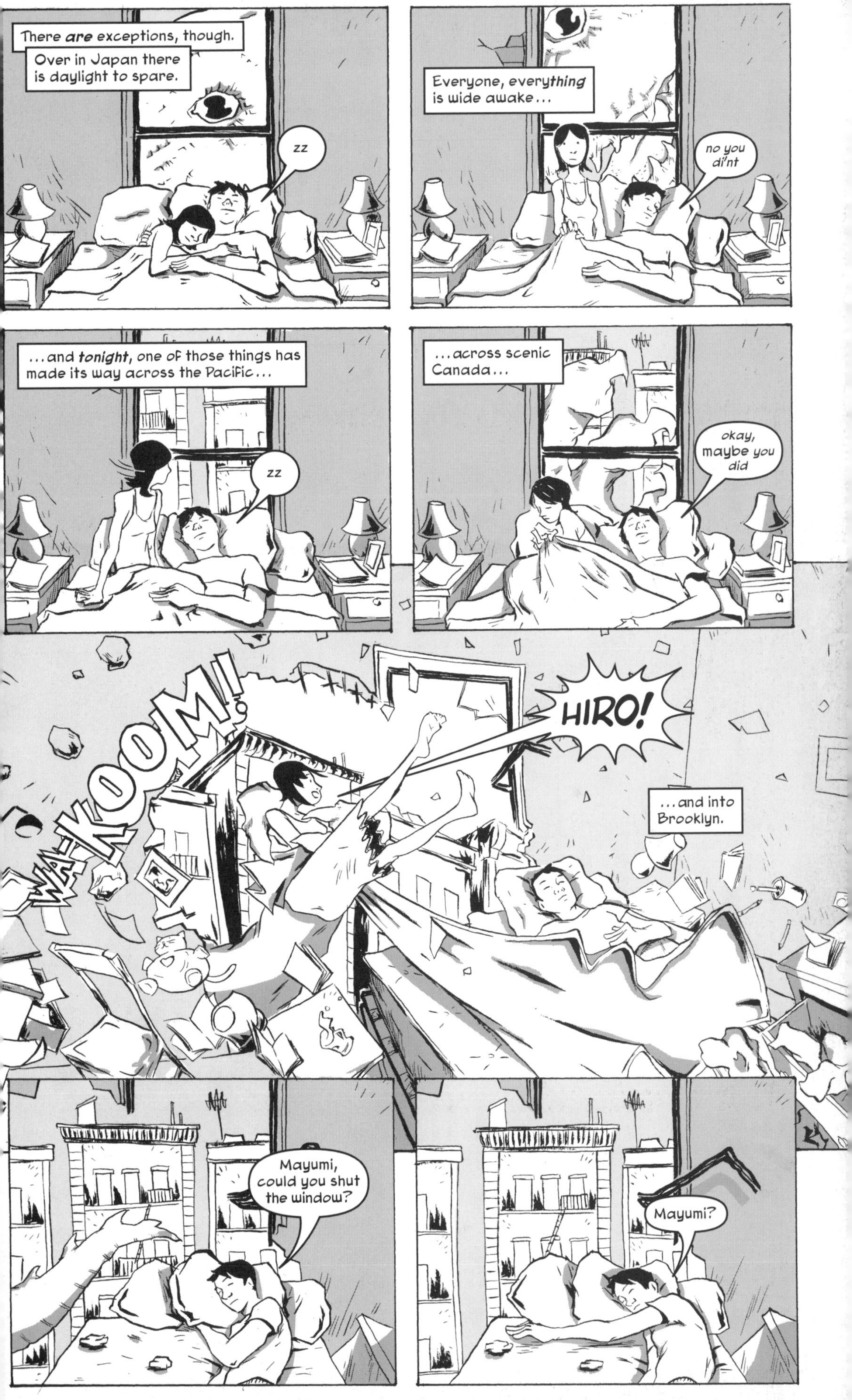
There *are* exceptions, though.
Over in Japan there is daylight to spare.
zz
Everyone, every*thing* is wide awake...
no you di'nt
...and *tonight*, one of those things has made its way across the Pacific...
zz
...across scenic Canada...
okay, maybe you did
WAKOOM!
HIRO!
...and into Brooklyn.
Mayumi, could you shut the window?
Mayumi?

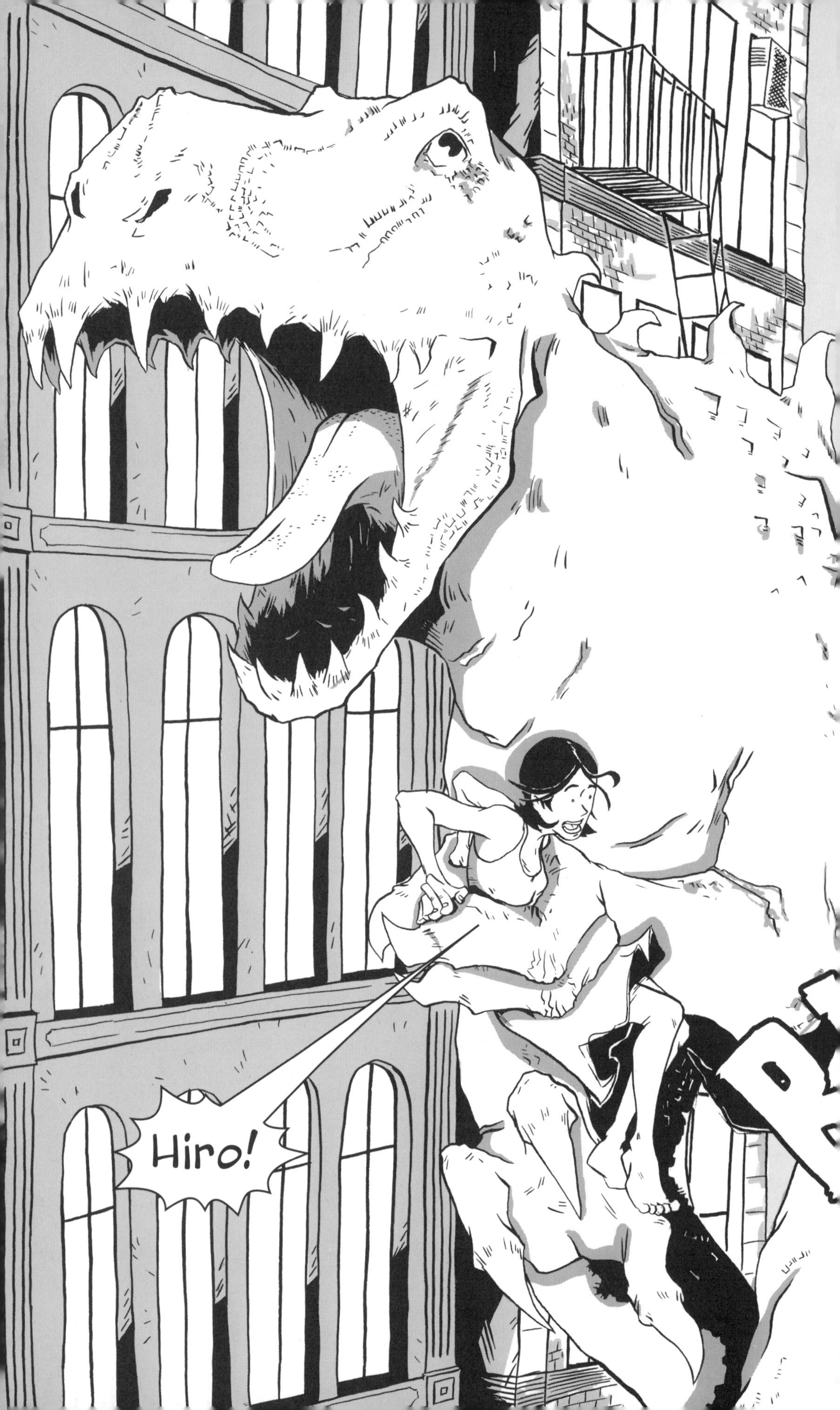
Hiro!

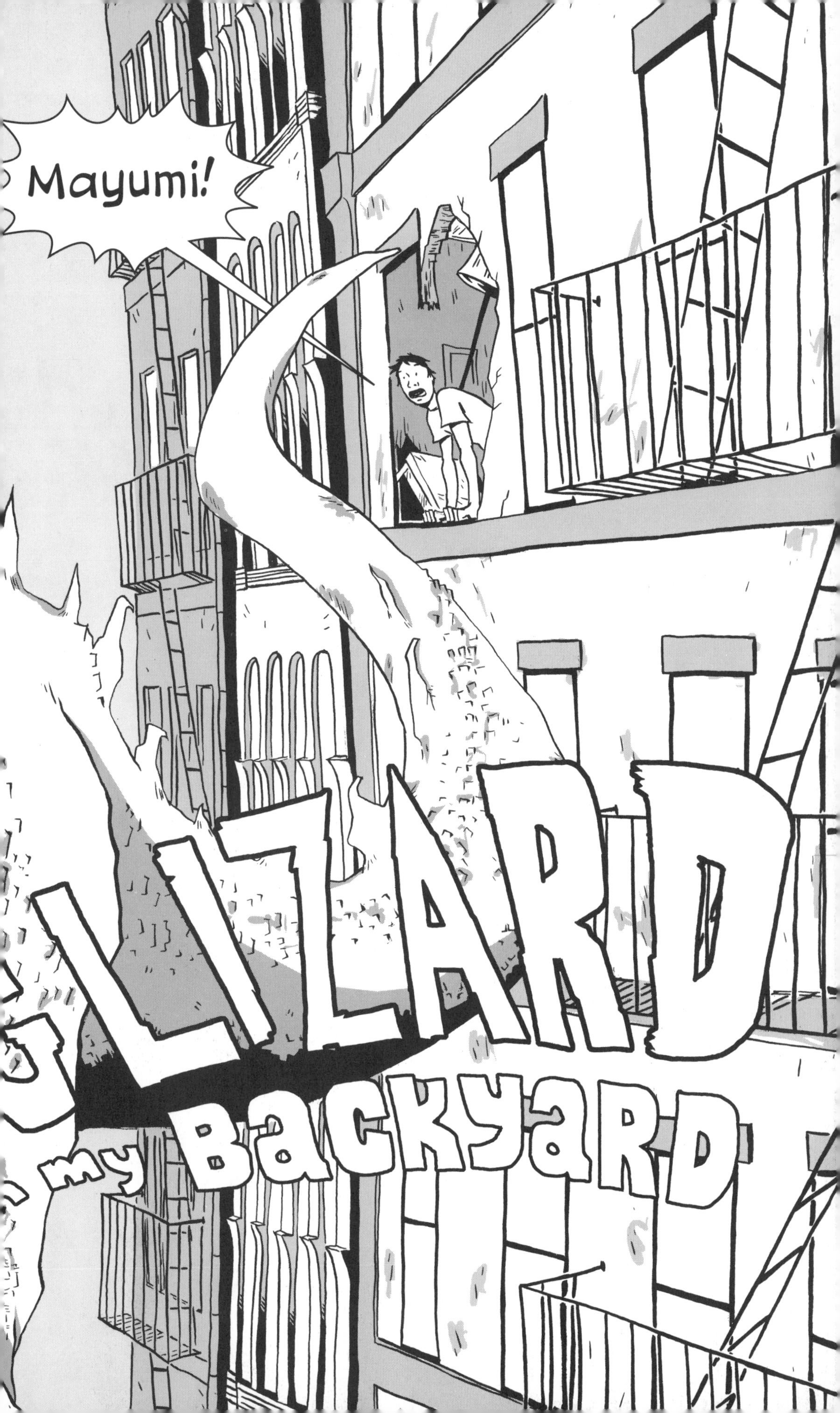
Mayumi!
LIZARD
my BACKYARD

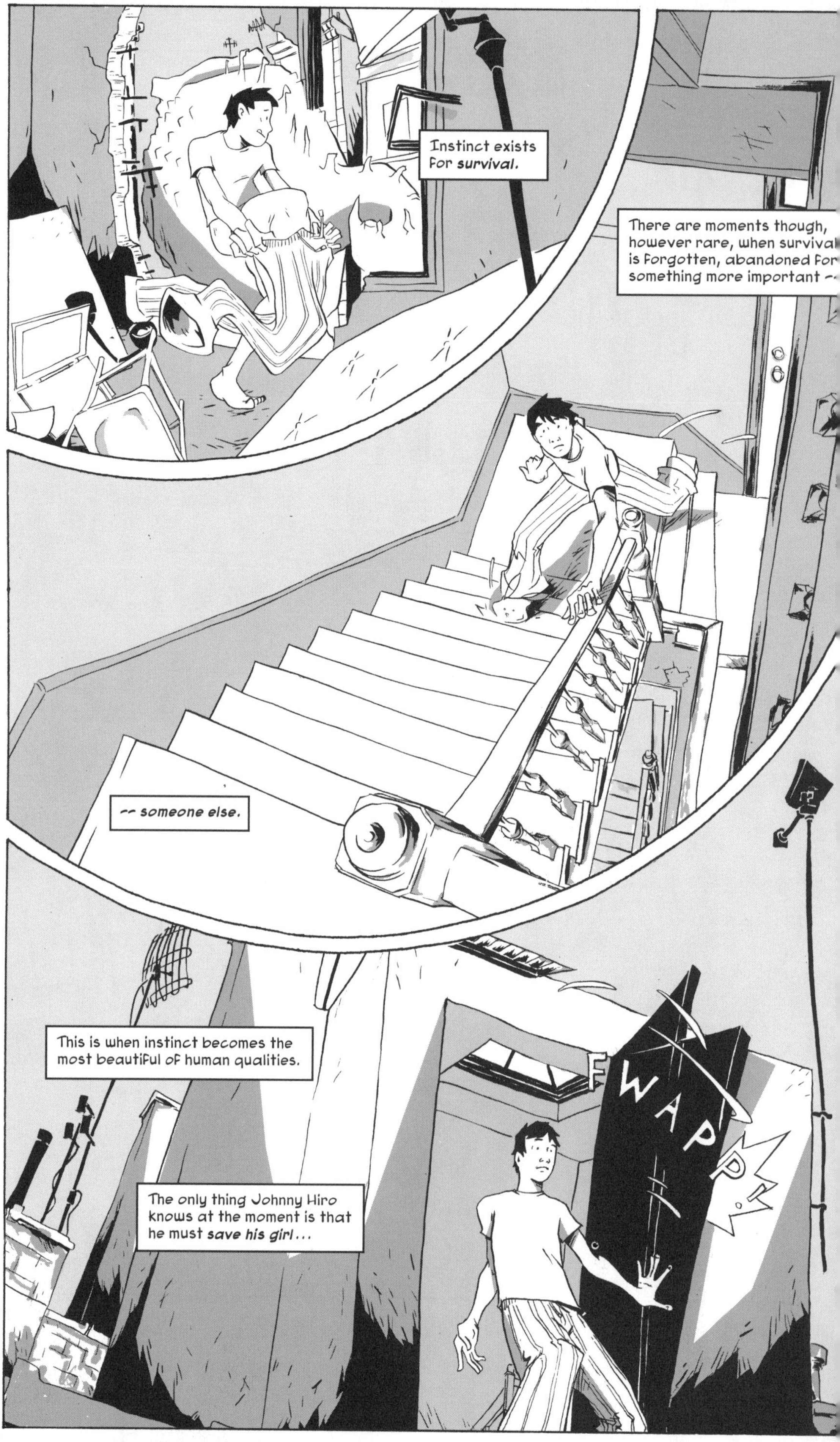
Instinct exists for *survival.*
There are moments though, however rare, when survival is forgotten, abandoned for something more important --
-- *someone else.*
This is when instinct becomes the most beautiful of human qualities.
The only thing Johnny Hiro knows at the moment is that he must *save his girl...*
FWAPP!

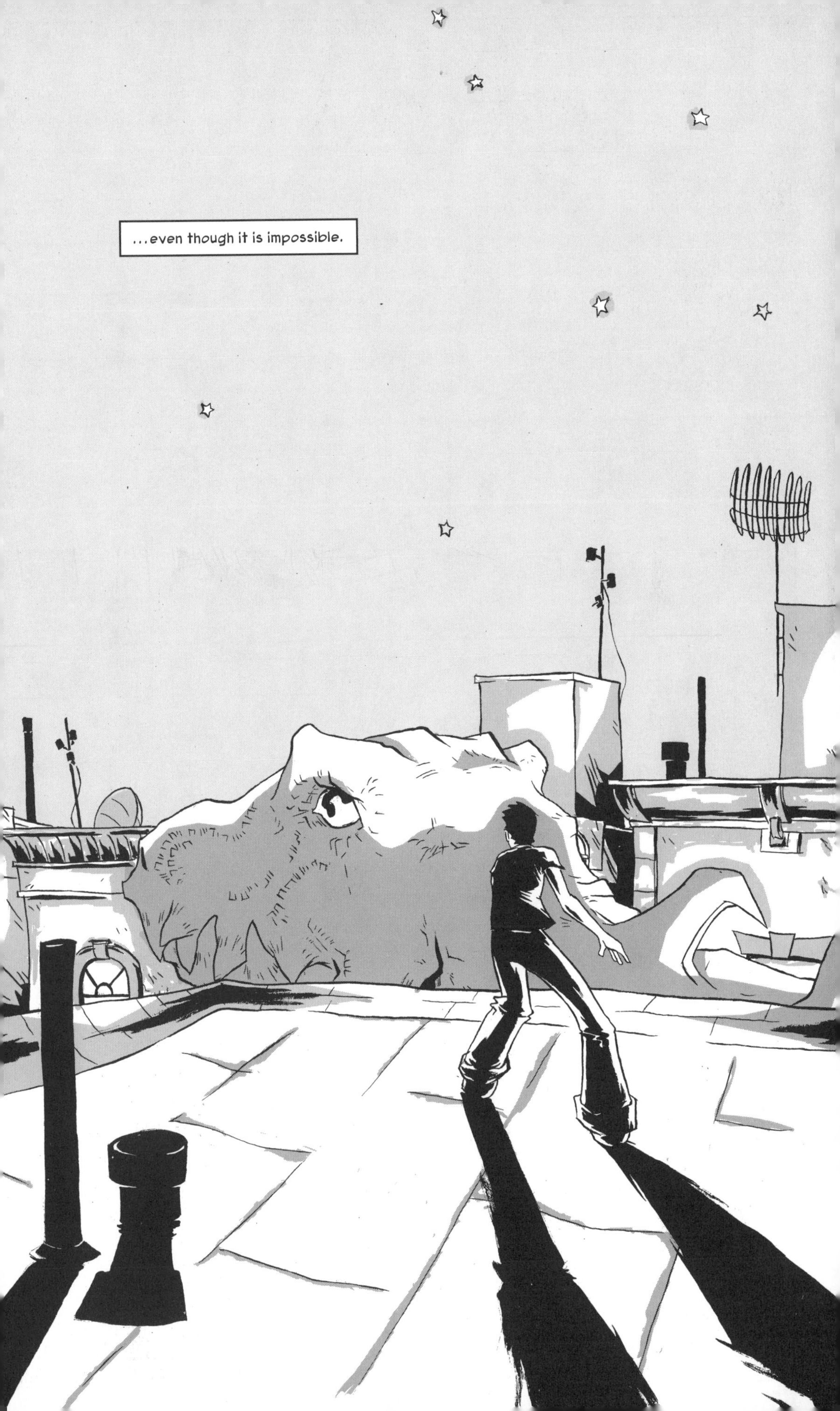
...even though it is impossible.

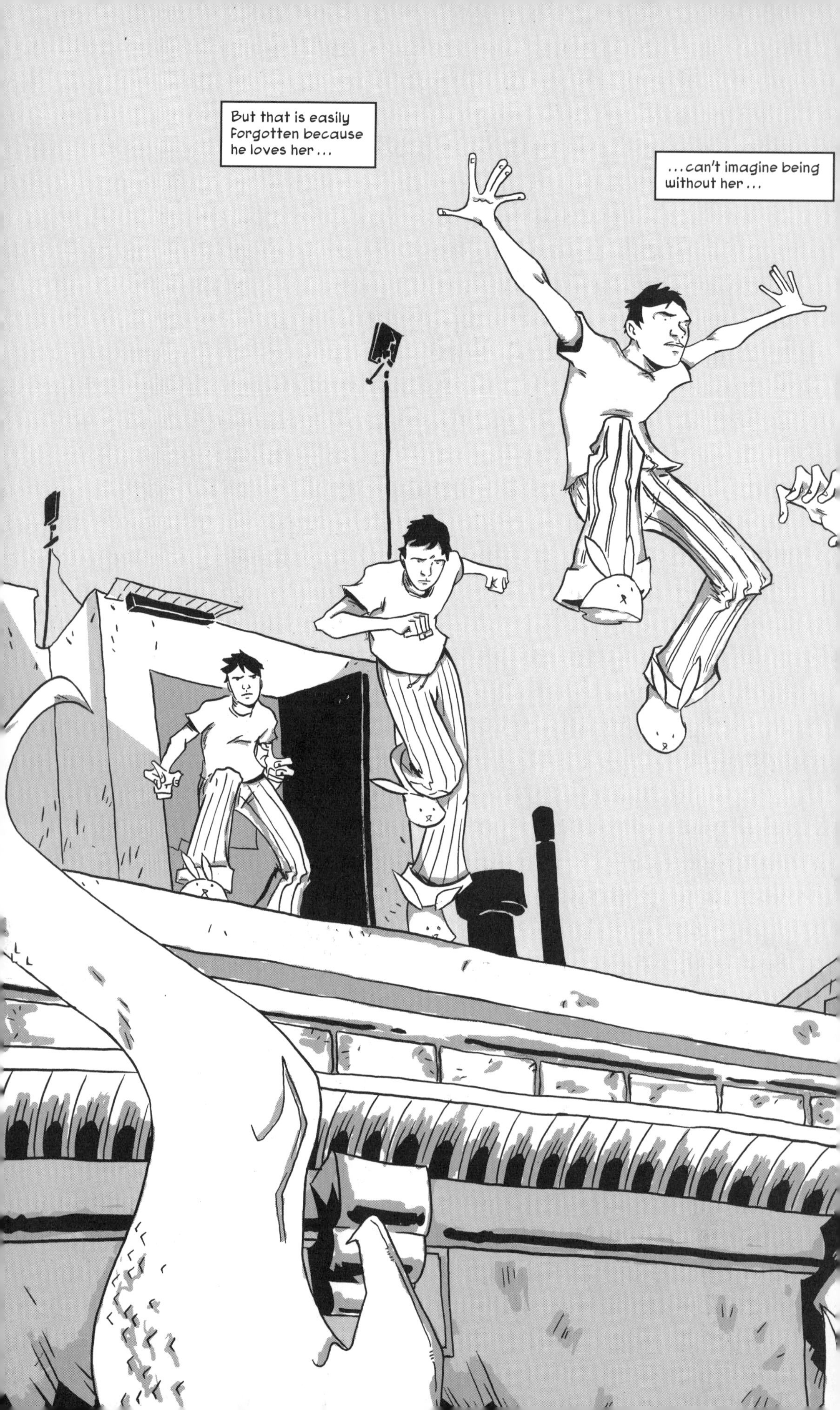
But that is easily forgotten because he loves her . . .
. . . can't imagine being without her . . .

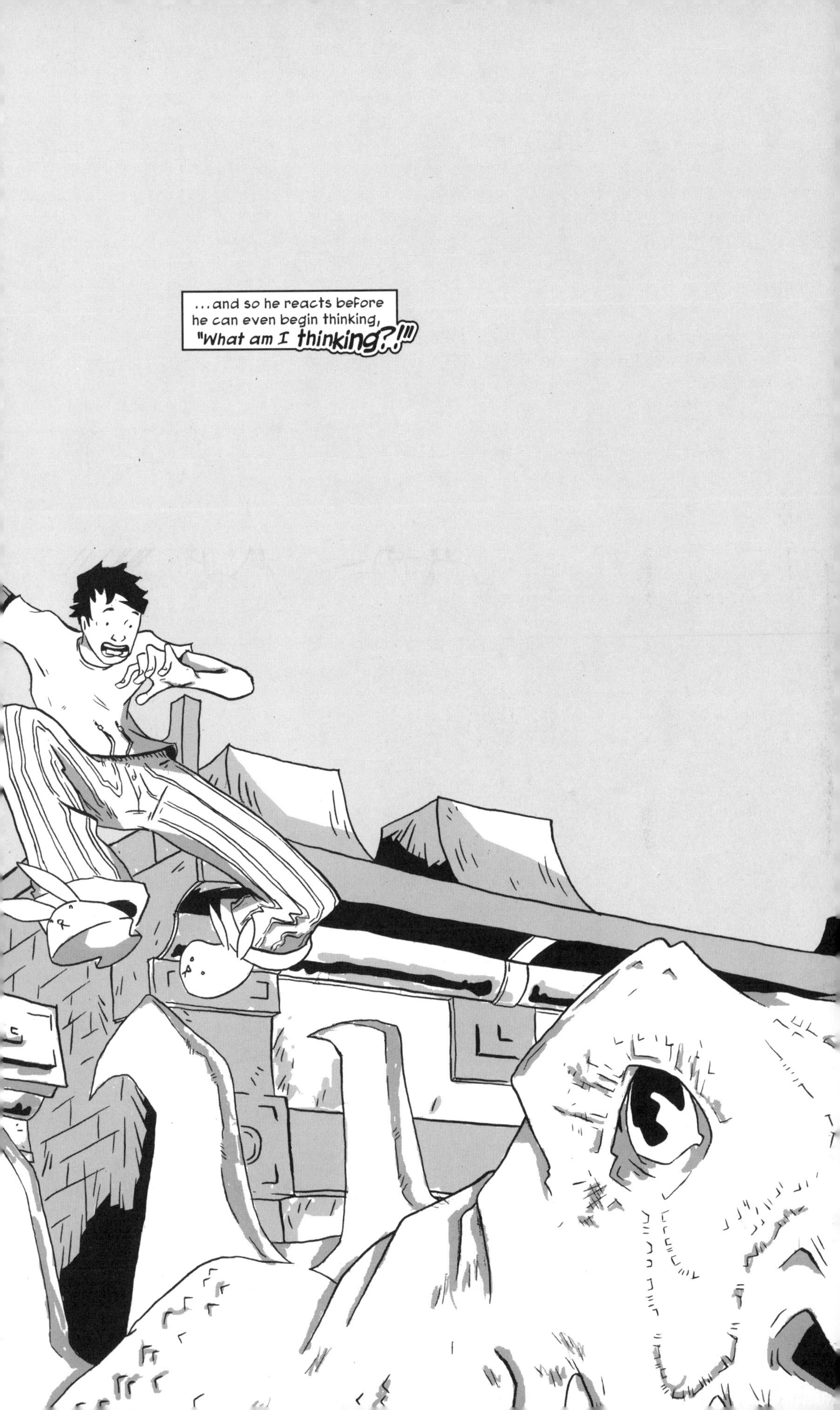
...and so he reacts before he can even begin thinking, "What am I thinking?!"

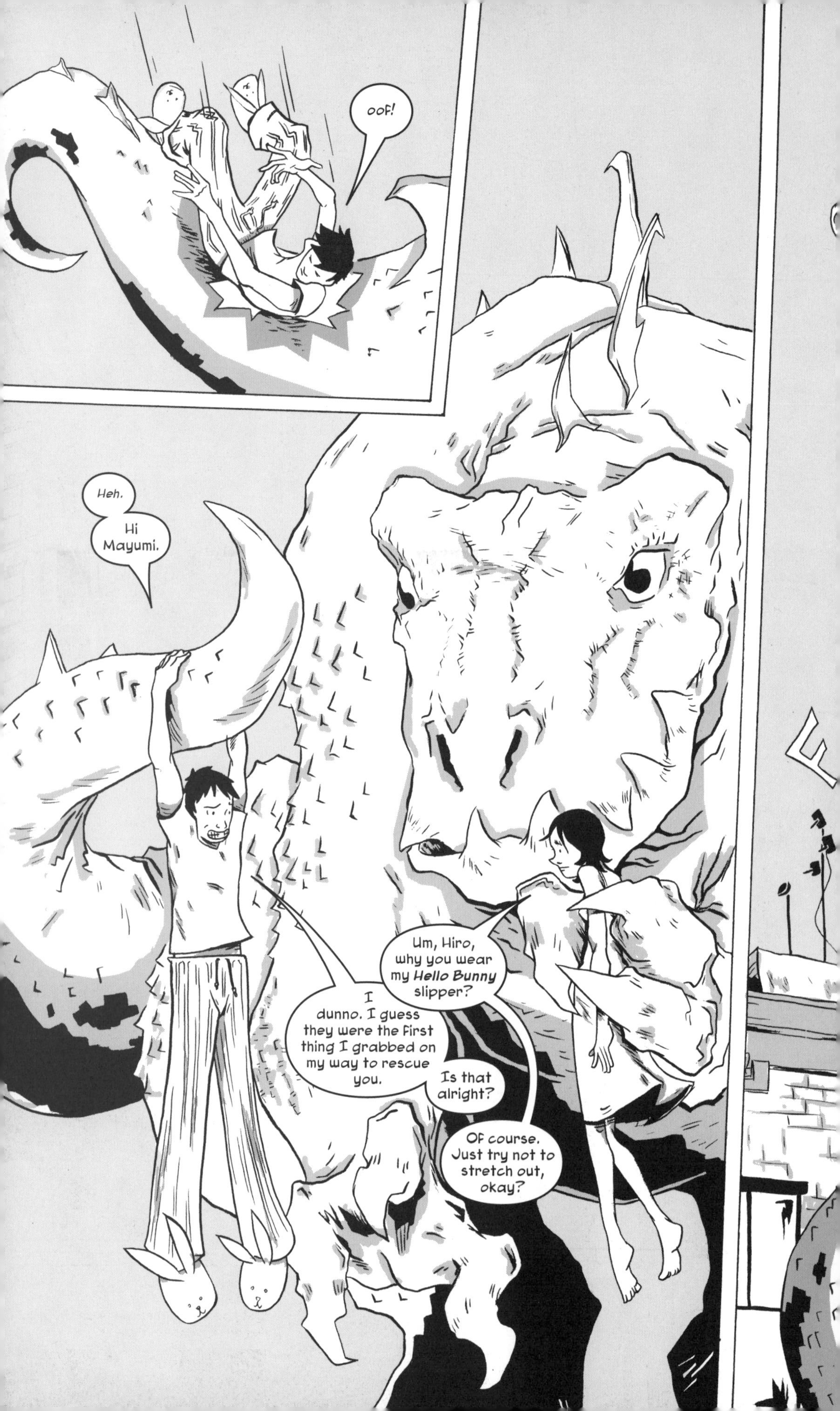
OOF!
Heh.
Hi Mayumi.
Um, Hiro, why you wear my *Hello Bunny* slipper?
I dunno. I guess they were the first thing I grabbed on my way to rescue you.
Is that alright?
Of course. Just try not to stretch out, okay?

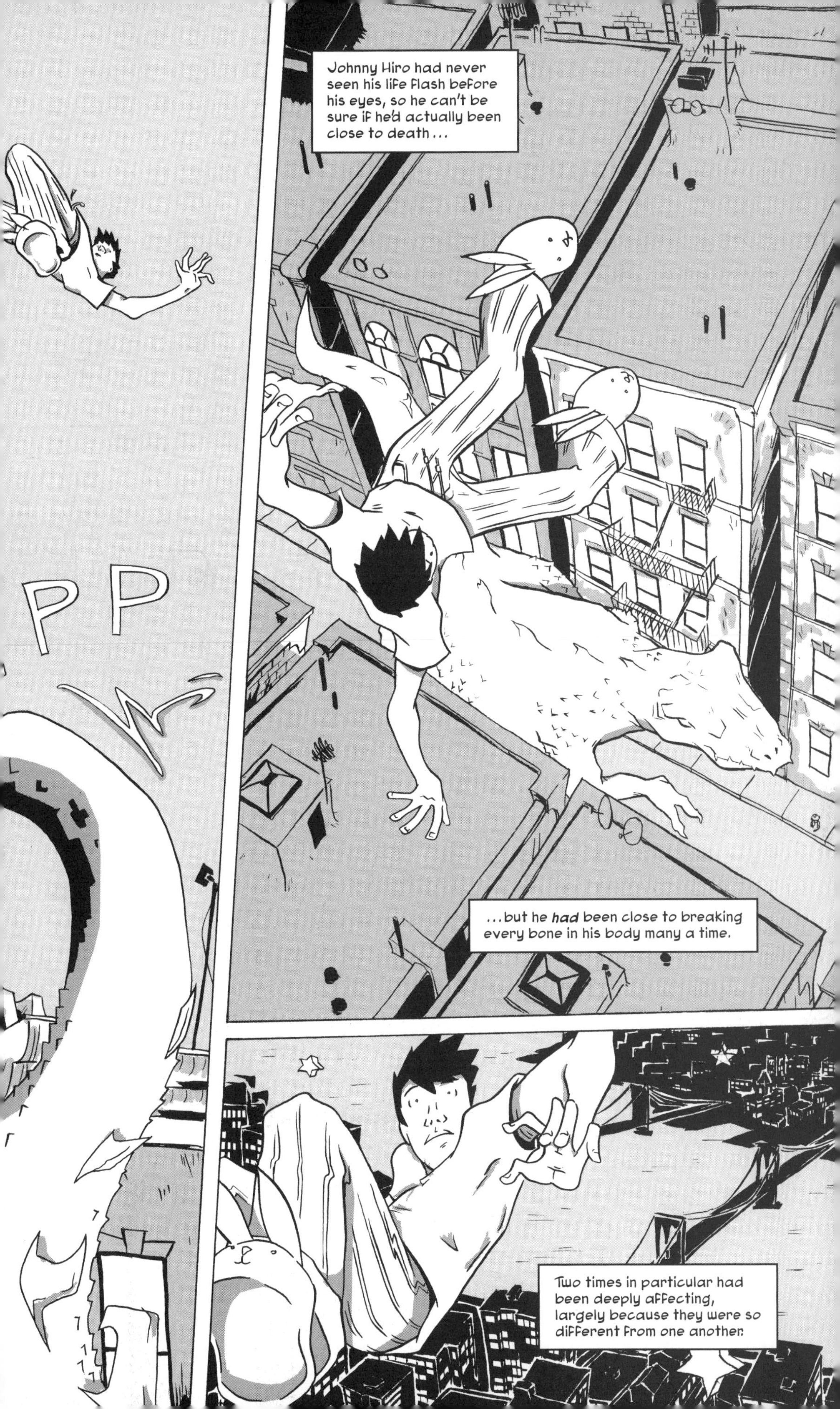

Johnny Hiro had never seen his life flash before his eyes, so he can't be sure if he'd actually been close to death...
PP
...but he *had* been close to breaking every bone in his body many a time.
Two times in particular had been deeply affecting, largely because they were so different from one another.

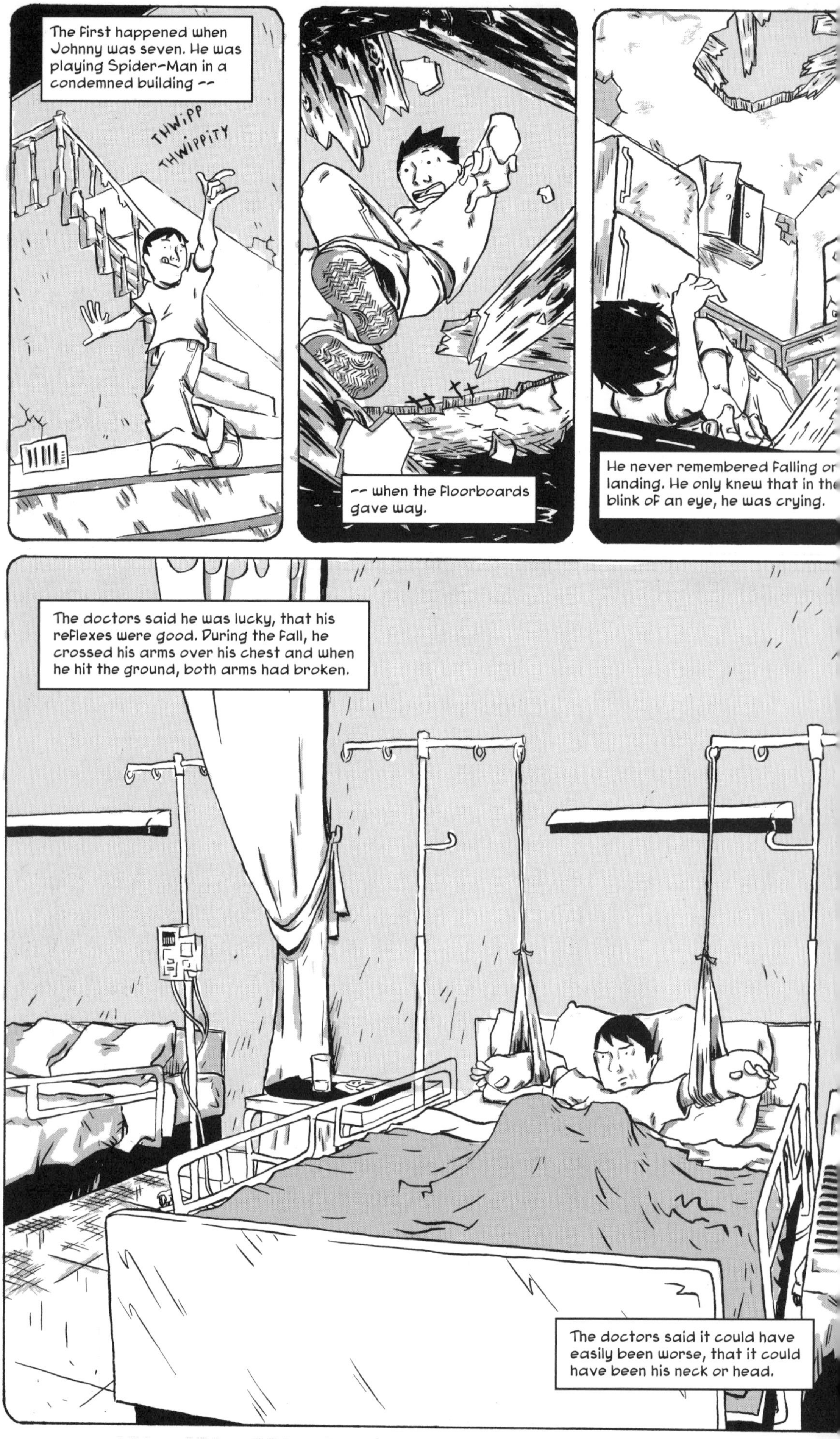
The first happened when Johnny was seven. He was playing Spider-Man in a condemned building --
THWIPP
THWIPPITY
-- when the floorboards gave way.
He never remembered falling or landing. He only knew that in the blink of an eye, he was crying.
The doctors said he was lucky, that his reflexes were good. During the fall, he crossed his arms over his chest and when he hit the ground, both arms had broken.
The doctors said it could have easily been worse, that it could have been his neck or head.

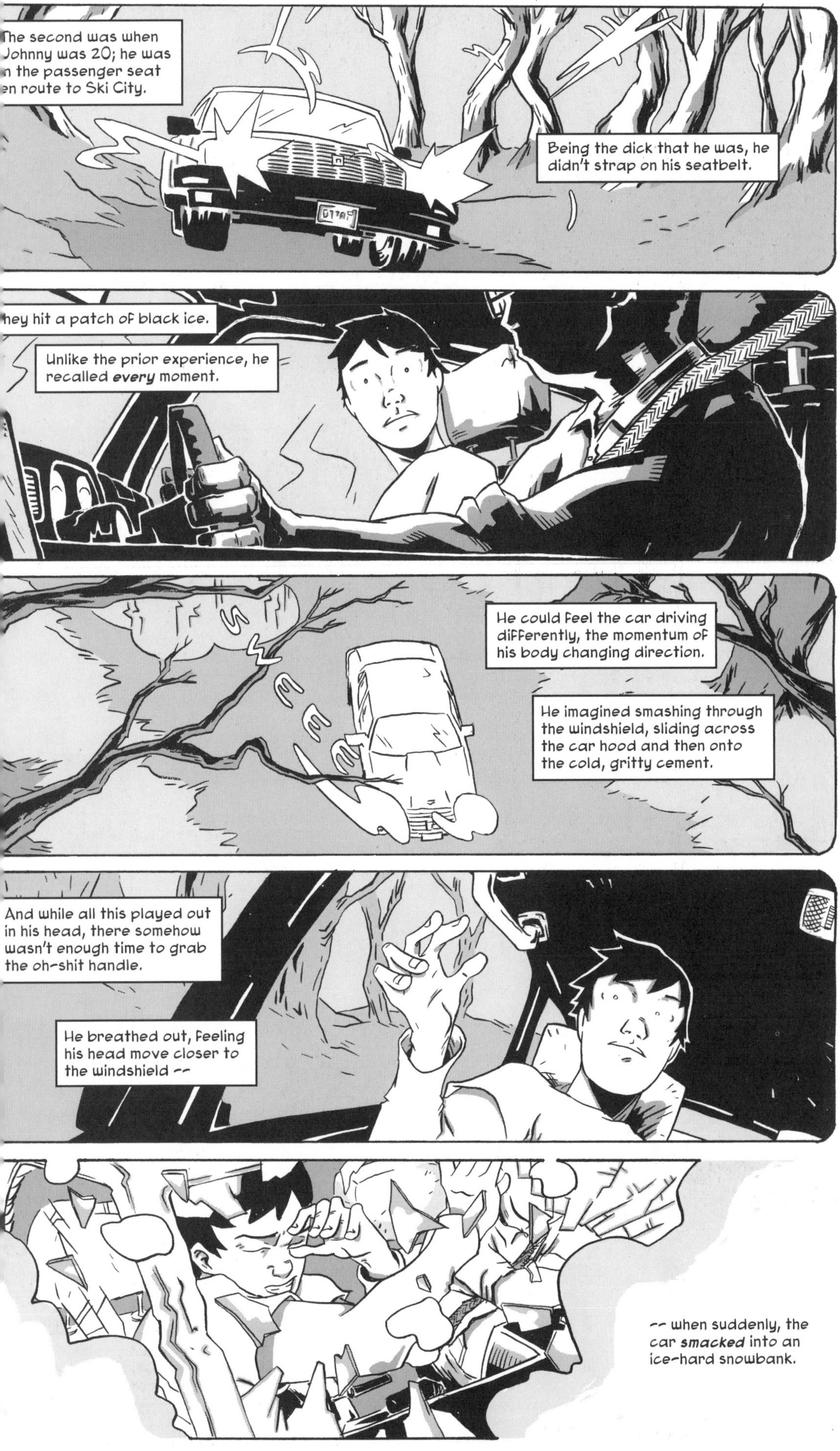
The second was when Johnny was 20; he was in the passenger seat en route to Ski City.
Being the dick that he was, he didn't strap on his seatbelt.
hey hit a patch of black ice.
Unlike the prior experience, he recalled *every* moment.
He could feel the car driving differently, the momentum of his body changing direction.
He imagined smashing through the windshield, sliding across the car hood and then onto the cold, gritty cement.
And while all this played out in his head, there somehow wasn't enough time to grab the oh-shit handle.
He breathed out, feeling his head move closer to the windshield --
-- when suddenly, the car *smacked* into an ice-hard snowbank.

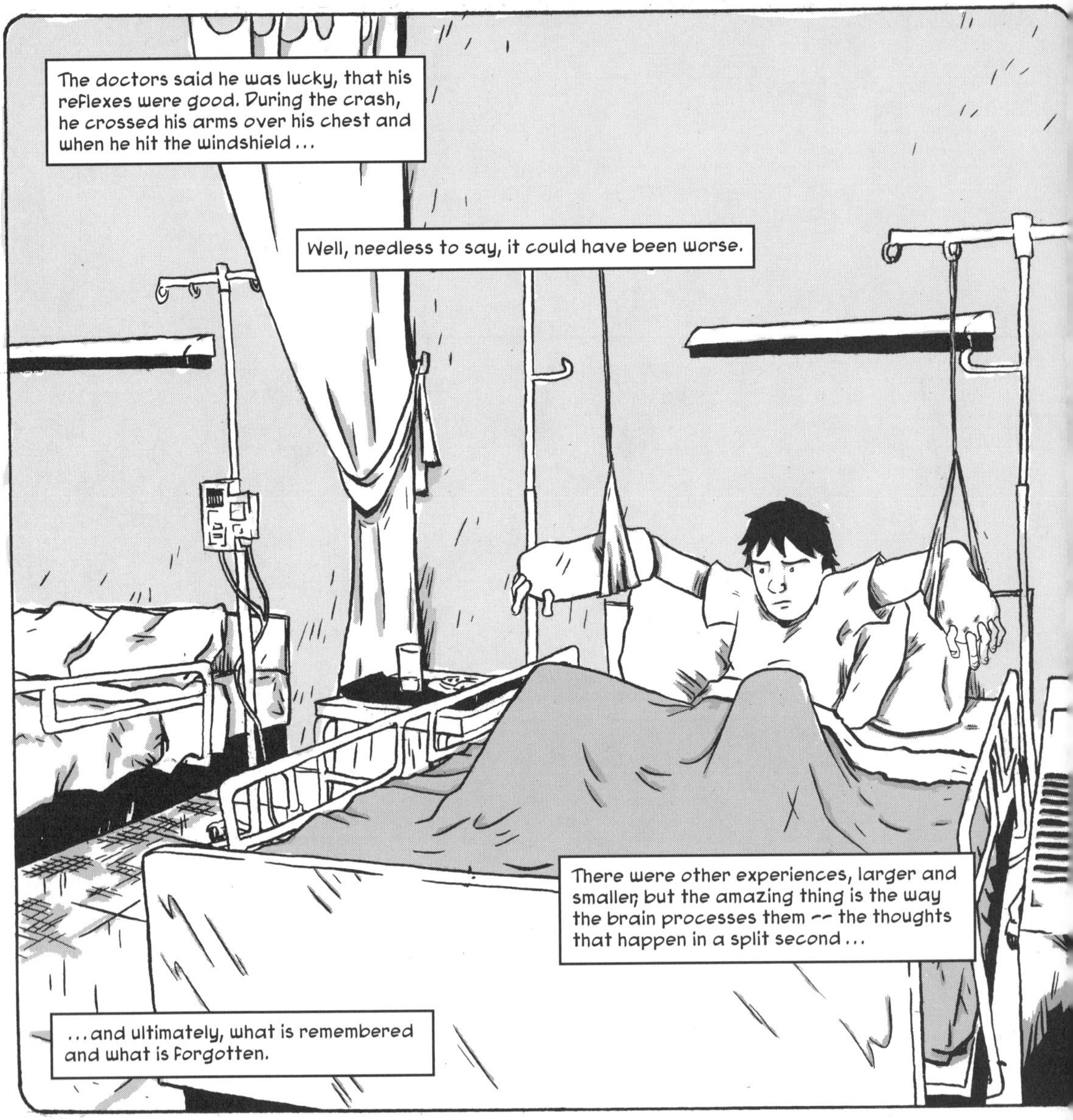
The doctors said he was lucky, that his reflexes were good. During the crash, he crossed his arms over his chest and when he hit the windshield . . .
Well, needless to say, it could have been worse.
There were other experiences, larger and smaller, but the amazing thing is the way the brain processes them -- the thoughts that happen in a split second . . .
. . . and ultimately, what is remembered and what is forgotten.

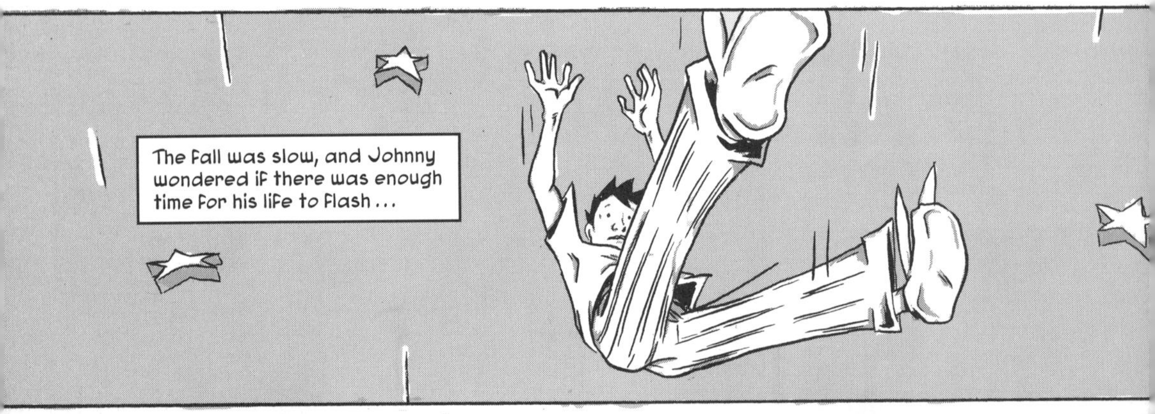
The fall was slow, and Johnny wondered if there was enough time for his life to flash . . .

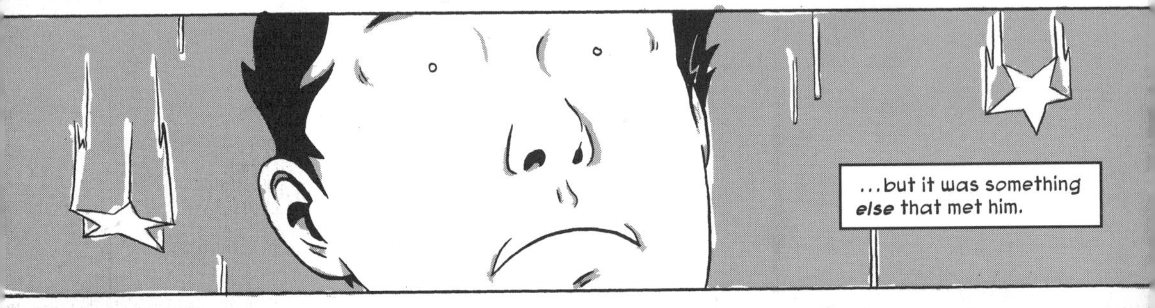
. . . but it was something *else* that met him.

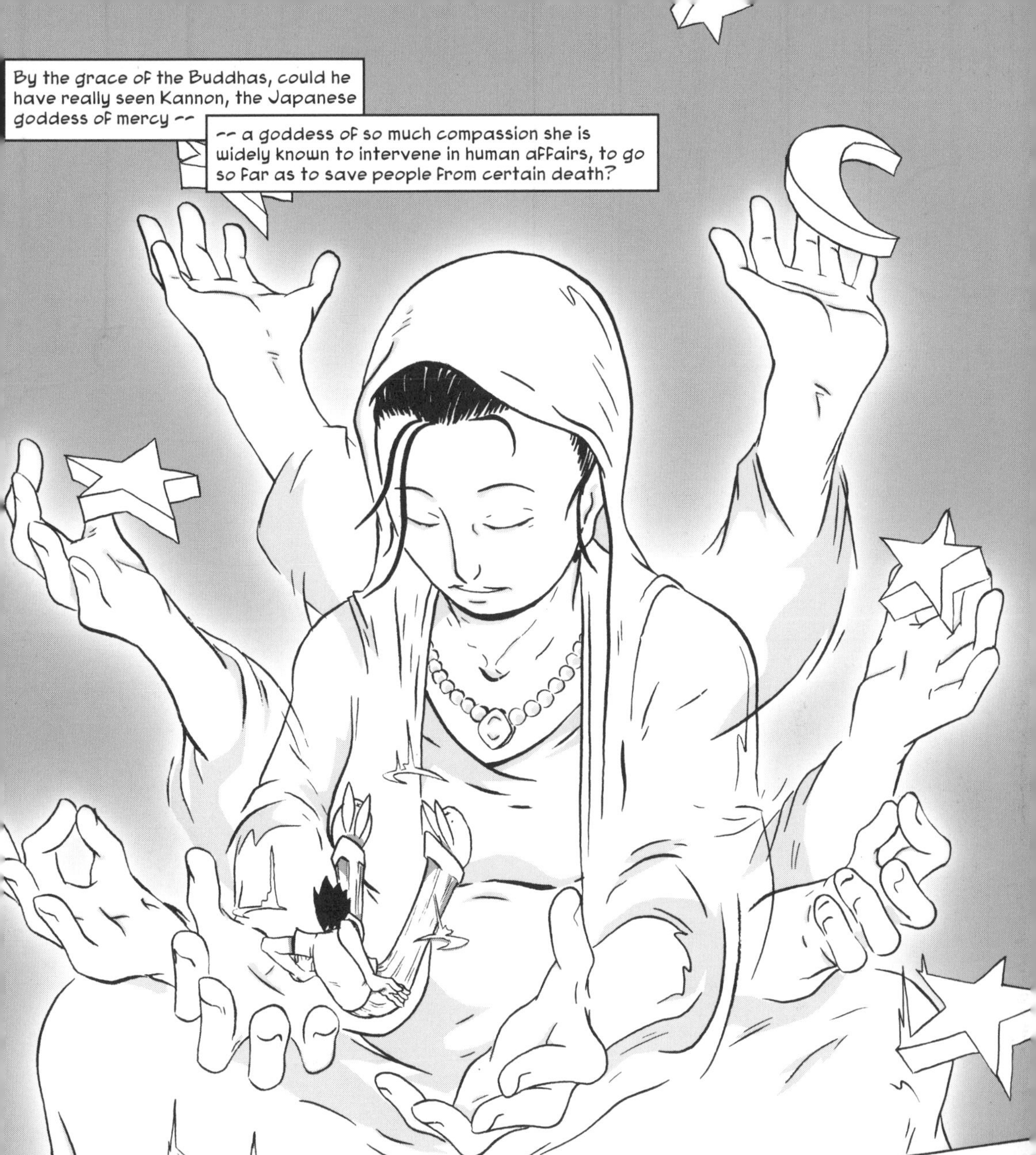
By the grace of the Buddhas, could he have really seen Kannon, the Japanese goddess of mercy --
-- a goddess of so much compassion she is widely known to intervene in human affairs, to go so far as to save people from certain death?

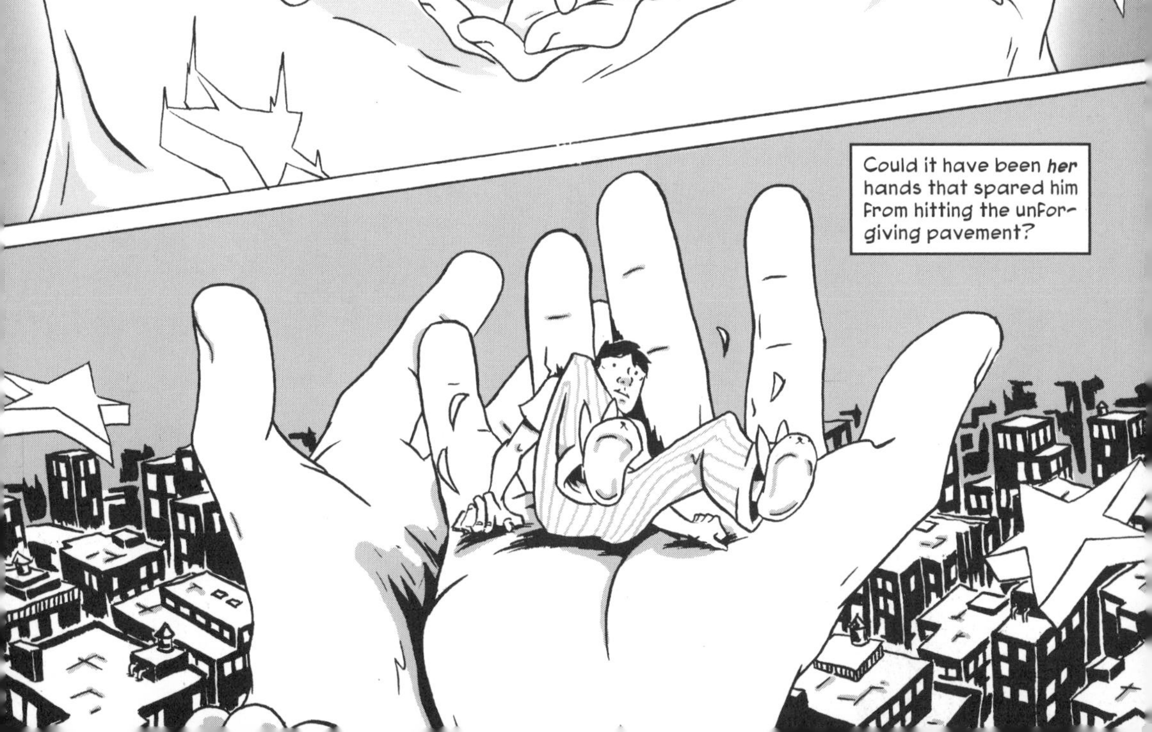
Could it have been ***her*** hands that spared him from hitting the unforgiving pavement?

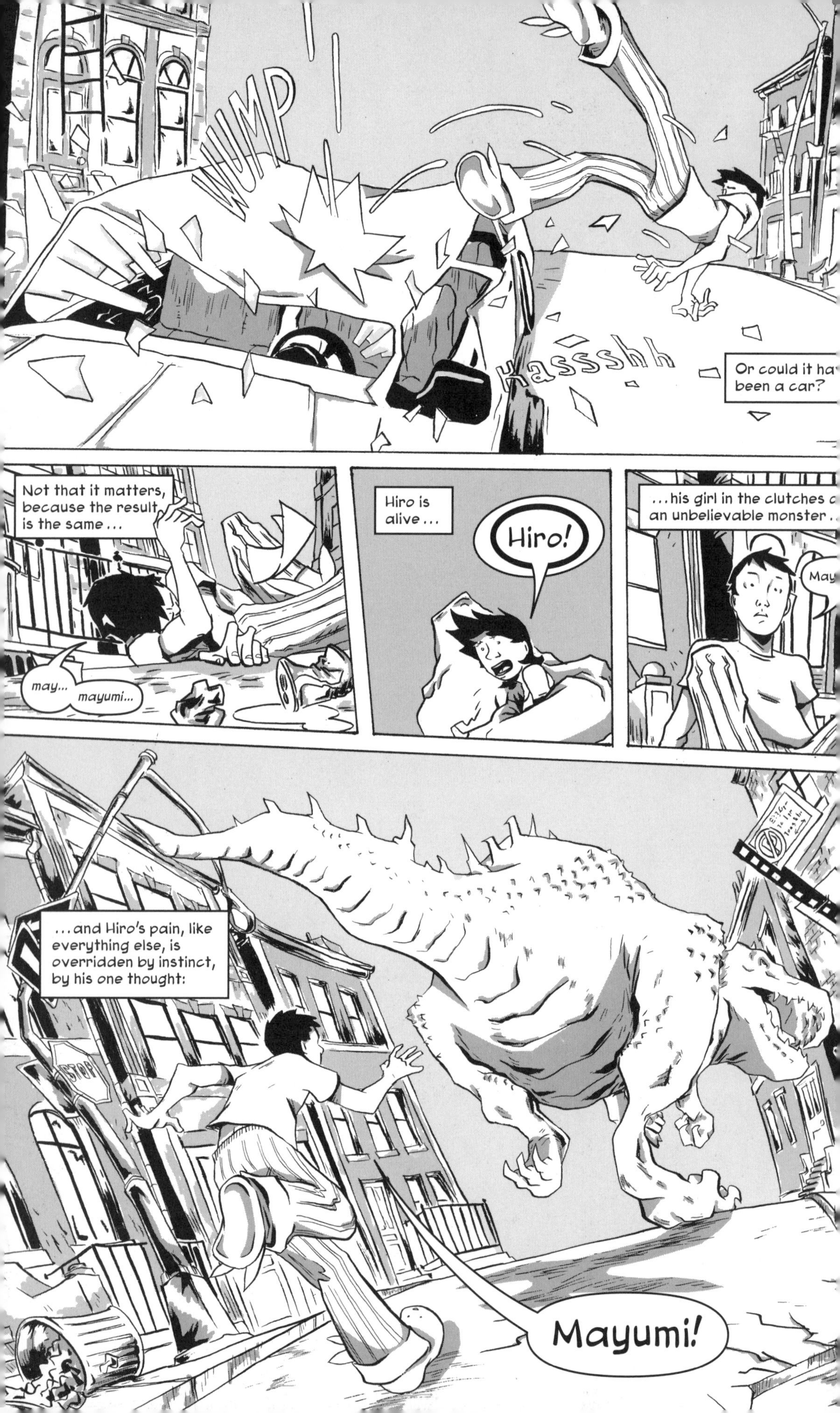
WUMP
kassshh
Or could it ha
been a car?
Not that it matters, because the result is the same …
may… mayumi…
Hiro is alive …
Hiro!
…his girl in the clutches o
an unbelievable monster …
May
…and Hiro's pain, like everything else, is overridden by instinct, by his one thought:
STOP
Mayumi!

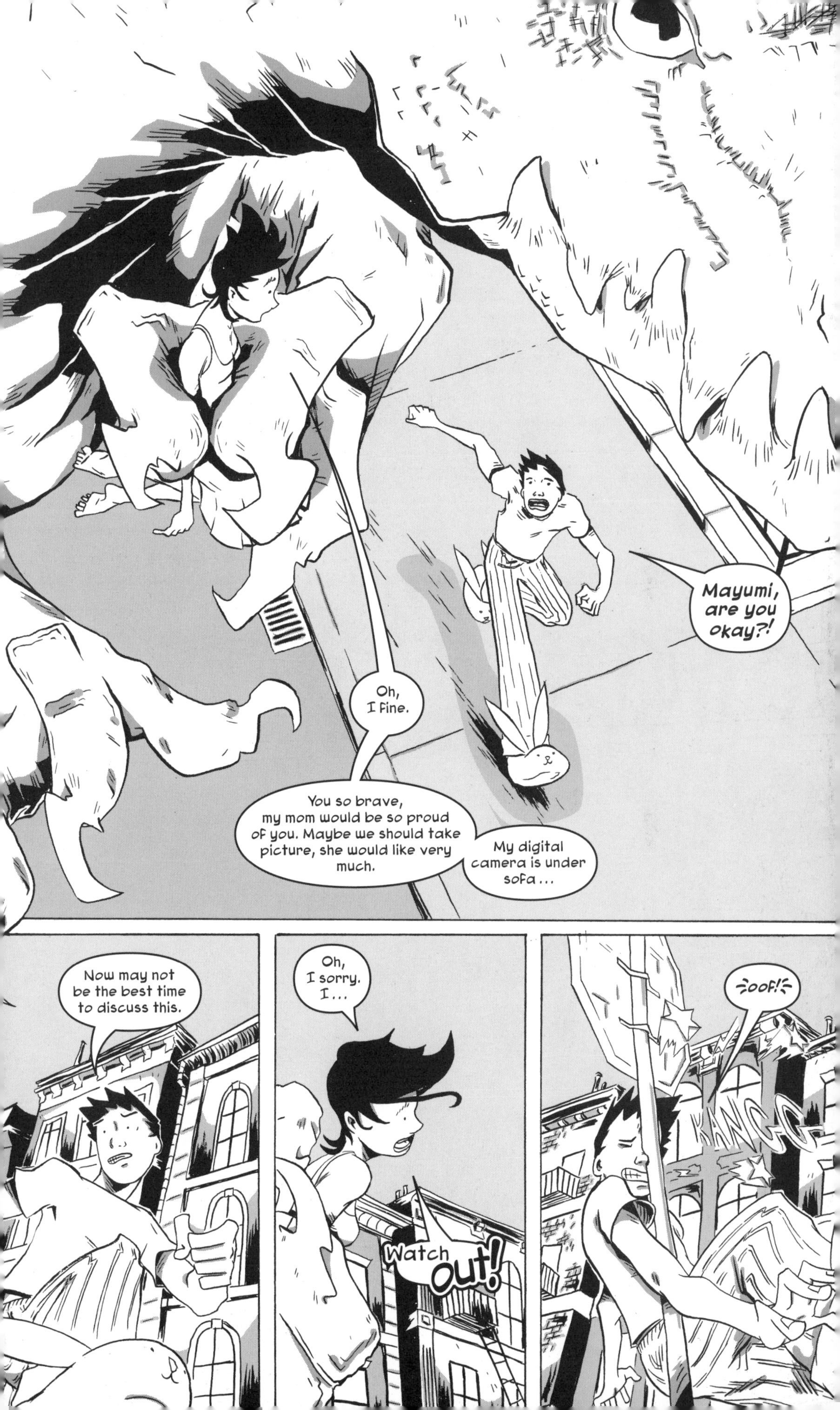
Mayumi, are you okay?!
Oh, I fine.
You so brave, my mom would be so proud of you. Maybe we should take picture, she would like very much.
My digital camera is under sofa...
Now may not be the best time to discuss this.
Oh, I sorry. I...
Watch out!
oof!

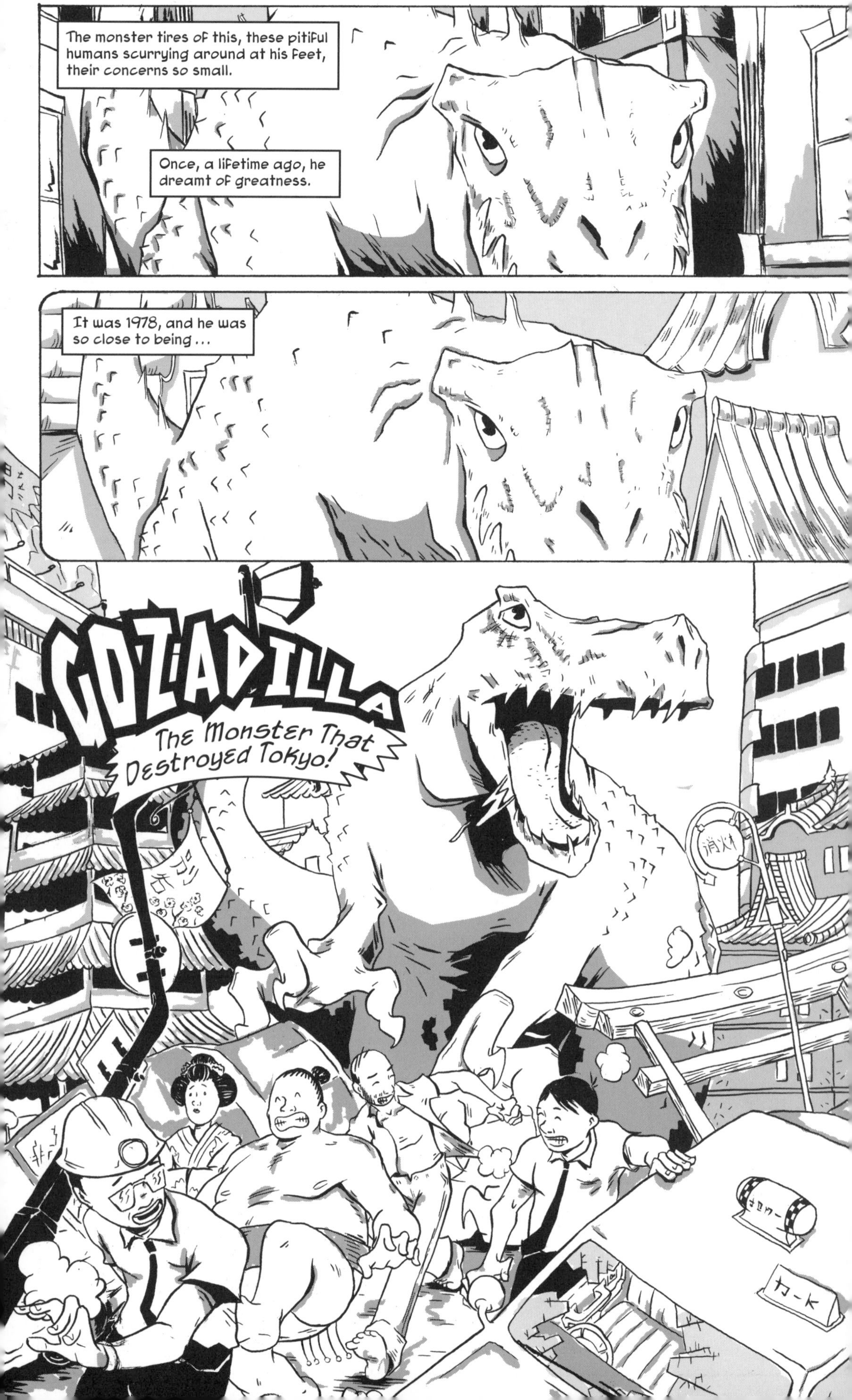
The monster tires of this, these pitiful humans scurrying around at his feet, their concerns so small.
Once, a lifetime ago, he dreamt of greatness.
It was 1978, and he was so close to being ...
..GOZiADILLA
The Monster That Destroyed Tokyo!

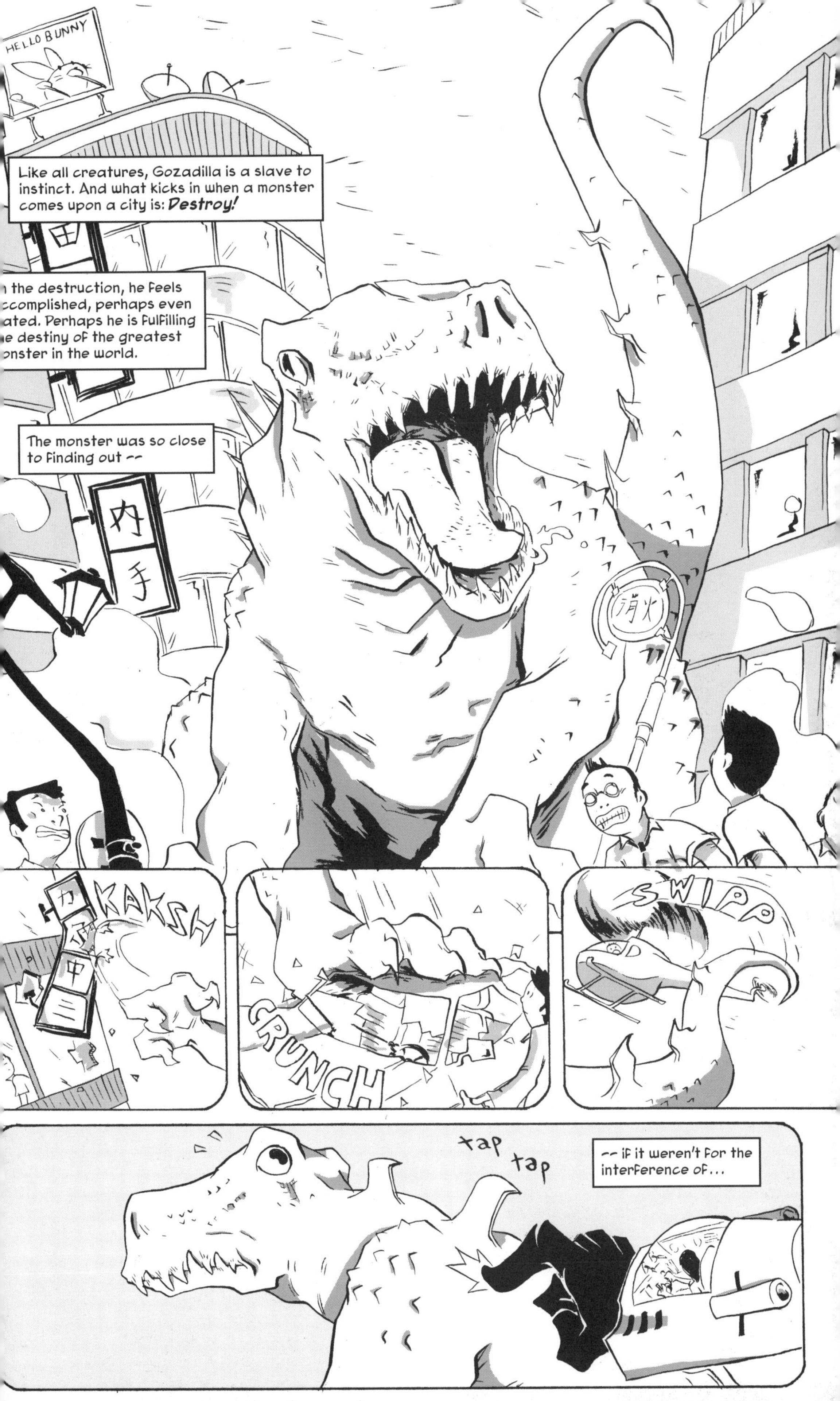
HELLO BUNNY
Like all creatures, Gozadilla is a slave to instinct. And what kicks in when a monster comes upon a city is: ***Destroy!***
n the destruction, he feels ccomplished, perhaps even ated. Perhaps he is fulfilling e destiny of the greatest onster in the world.
The monster was so close to finding out --
KAKSH
CRUNCH
SWIPP
tap
tap
-- if it weren't for the interference of...

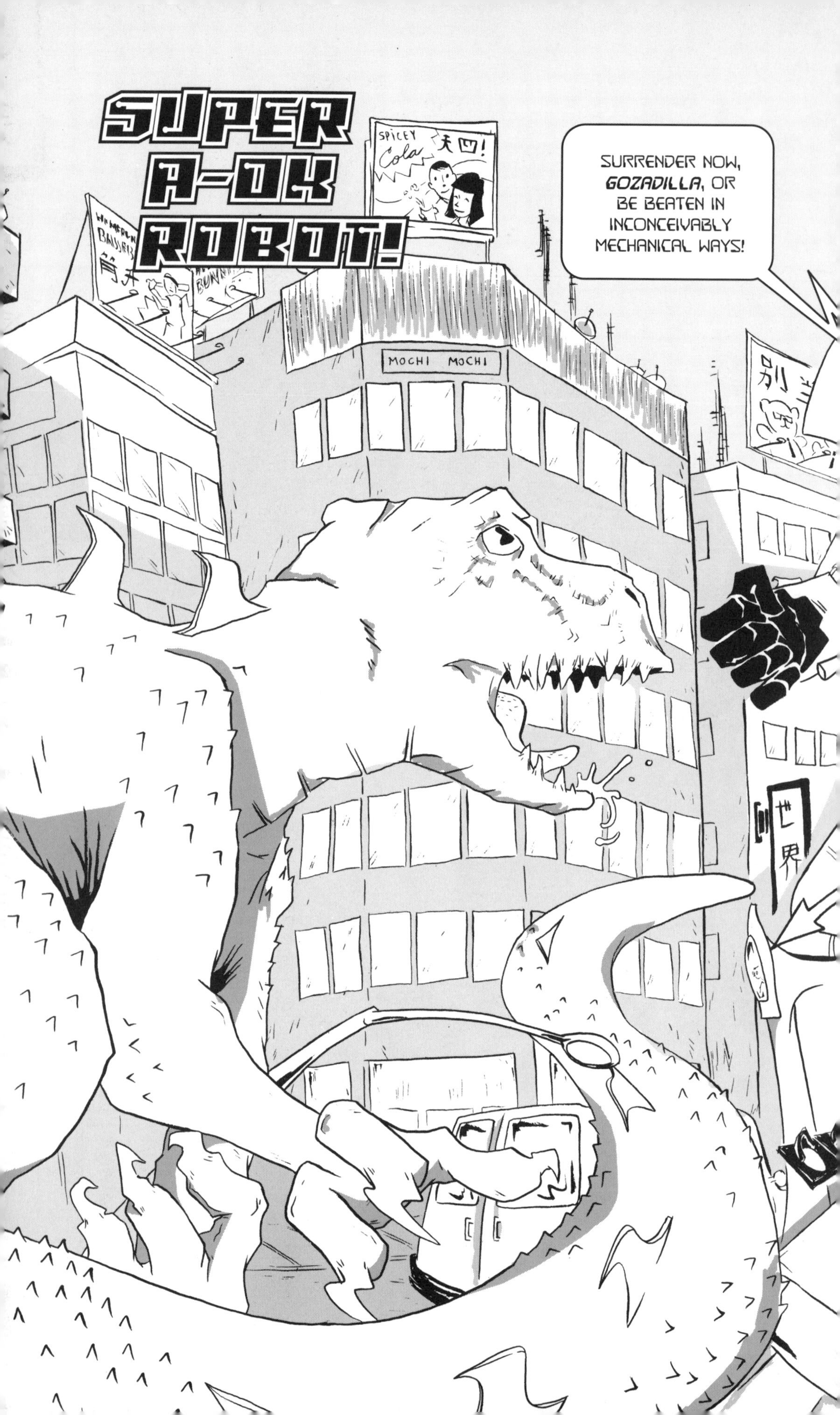
SUPER A-OK ROBOT!
SPICEY
Cola
MOCHI MOCHI
SURRENDER NOW, GOZADILLA, OR BE BEATEN IN INCONCEIVABLY MECHANICAL WAYS!
世界

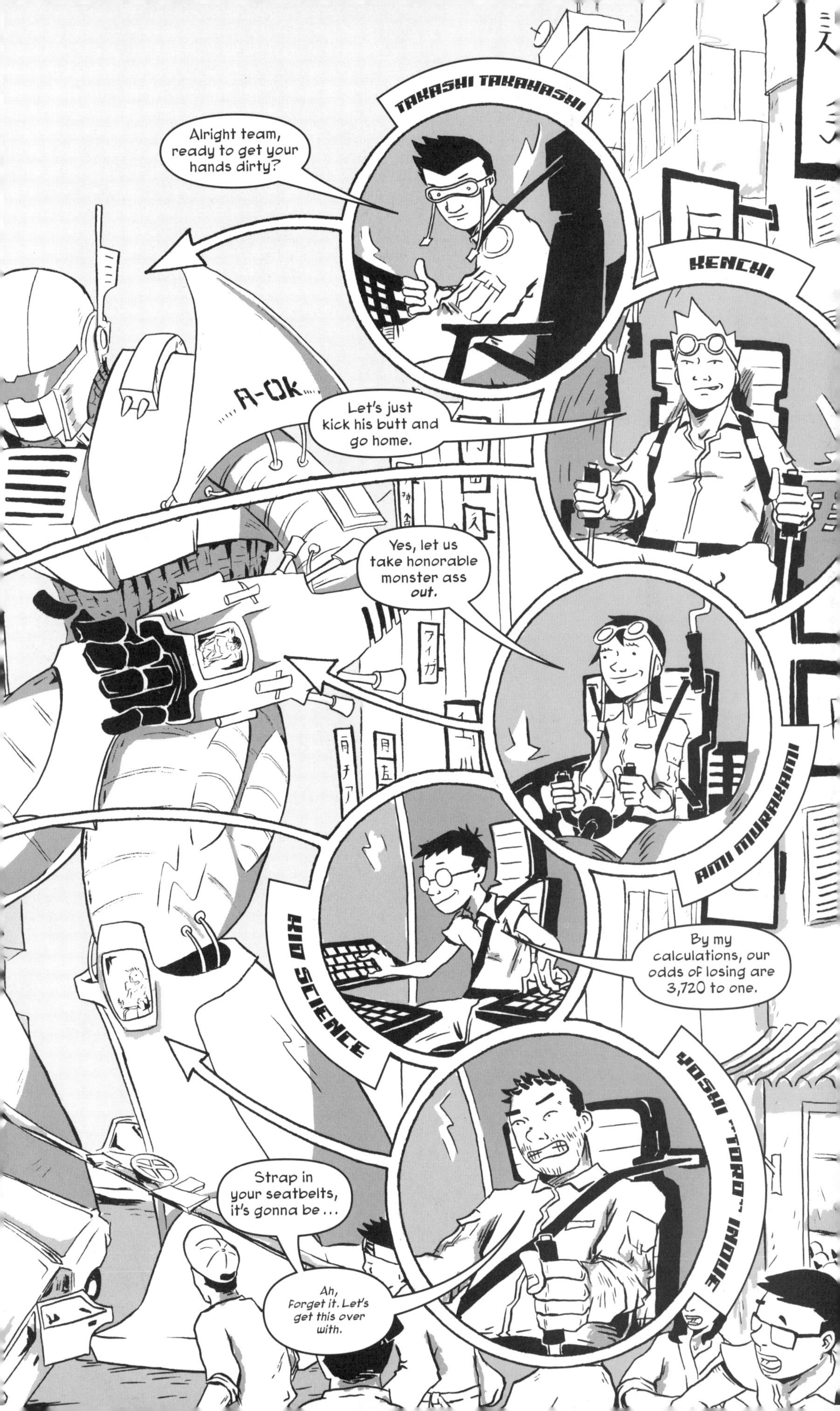
TAKASHI TAKAHASHI
Alright team, ready to get your hands dirty?
A-OK
KENCHI
Let's just kick his butt and go home.
Yes, let us take honorable monster ass *out.*
AMI MURAKAMI
KID SCIENCE
By my calculations, our odds of losing are 3,720 to one.
YOSHI "TORO" INOUE
Strap in your seatbelts, it's gonna be . . .
Ah, forget it. Let's get this over with.

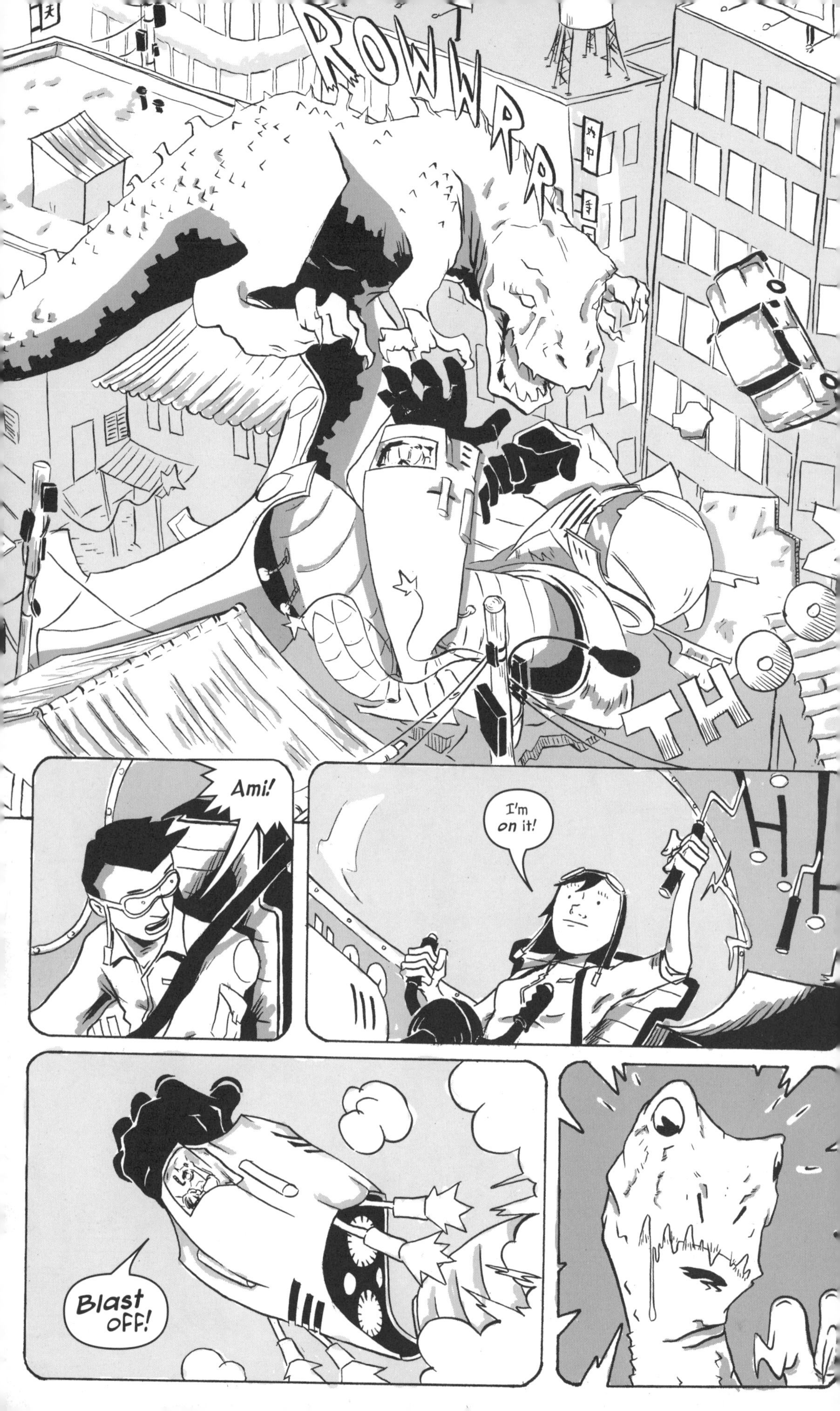
ROWWRR
THOOOO
Ami!
I'm on it!
Blast off!

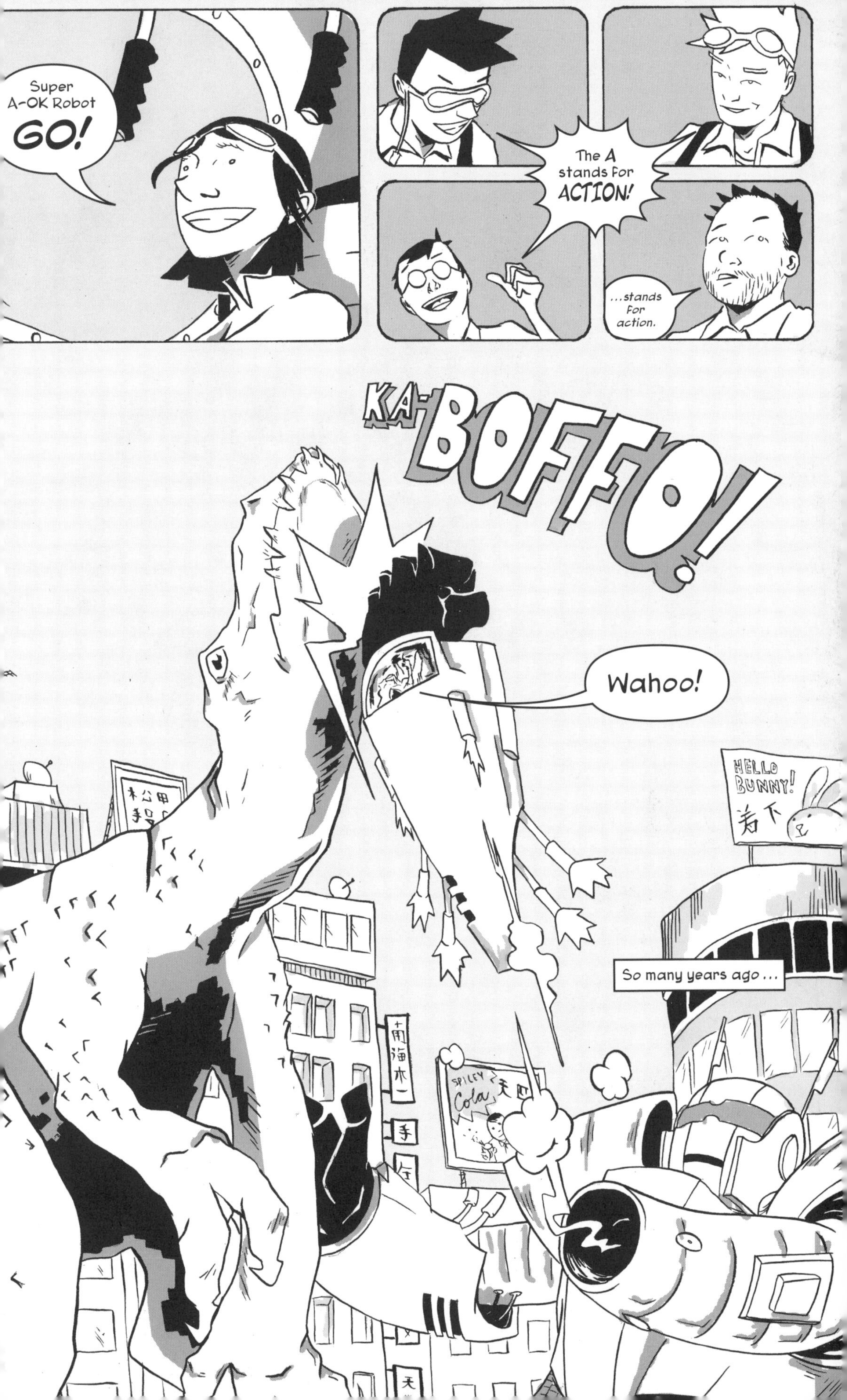
Super A-OK Robot GO!
The A stands for ACTION!
...stands for action.
KA-BOFFO!
Wahoo!
HELLO BUNNY!
SPILEY Cola
So many years ago...

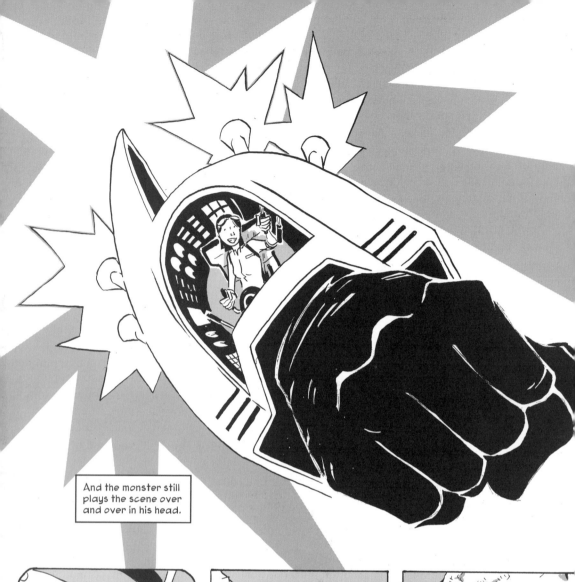

And the monster still plays the scene over and over in his head.

He remembers that confident smirk.

And now the mother's actions will hold dire consequences for the daughter.

For Gozadilla, this is a story of *revenge*.

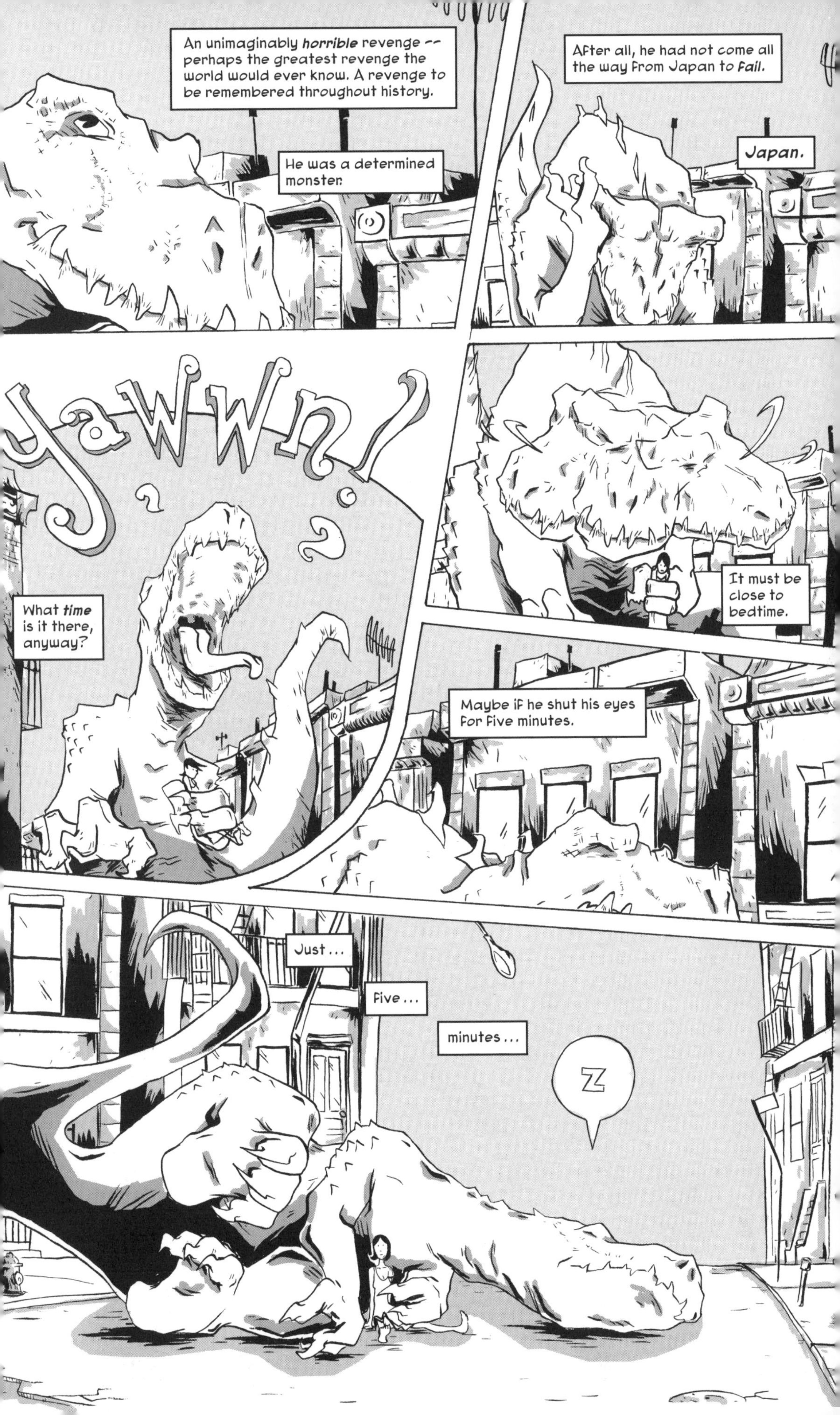
An unimaginably **horrible** revenge -- perhaps the greatest revenge the world would ever know. A revenge to be remembered throughout history.
He was a determined monster.
After all, he had not come all the way from Japan to **fail.**
Japan.
yawwn!
What *time* is it there, anyway?
It must be close to bedtime.
Maybe if he shut his eyes for five minutes.
Just...
five...
minutes...
Z

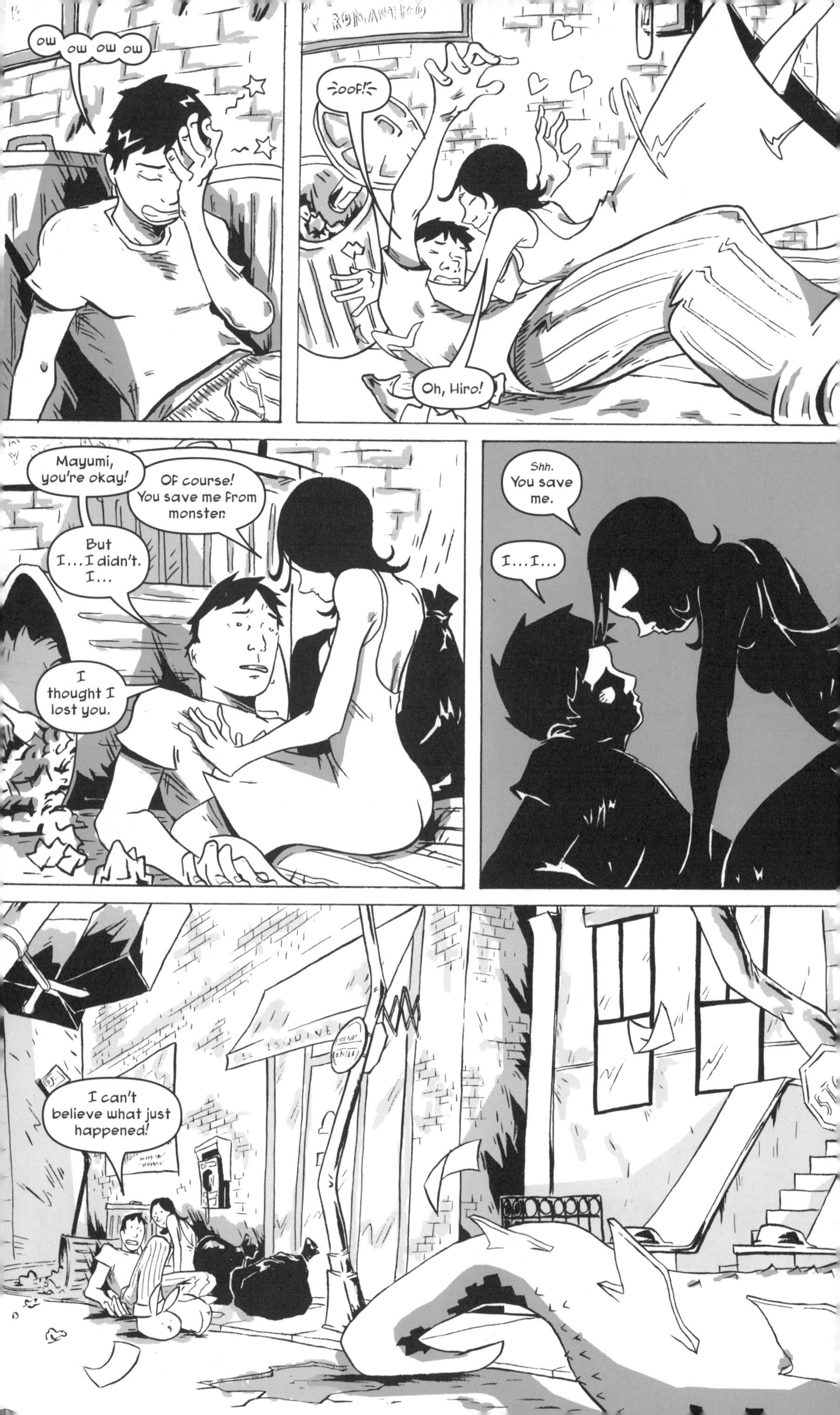
ow
ow ow ow
OOF!
Oh, Hiro!
Mayumi, you're okay!
Of course! You save me from monster.
But I... I didn't. I...
I thought I lost you.
Shh. You save me.
I... I...
I can't believe what just happened!

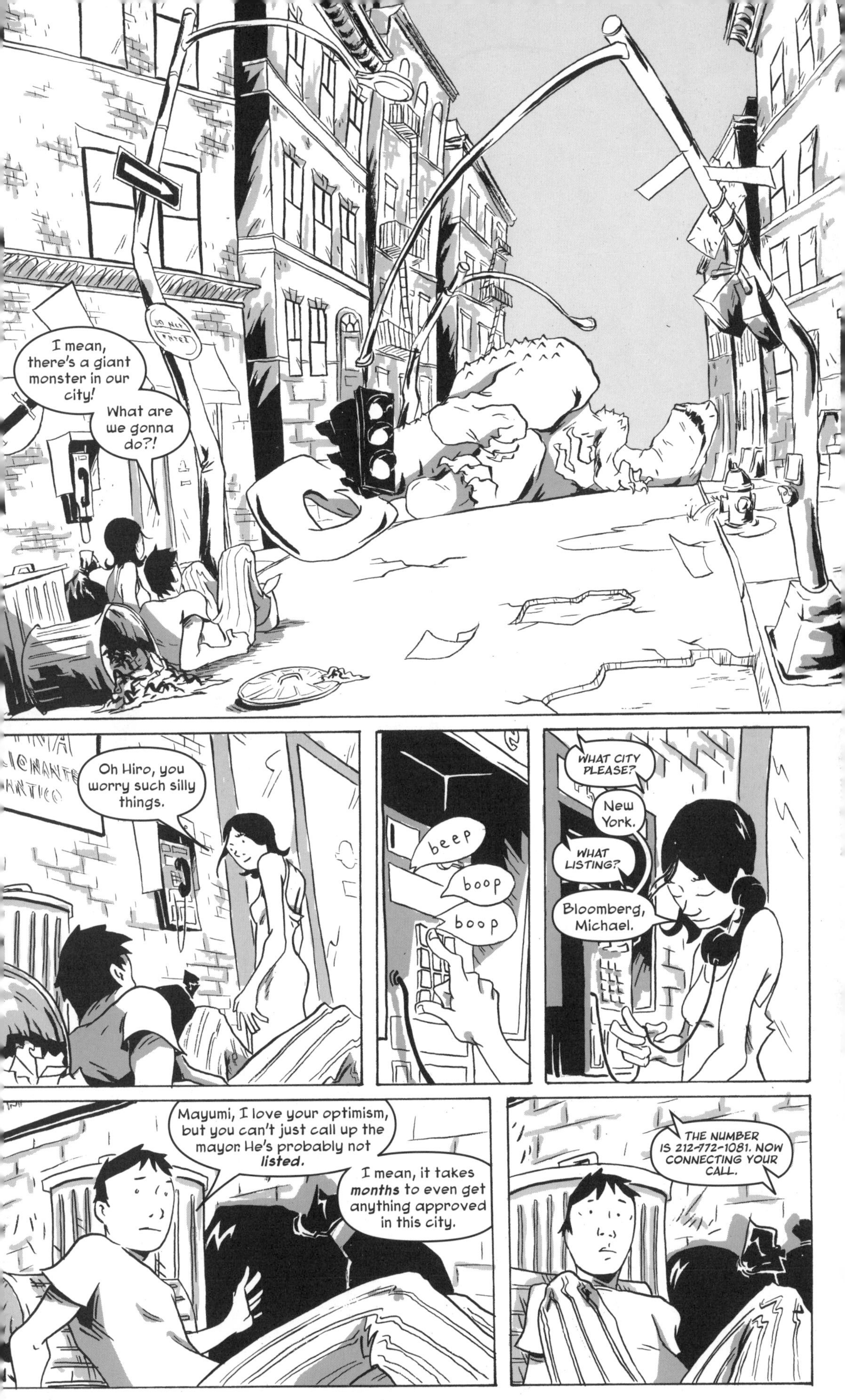
I mean, there's a giant monster in our city!
What are we gonna do?!
Oh Hiro, you worry such silly things.
beep
boop
boop
WHAT CITY PLEASE?
New York.
WHAT LISTING?
Bloomberg, Michael.
Mayumi, I love your optimism, but you can't just call up the mayor. He's probably not *listed*.
I mean, it takes *months* to even get anything approved in this city.
THE NUMBER IS 212-772-1081. NOW CONNECTING YOUR CALL.

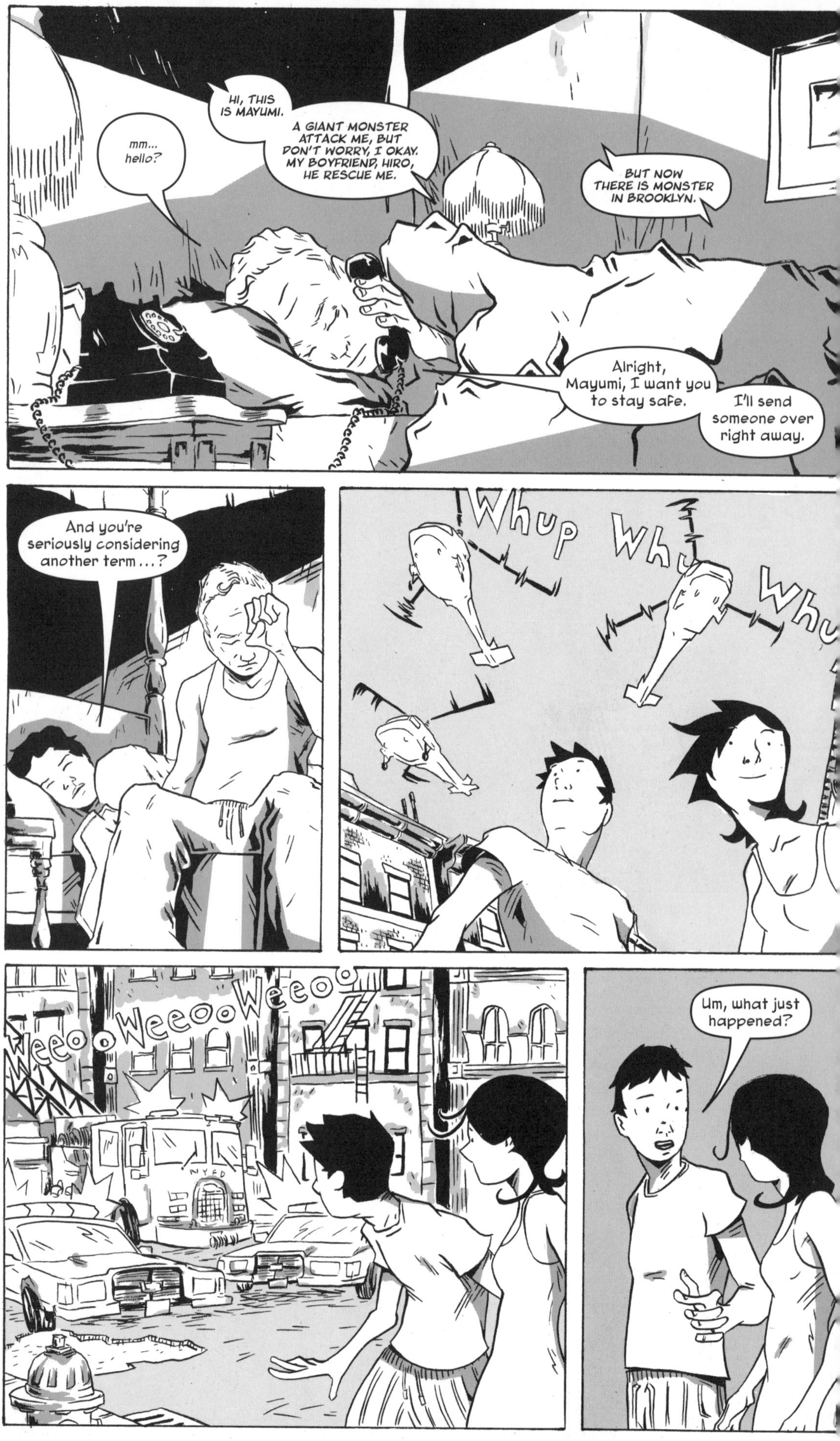

mm...
hello?
HI, THIS
IS MAYUMI.
A GIANT MONSTER
ATTACK ME, BUT
DON'T WORRY, I OKAY.
MY BOYFRIEND, HIRO,
HE RESCUE ME.
BUT NOW
THERE IS MONSTER
IN BROOKLYN.
Alright,
Mayumi, I want you
to stay safe.
I'll send
someone over
right away.
And you're
seriously considering
another term . . . ?
Whup
Whu
Whu
Weeo
Weeoo
Weeoo
NYFD
Um, what just
happened?

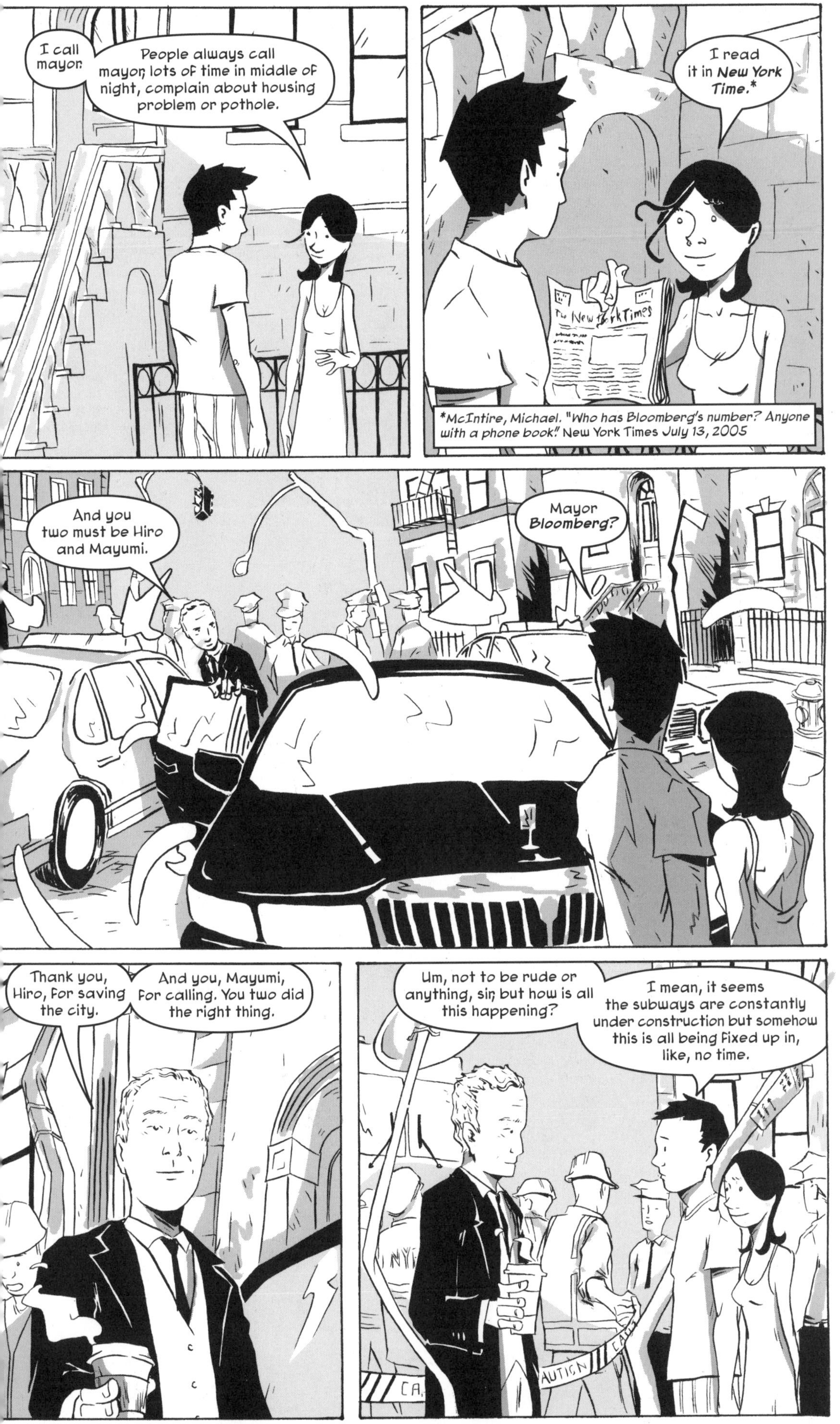
I call mayor.
People always call mayor, lots of time in middle of night, complain about housing problem or pothole.
I read it in **New York Time.***
The New York Times
*McIntire, Michael. "Who has Bloomberg's number? Anyone with a phone book." New York Times July 13, 2005
And you two must be Hiro and Mayumi.
Mayor *Bloomberg?*
Thank you, Hiro, for saving the city.
And you, Mayumi, for calling. You two did the right thing.
Um, not to be rude or anything, sir, but how is all this happening?
I mean, it seems the subways are constantly under construction but somehow this is all being fixed up in, like, no time.
CAUTION

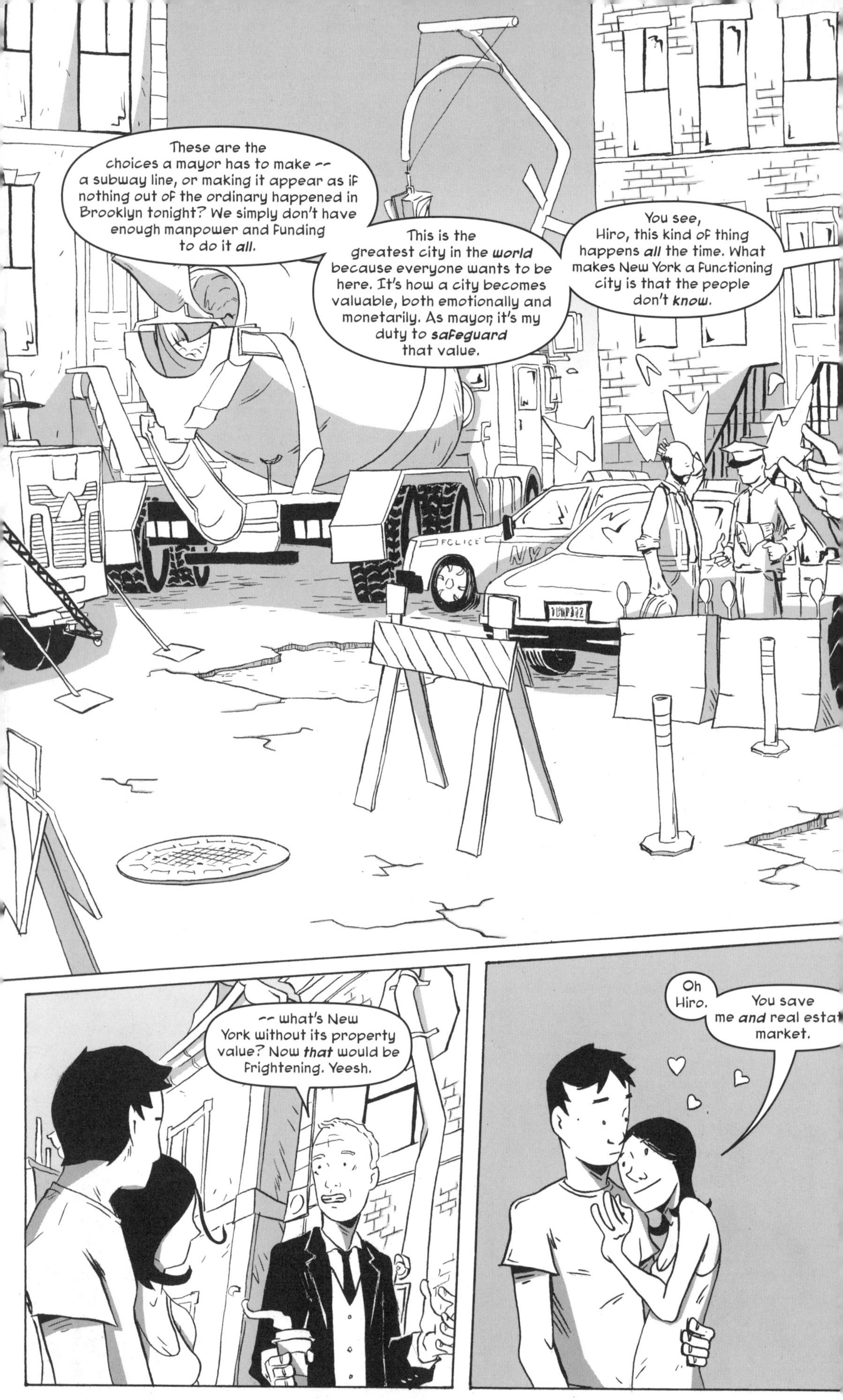
These are the choices a mayor has to make -- a subway line, or making it appear as if nothing out of the ordinary happened in Brooklyn tonight? We simply don't have enough manpower and funding to do it *all*.
This is the greatest city in the *world* because everyone wants to be here. It's how a city becomes valuable, both emotionally and monetarily. As mayor, it's my duty to *safeguard* that value.
You see, Hiro, this kind of thing happens *all* the time. What makes New York a functioning city is that the people don't *know*.
POLICE
NYP
-- what's New York without its property value? Now *that* would be frightening. Yeesh.
Oh Hiro.
You save me *and* real estat market.

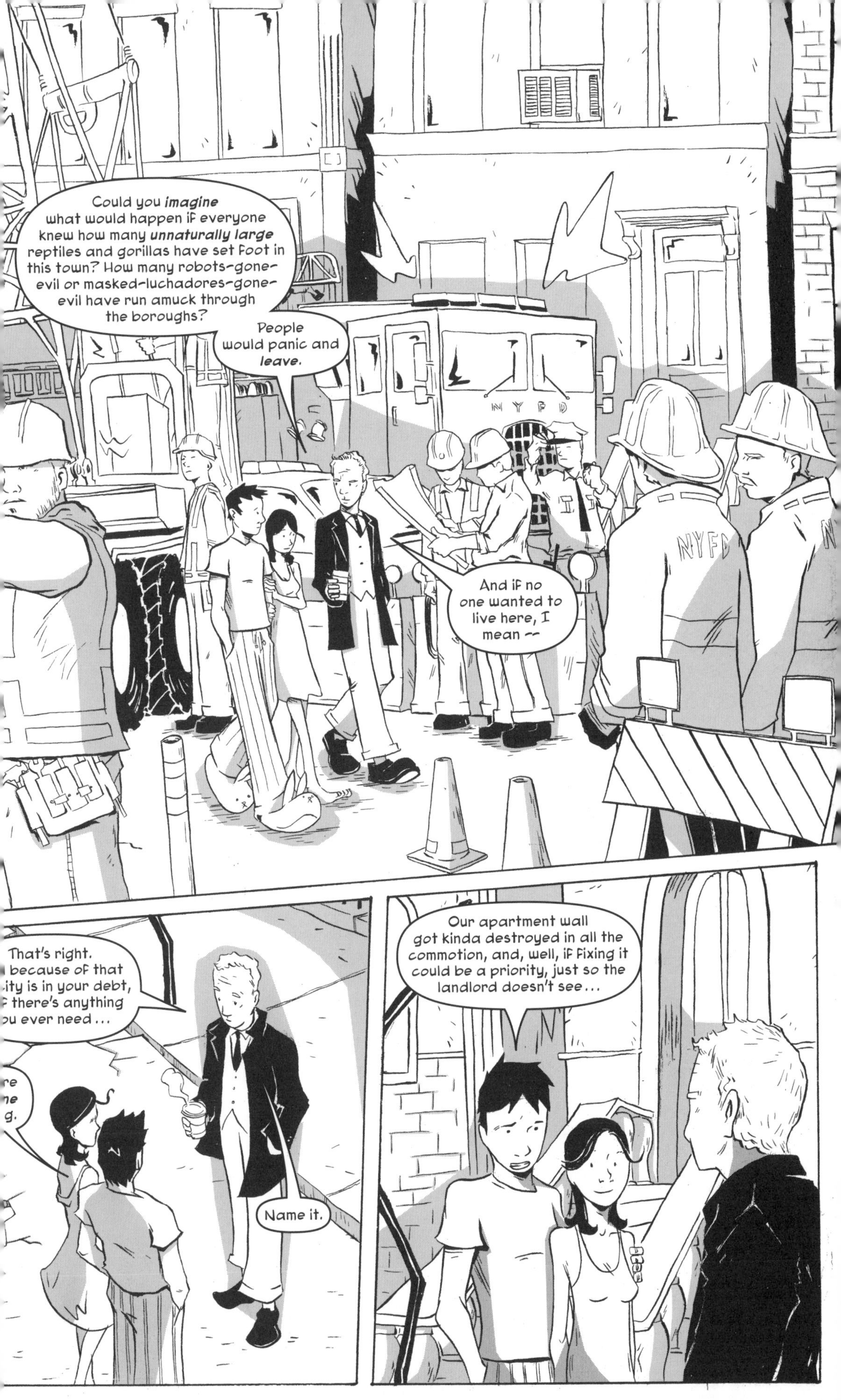

Could you *imagine* what would happen if everyone knew how many *unnaturally large* reptiles and gorillas have set foot in this town? How many robots-gone-evil or masked-luchadores-gone-evil have run amuck through the boroughs?
People would panic and *leave.*
And if no one wanted to live here, I mean --
That's right.
because of that
ity is in your debt,
there's anything
ou ever need...
Name it.
Our apartment wall got kinda destroyed in all the commotion, and, well, if fixing it could be a priority, just so the landlord doesn't see...
NYFD

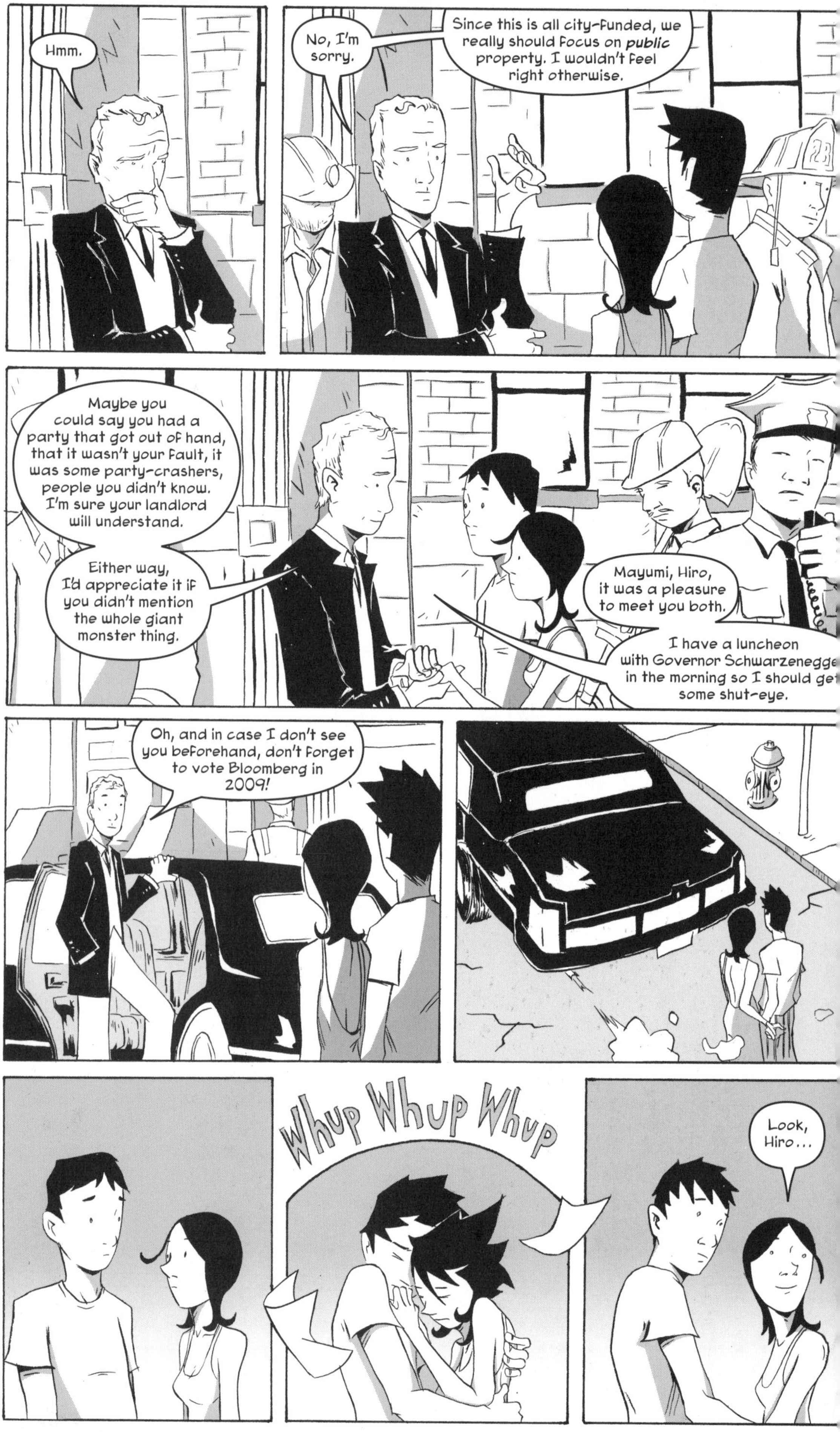
Hmm.
No, I'm sorry.
Since this is all city-funded, we really should focus on *public* property. I wouldn't feel right otherwise.
Maybe you could say you had a party that got out of hand, that it wasn't your fault, it was some party-crashers, people you didn't know. I'm sure your landlord will understand.
Either way, I'd appreciate it if you didn't mention the whole giant monster thing.
Mayumi, Hiro, it was a pleasure to meet you both.
I have a luncheon with Governor Schwarzenegge in the morning so I should get some shut-eye.
Oh, and in case I don't see you beforehand, don't forget to vote Bloomberg in 2009!
Whup Whup Whup
Look, Hiro...

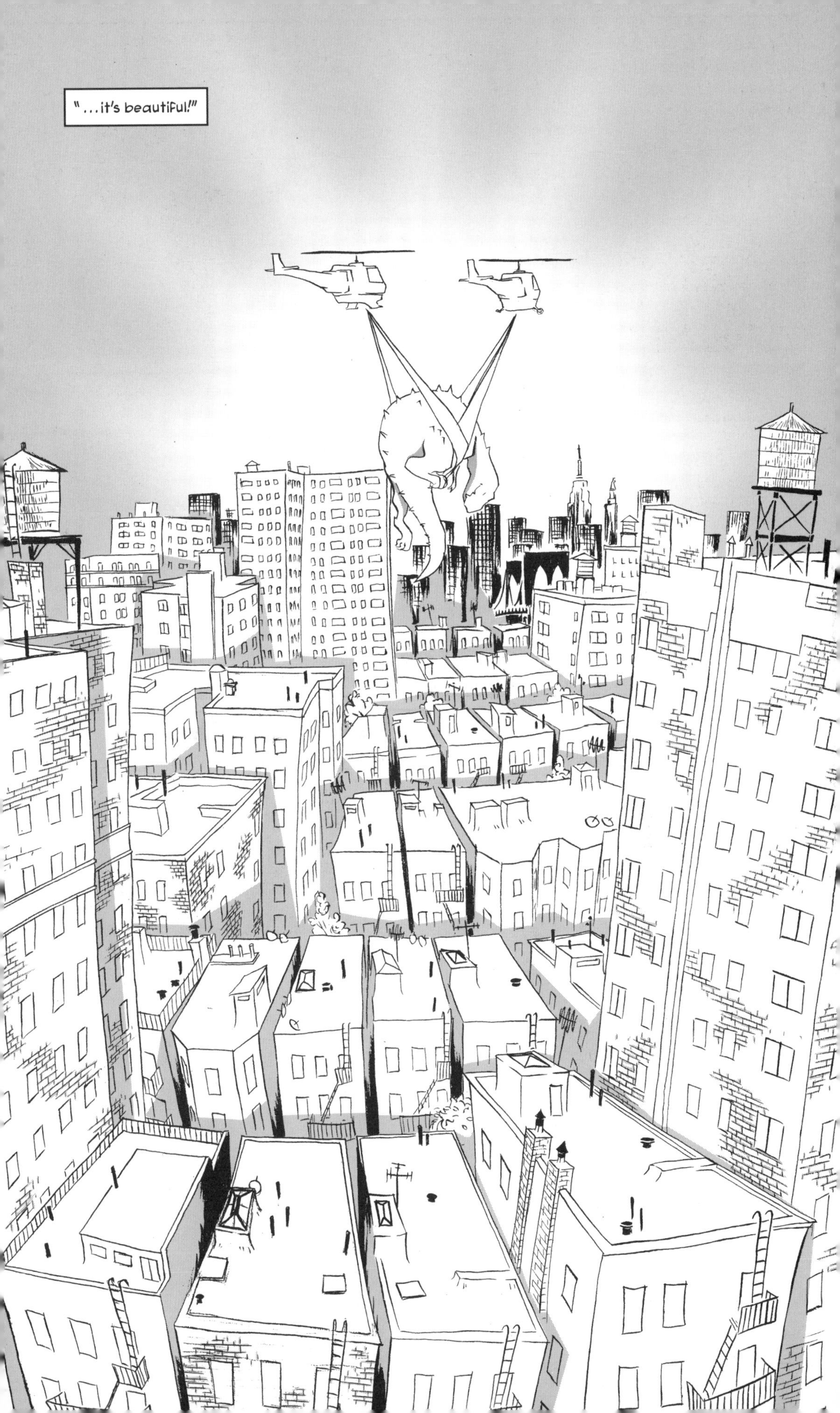
"...it's beautiful!"

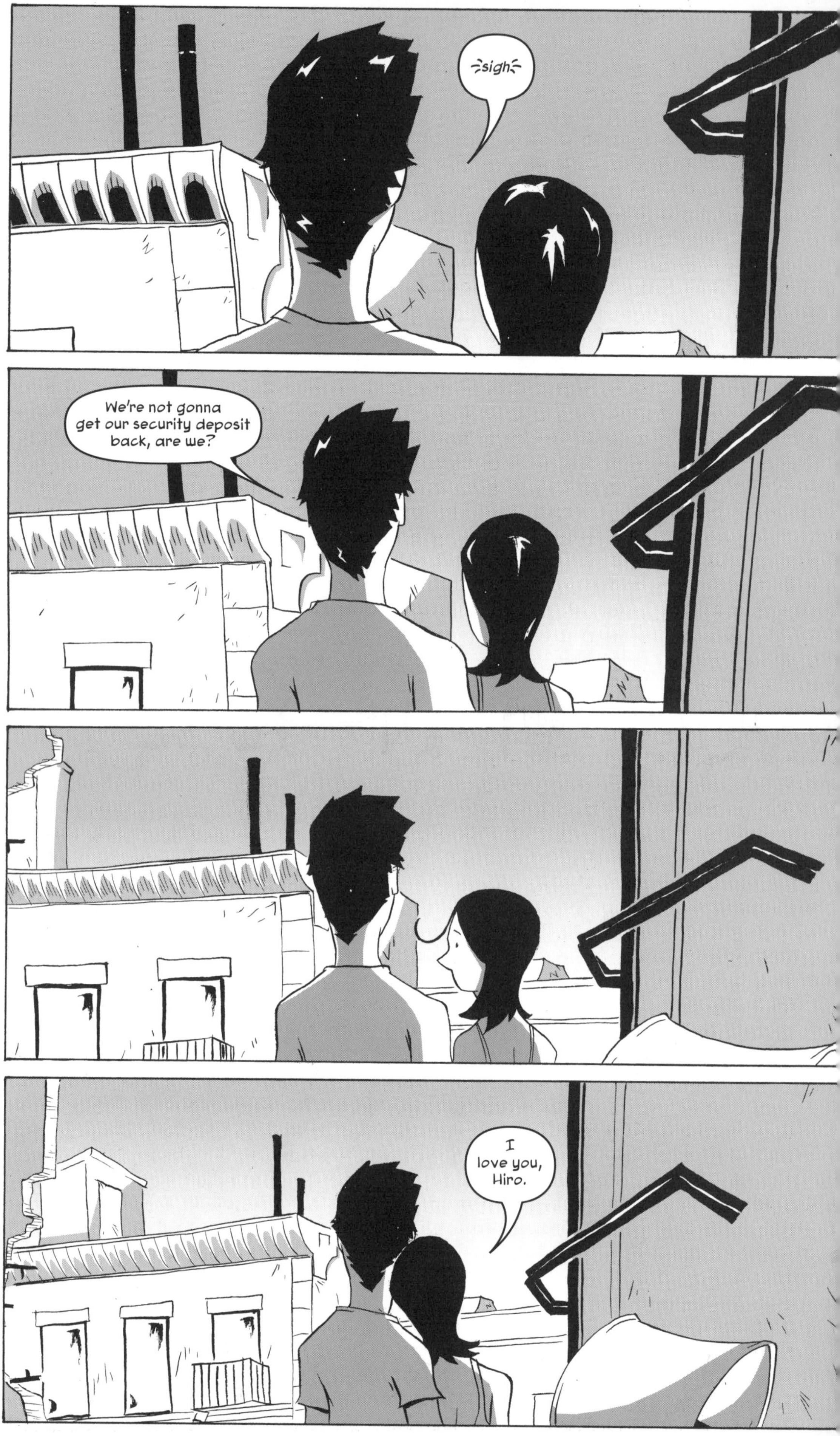
sigh
We're not gonna get our security deposit back, are we?
I love you, Hiro.

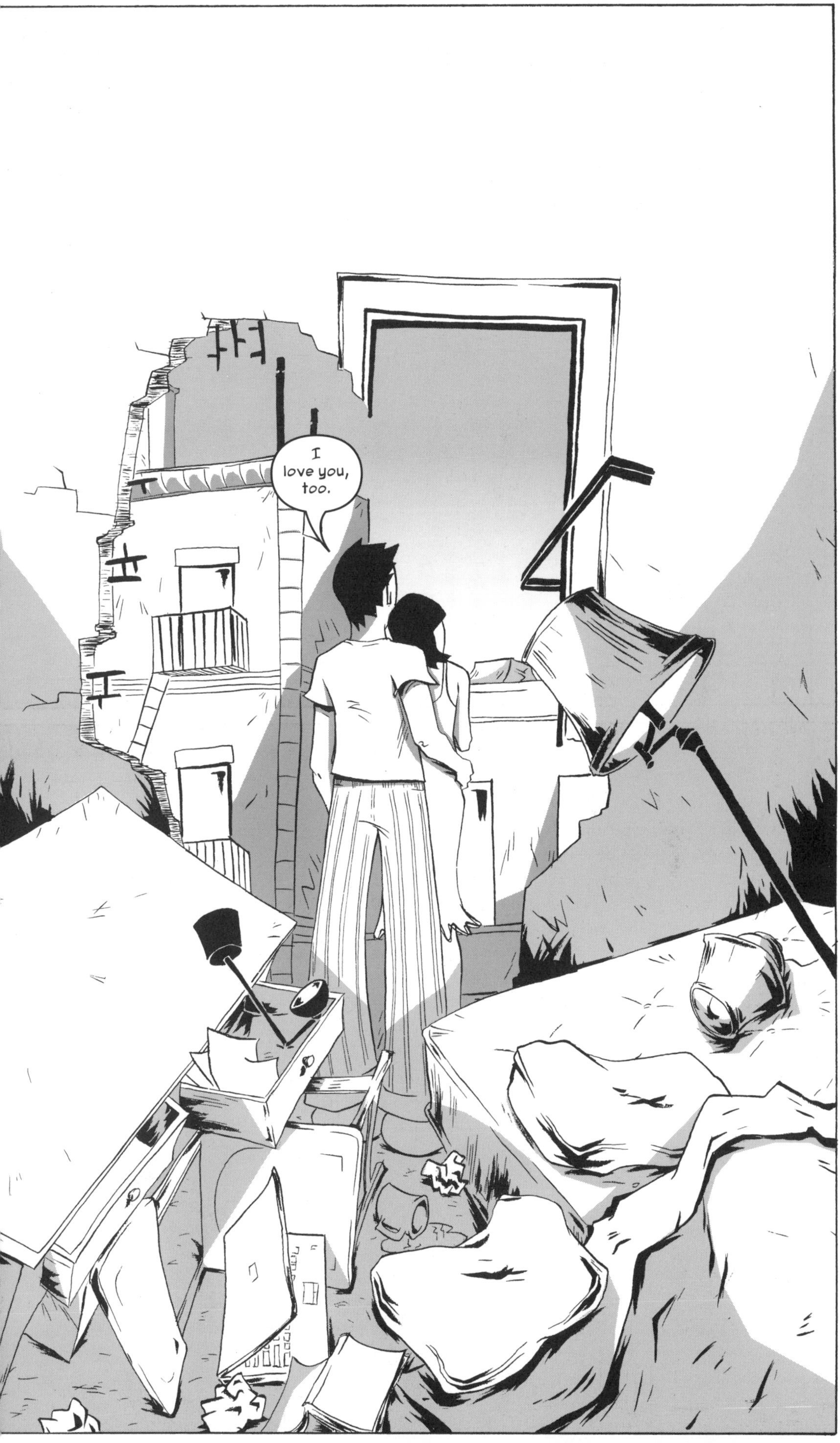
I love you, too.

伊勢えびの操業

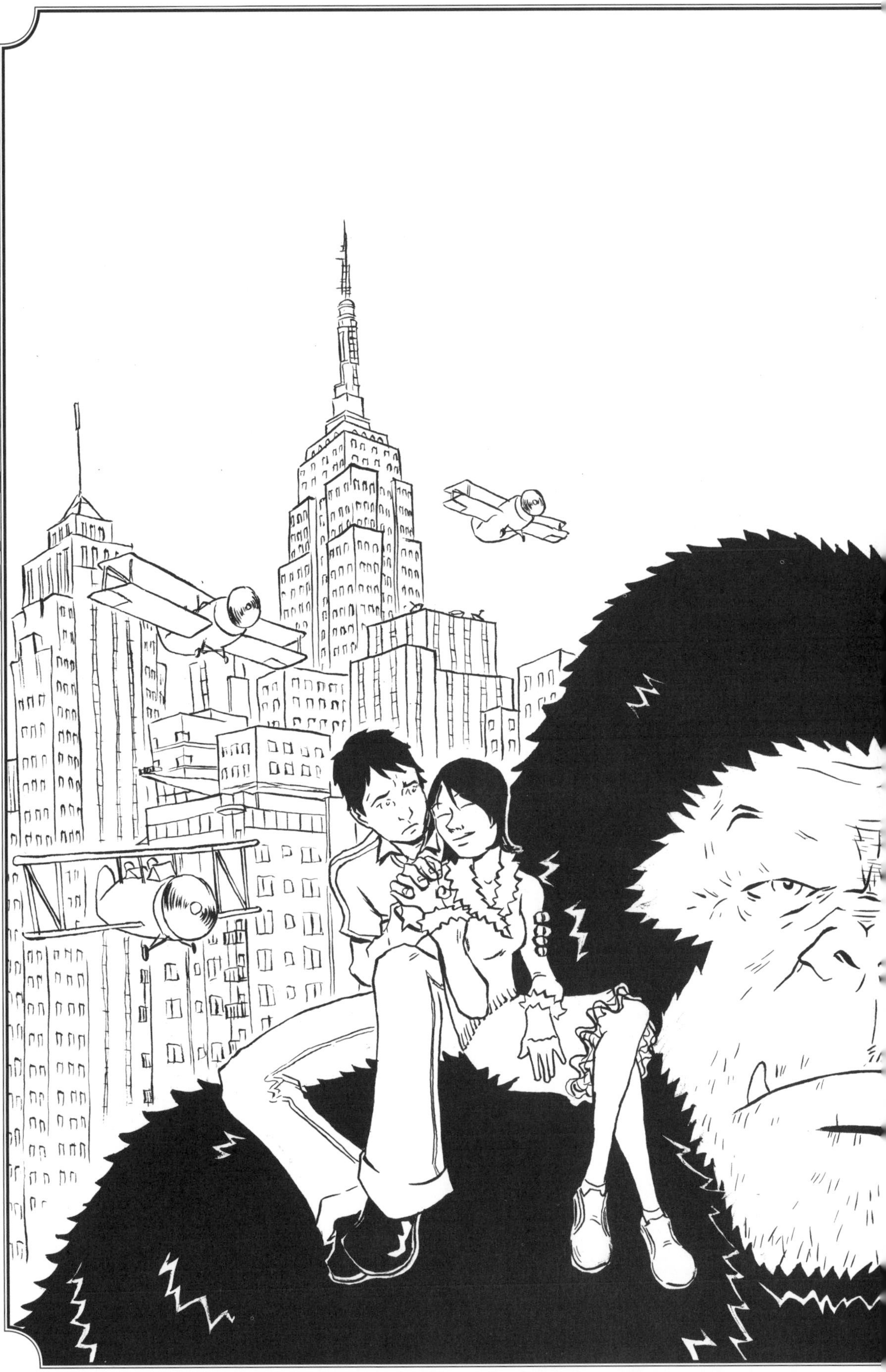

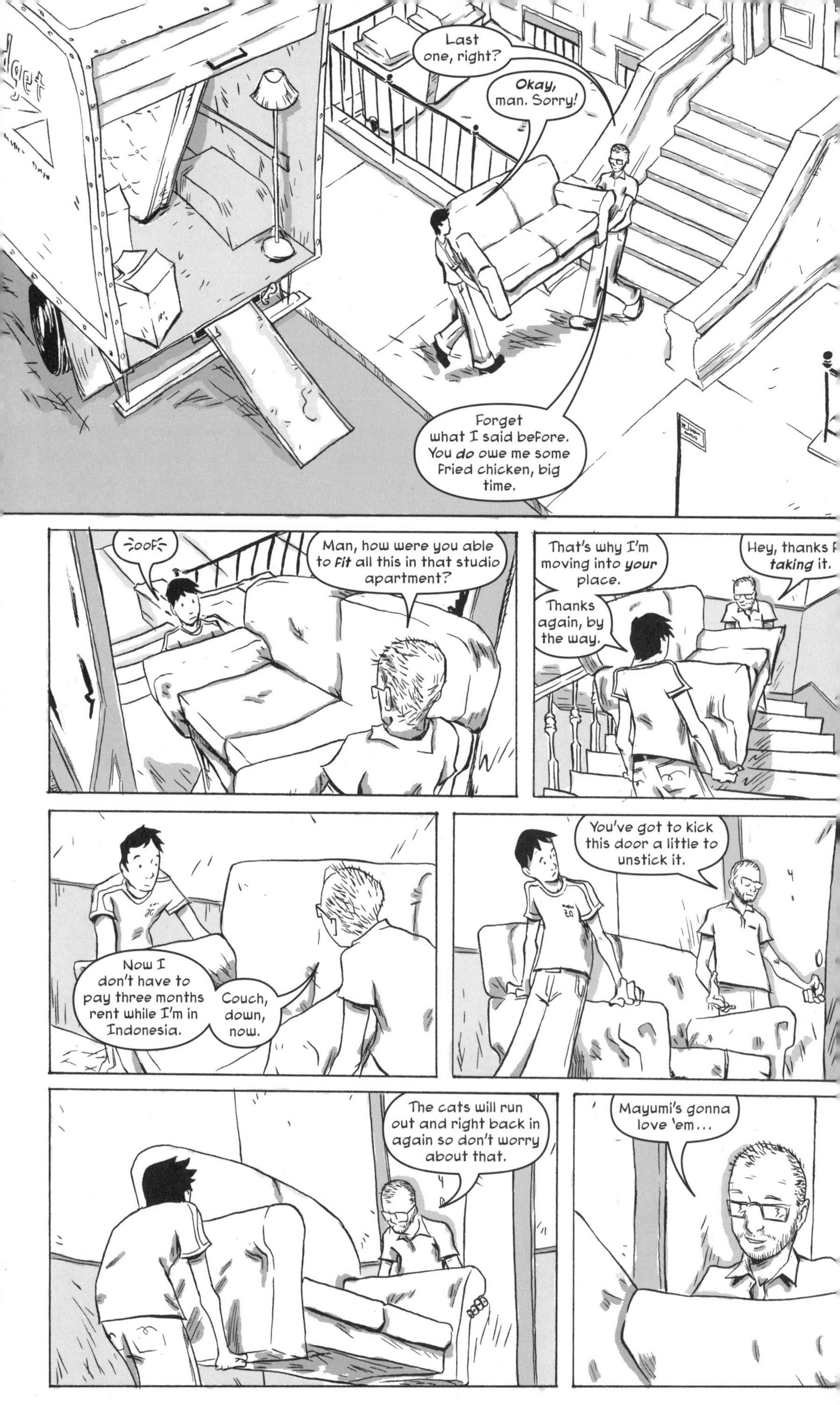
Last one, right?
Okay, man. Sorry!
Forget what I said before. You *do* owe me some fried chicken, big time.
oof
Man, how were you able to *fit* all this in that studio apartment?
That's why I'm moving into *your* place.
Thanks again, by the way.
Hey, thanks
taking it.
Now I don't have to pay three months rent while I'm in Indonesia.
Couch, down, now.
You've got to kick this door a little to unstick it.
The cats will run out and right back in again so don't worry about that.
Mayumi's gonna love 'em...

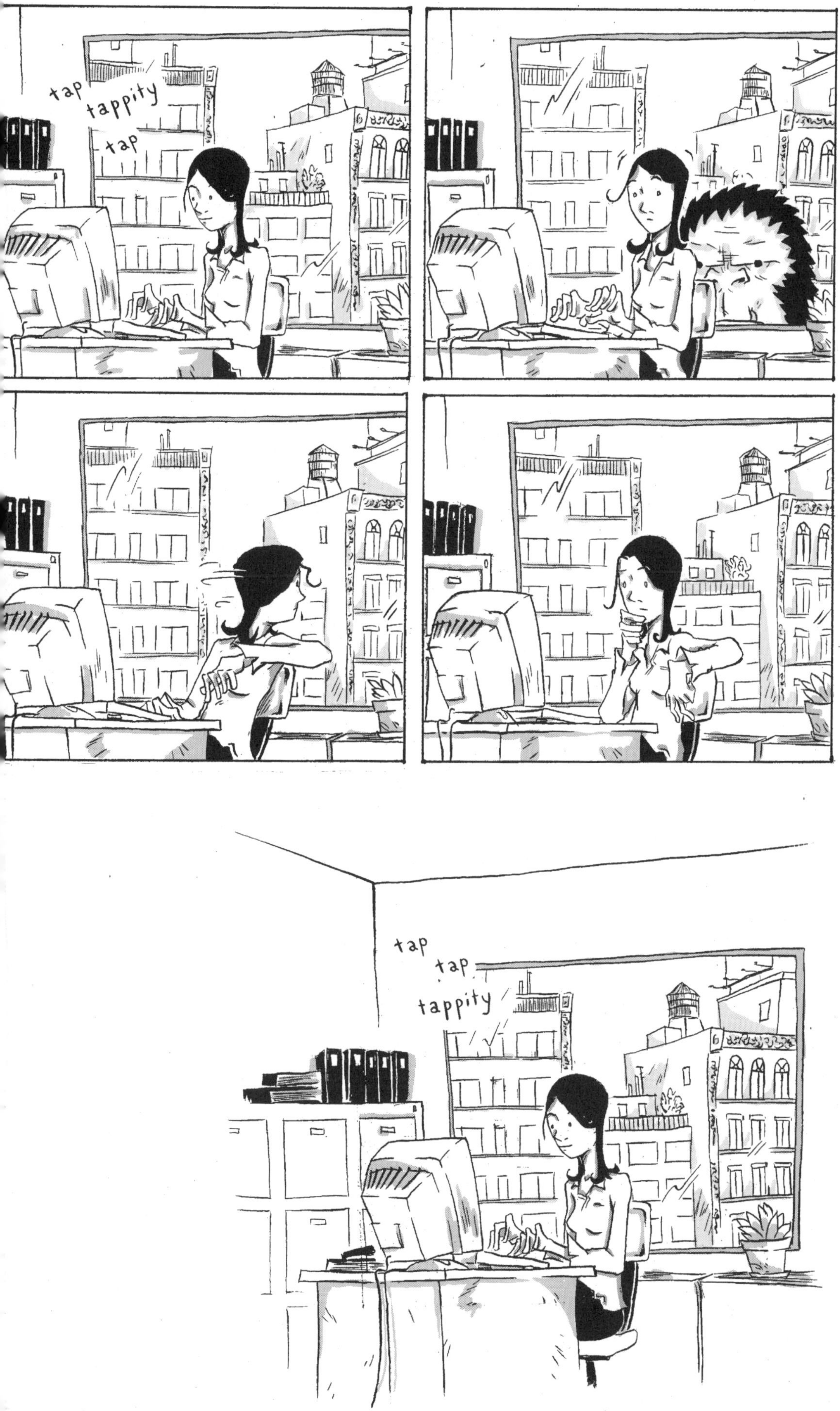
tap
tappity
tap
tap
tap
tappity

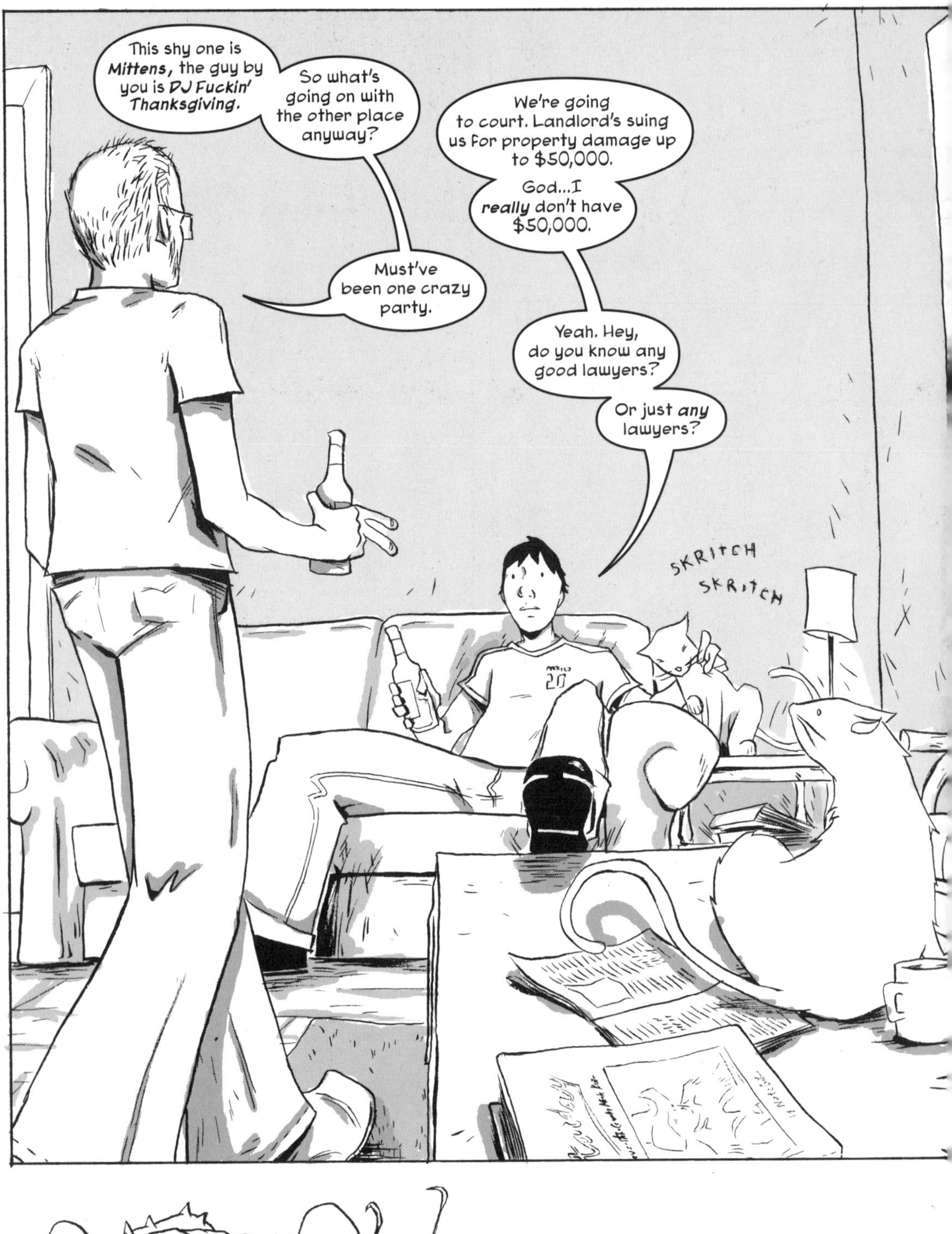

This shy one is *Mittens*, the guy by you is *DJ Fuckin' Thanksgiving.*
So what's going on with the other place anyway?
We're going to court. Landlord's suing us for property damage up to $50,000.
God...I *really* don't have $50,000.
Must've been one crazy party.
Yeah. Hey, do you know any good lawyers?
Or just *any* lawyers?
SKRITCH
SKRITCH

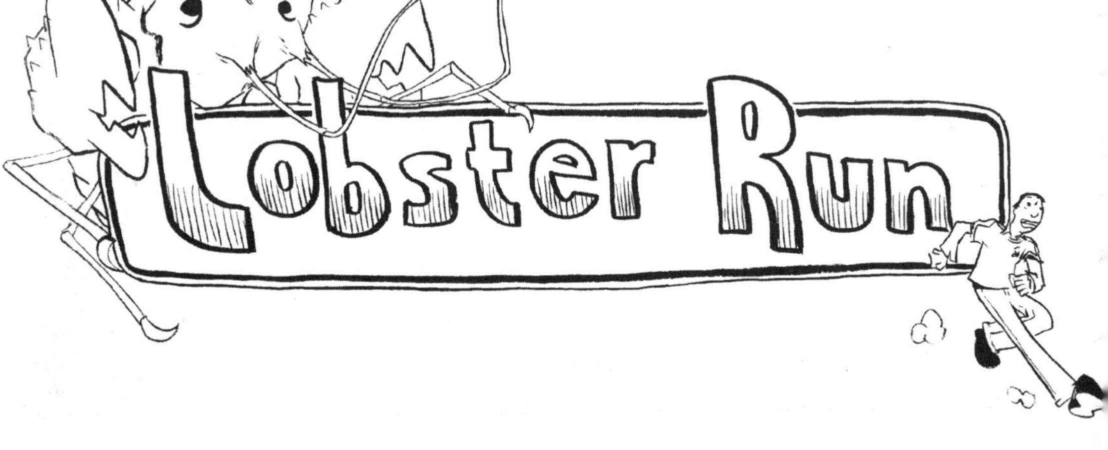

Lobster Run

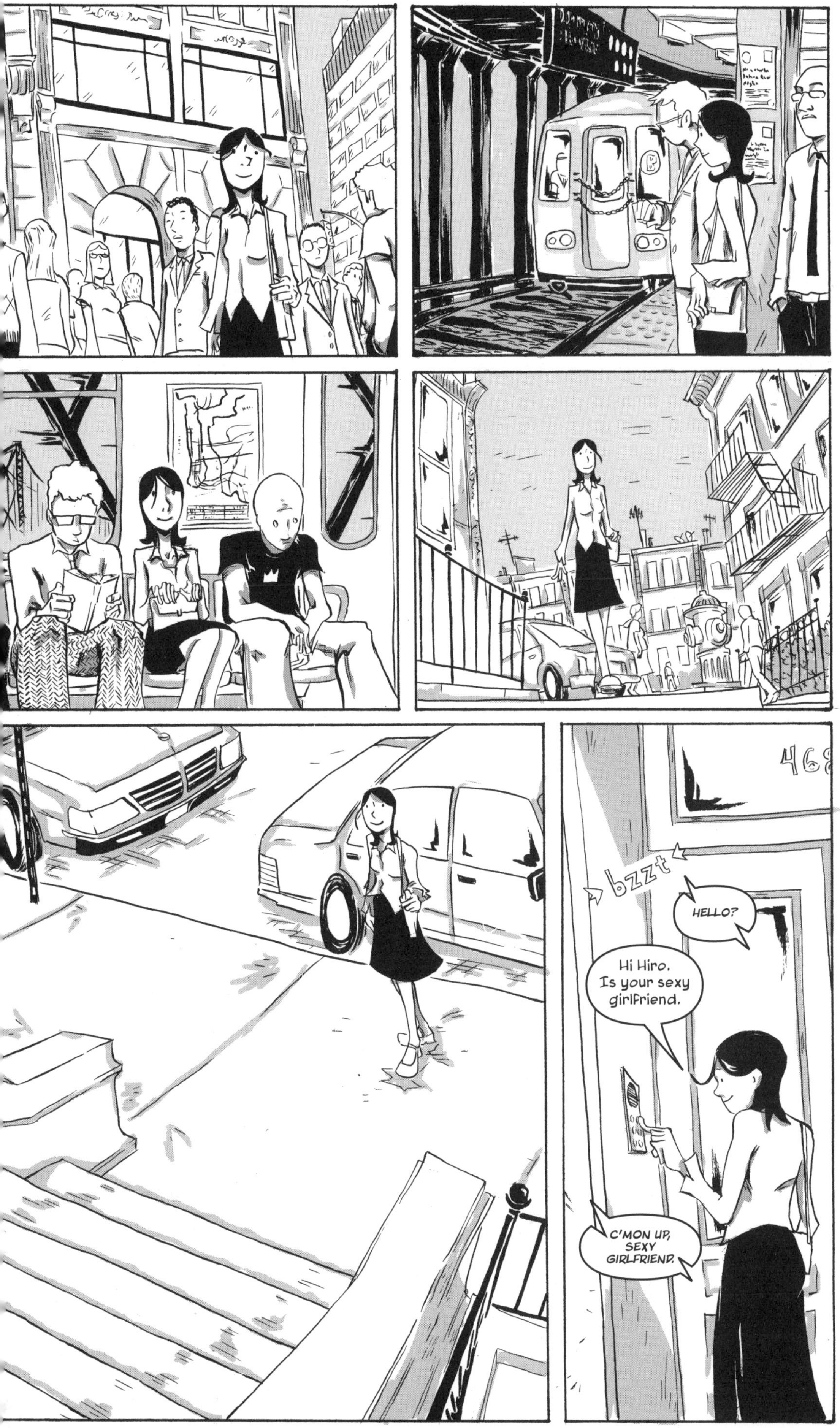

468
bzzt
HELLO?
Hi Hiro. Is your sexy girlfriend.
C'MON UP, SEXY GIRLFRIEND.

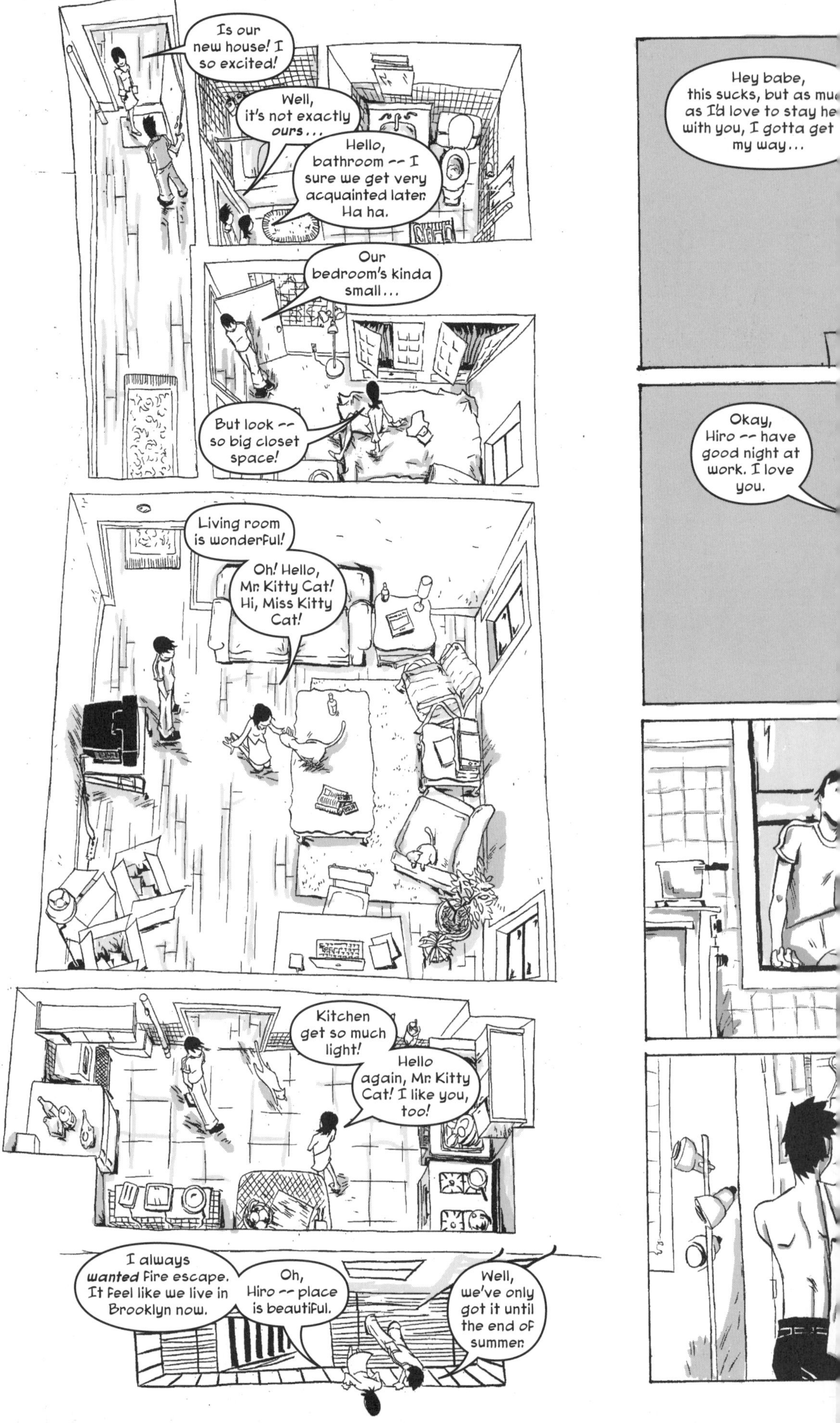
Is our new house! I so excited!
Well, it's not exactly *ours*...
Hello, bathroom -- I sure we get very acquainted later. Ha ha.
Our bedroom's kinda small...
But look -- so big closet space!
Living room is wonderful!
Oh! Hello, Mr. Kitty Cat! Hi, Miss Kitty Cat!
Kitchen get so much light!
Hello again, Mr. Kitty Cat! I like you, too!
I always *wanted* fire escape. It feel like we live in Brooklyn now.
Oh, Hiro -- place is beautiful.
Well, we've only got it until the end of summer.
Okay, Hiro -- have good night at work. I love you.

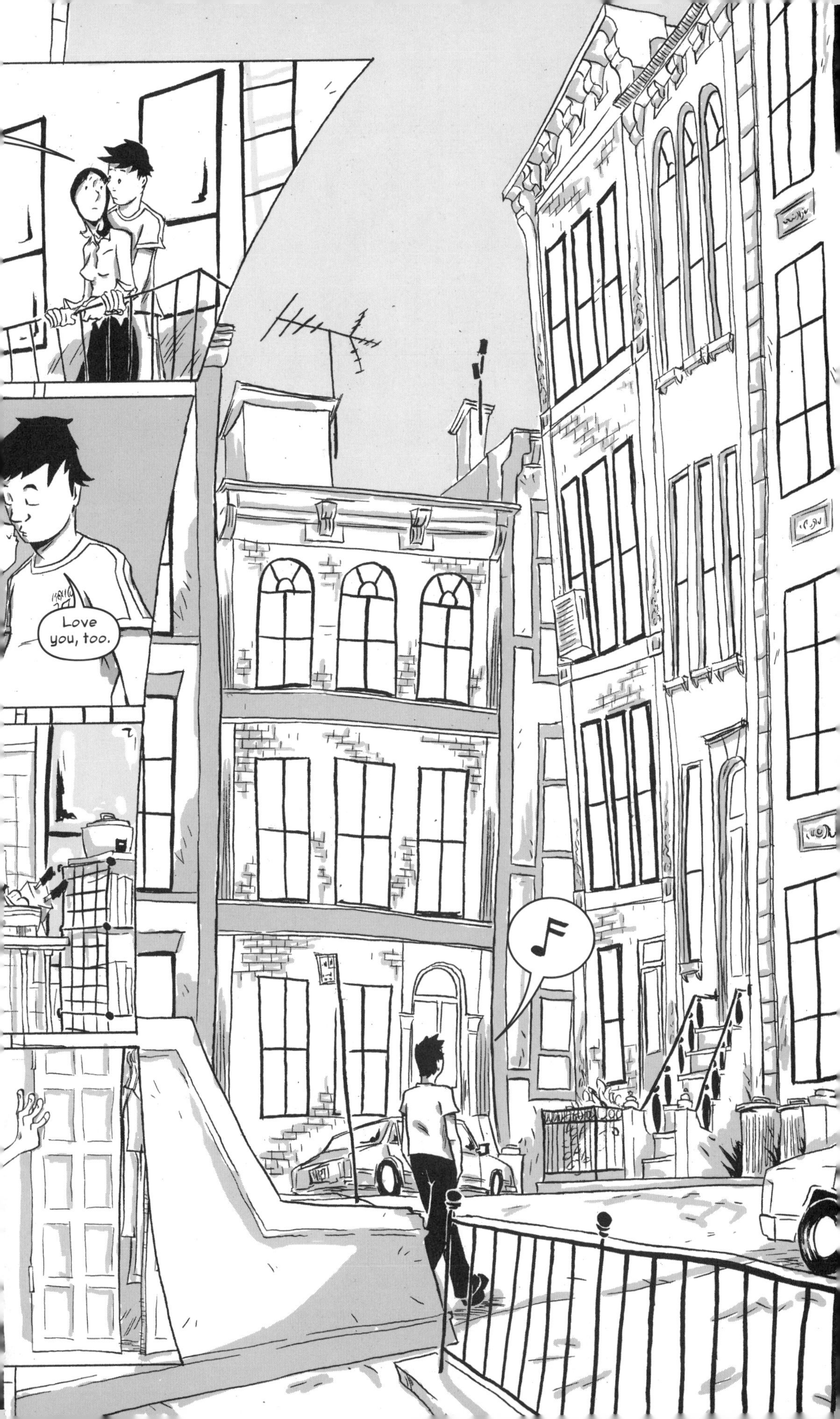
Love you, too.

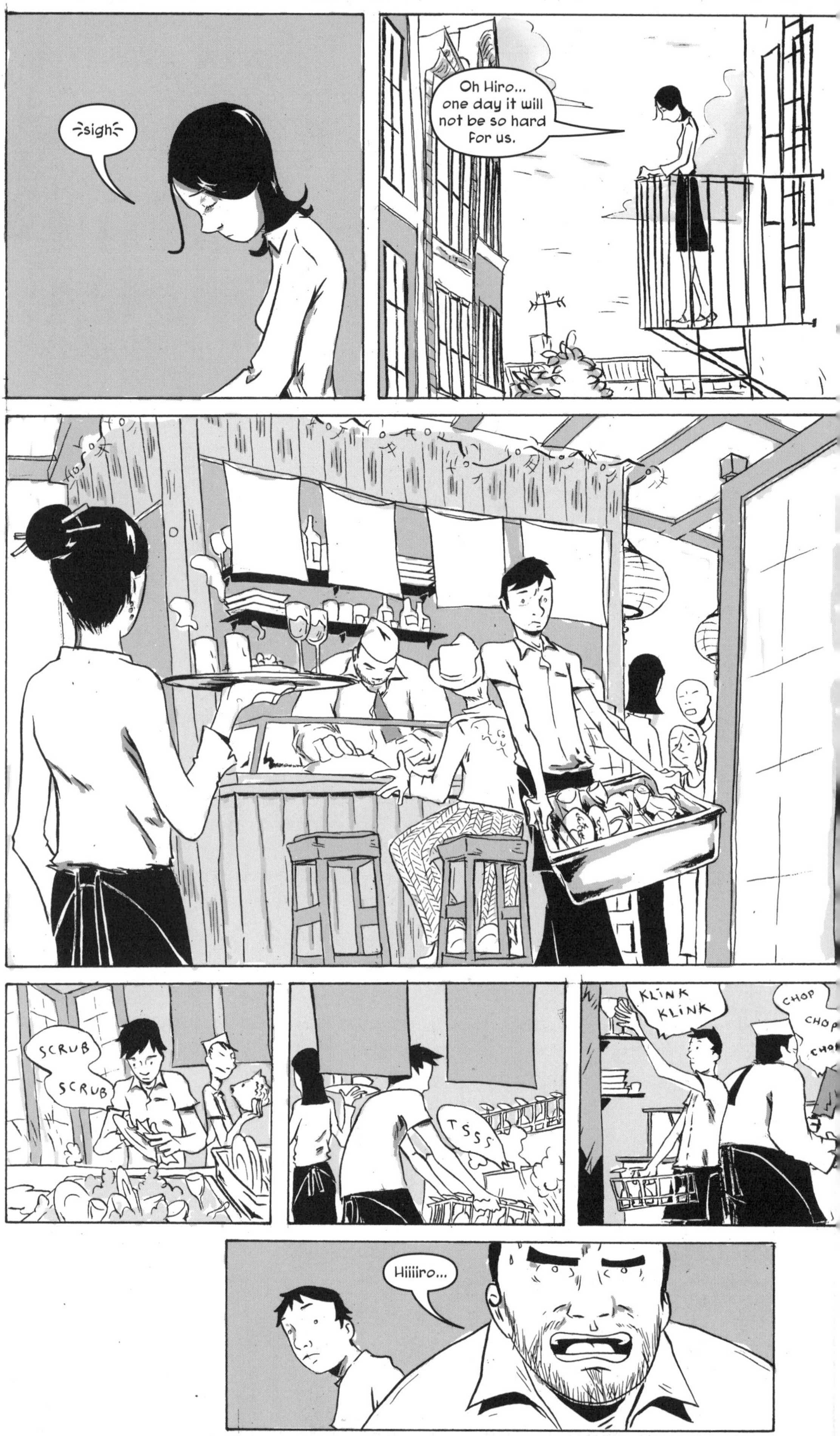
sigh
Oh Hiro... one day it will not be so hard for us.
SCRUB SCRUB
TSSS
KLINK KLINK
CHOP
CHOP
Hiiiiro...

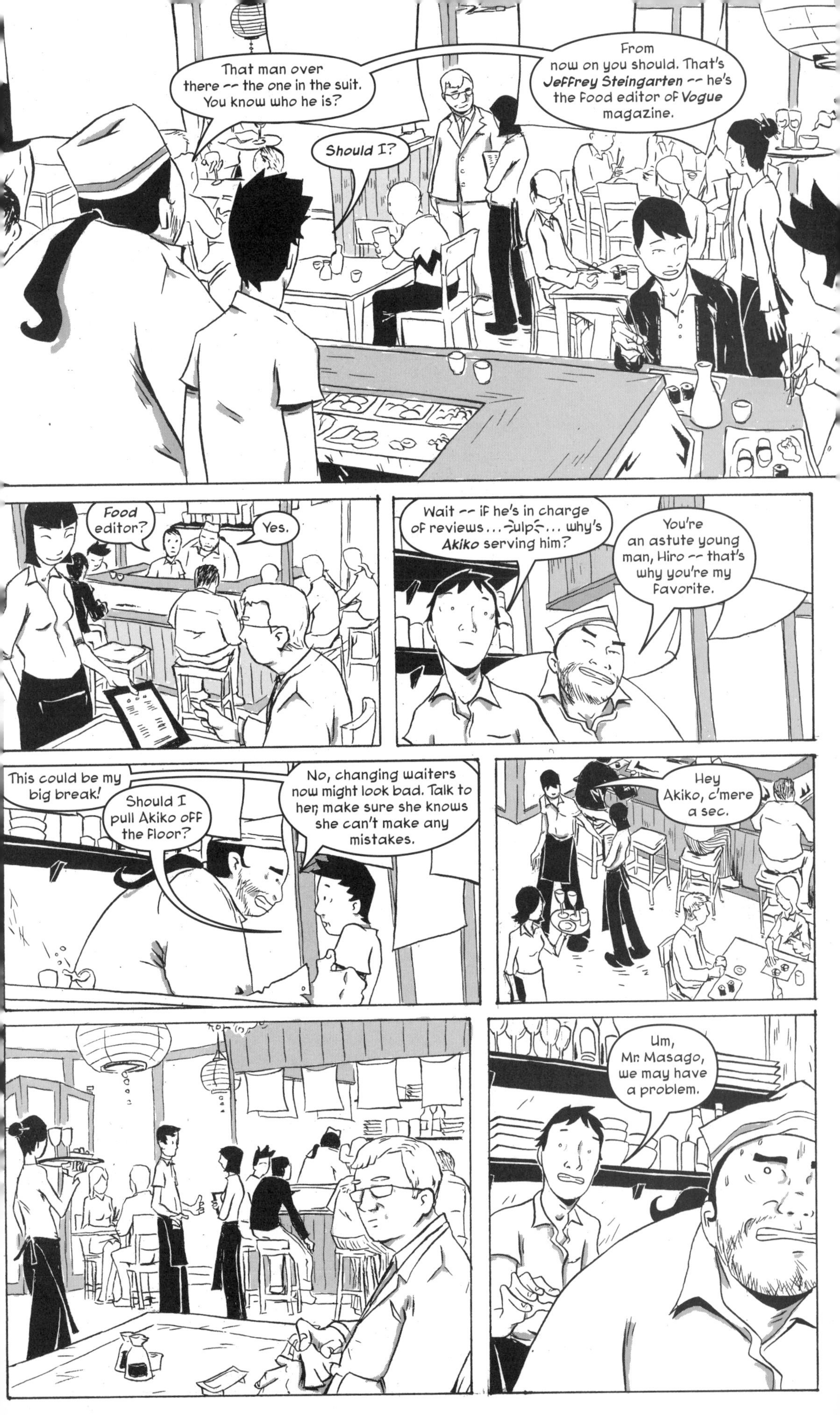
That man over there -- the one in the suit. You know who he is?
Should I?
From now on you should. That's Jeffrey Steingarten -- he's the food editor of Vogue magazine.
Food editor?
Yes.
Wait -- if he's in charge of reviews... gulp... why's Akiko serving him?
You're an astute young man, Hiro -- that's why you're my favorite.
This could be my big break!
Should I pull Akiko off the floor?
No, changing waiters now might look bad. Talk to her, make sure she knows she can't make any mistakes.
Hey Akiko, c'mere a sec.
Um, Mr. Masago, we may have a problem.

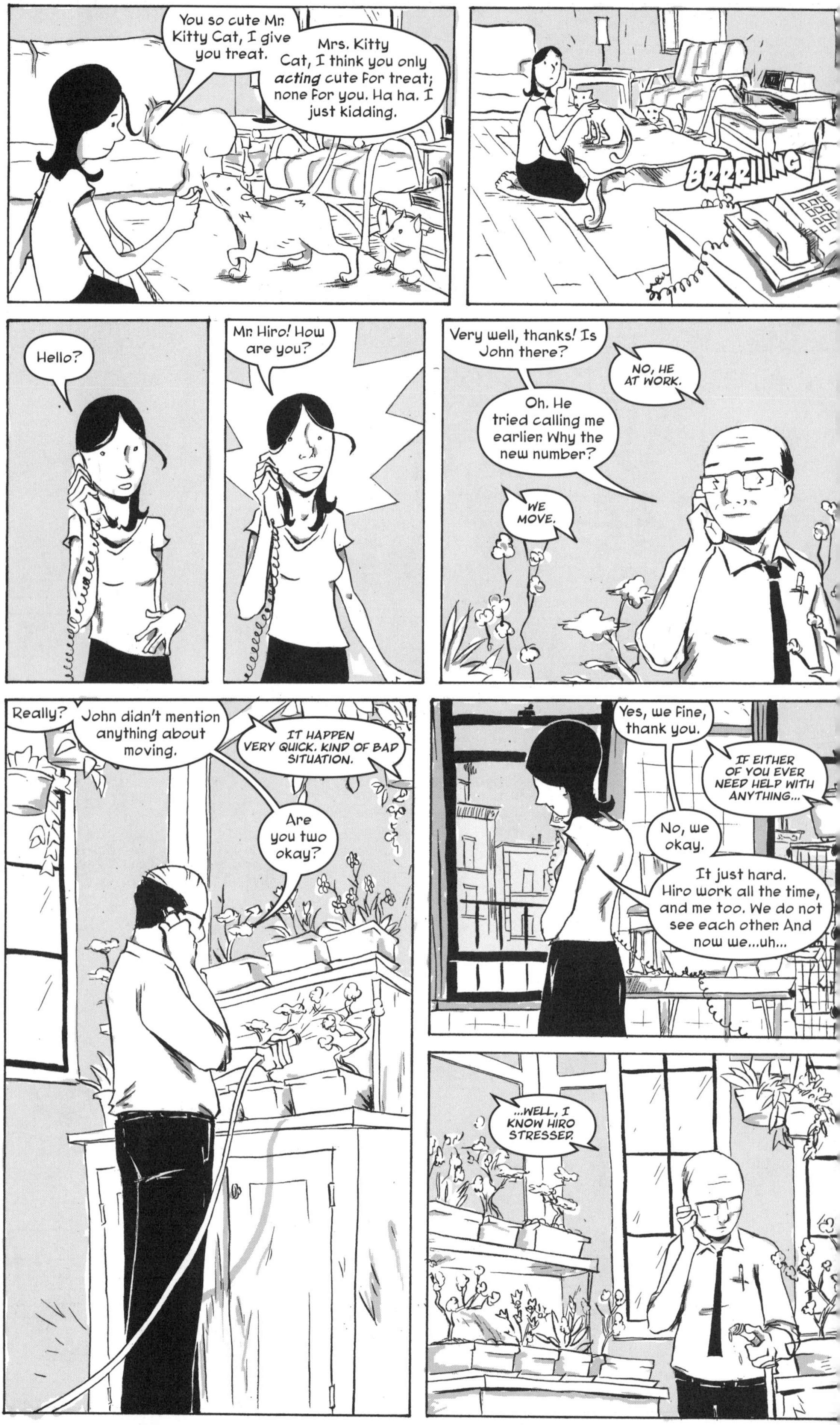

You so cute Mr. Kitty Cat, I give you treat.
Mrs. Kitty Cat, I think you only *acting* cute for treat; none for you. Ha ha. I just kidding.
BRRRIIING
Hello?
Mr. Hiro! How are you?
Very well, thanks! Is John there?
NO, HE AT WORK.
Oh. He tried calling me earlier. Why the new number?
WE MOVE.
Really?
John didn't mention anything about moving.
IT HAPPEN VERY QUICK. KIND OF BAD SITUATION.
Are you two okay?
Yes, we fine, thank you.
IF EITHER OF YOU EVER NEED HELP WITH ANYTHING...
No, we okay.
It just hard. Hiro work all the time, and me too. We do not see each other. And now we...uh...
...WELL, I KNOW HIRO STRESSED.

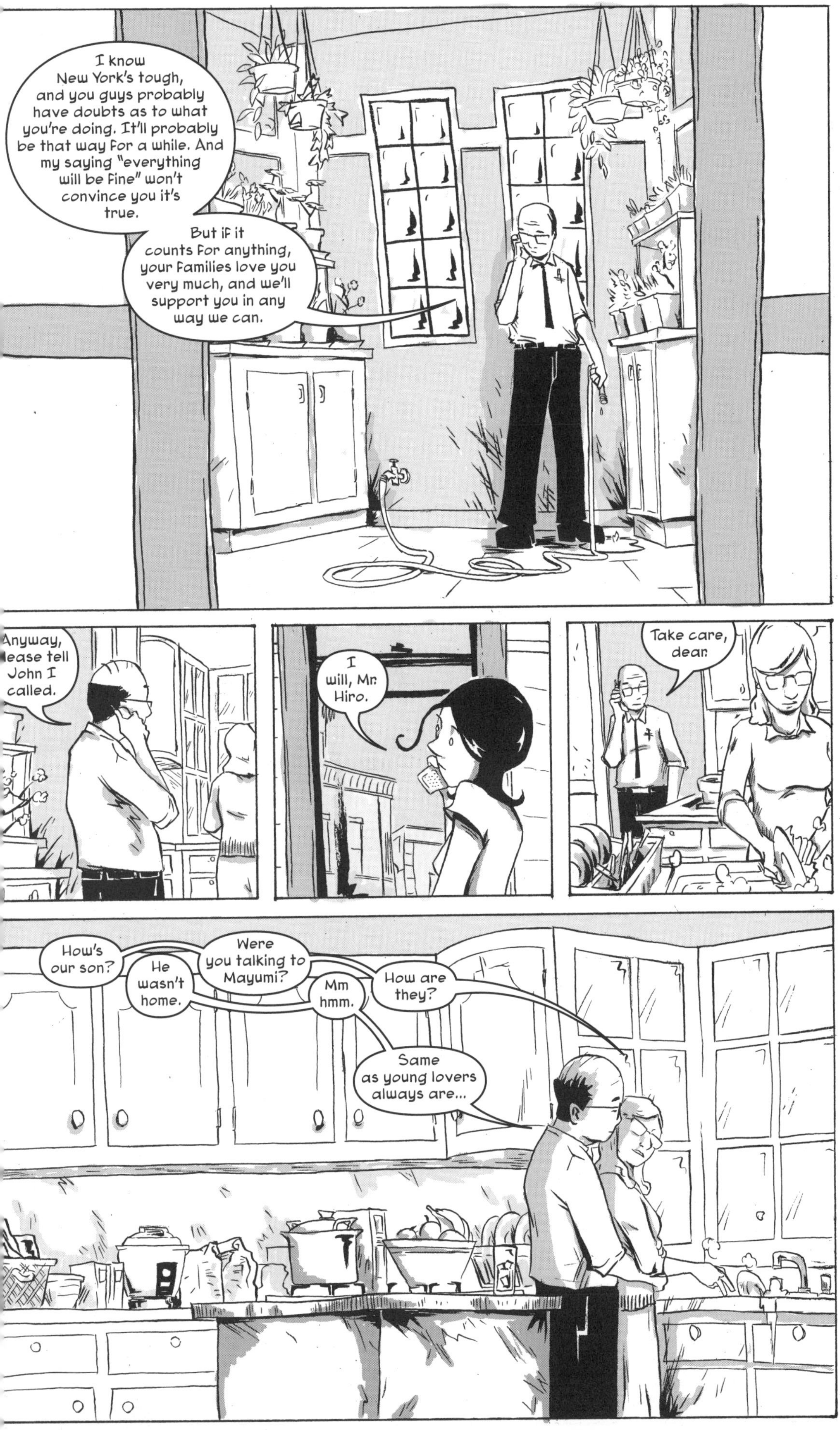
I know New York's tough, and you guys probably have doubts as to what you're doing. It'll probably be that way for a while. And my saying "everything will be fine" won't convince you it's true.
But if it counts for anything, your families love you very much, and we'll support you in any way we can.
Anyway, ease tell John I called.
I will, Mr. Hiro.
Take care, dear.
How's our son?
He wasn't home.
Were you talking to Mayumi?
Mm hmm.
How are they?
Same as young lovers always are...

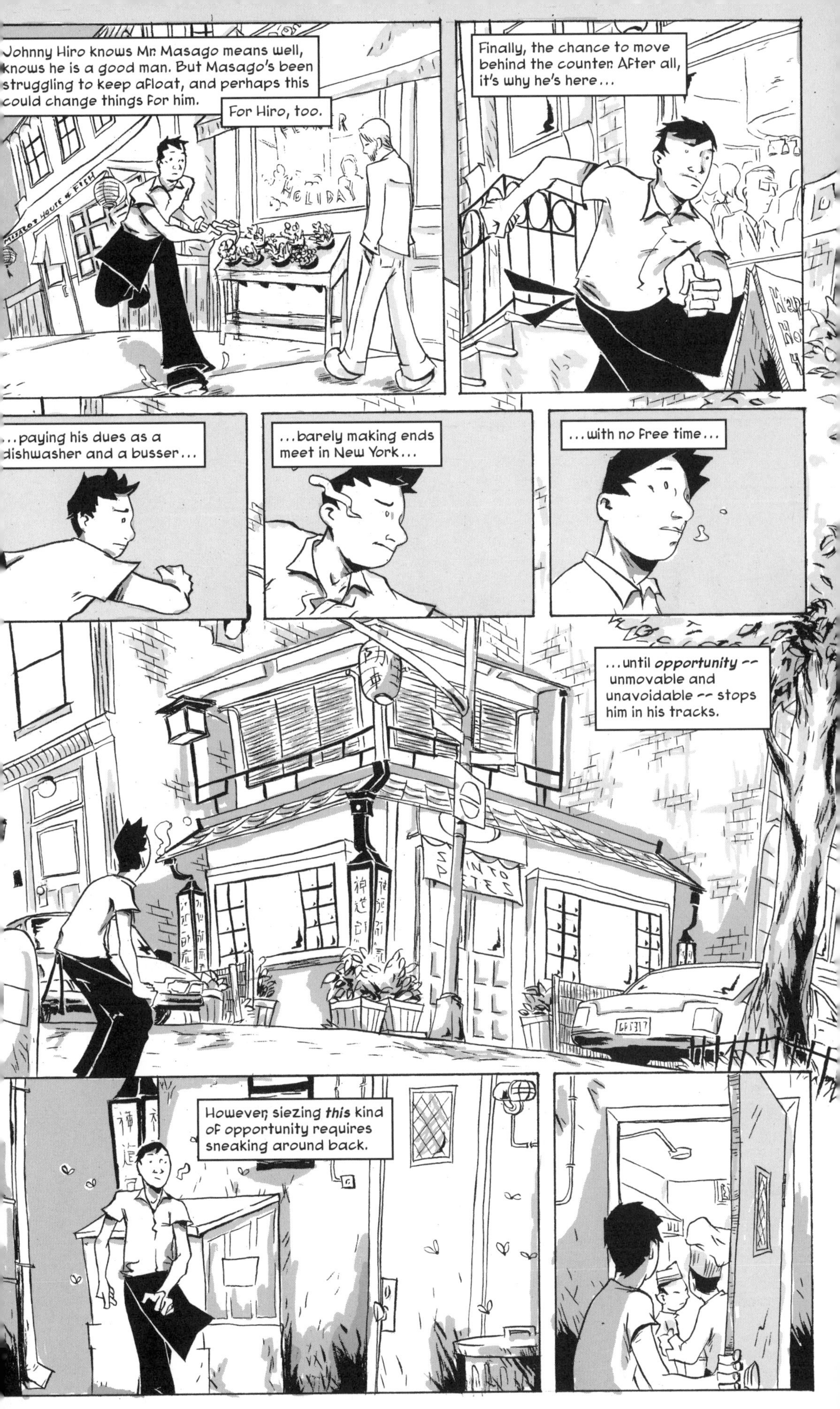
Johnny Hiro knows Mr. Masago means well, knows he is a good man. But Masago's been struggling to keep afloat, and perhaps this could change things for him.
For Hiro, too.
HOLIDAY
Finally, the chance to move behind the counter. After all, it's why he's here...
...paying his dues as a dishwasher and a busser...
...barely making ends meet in New York...
...with no free time...
...until *opportunity* -- unmovable and unavoidable -- stops him in his tracks.
However, siezing *this* kind of opportunity requires sneaking around back.

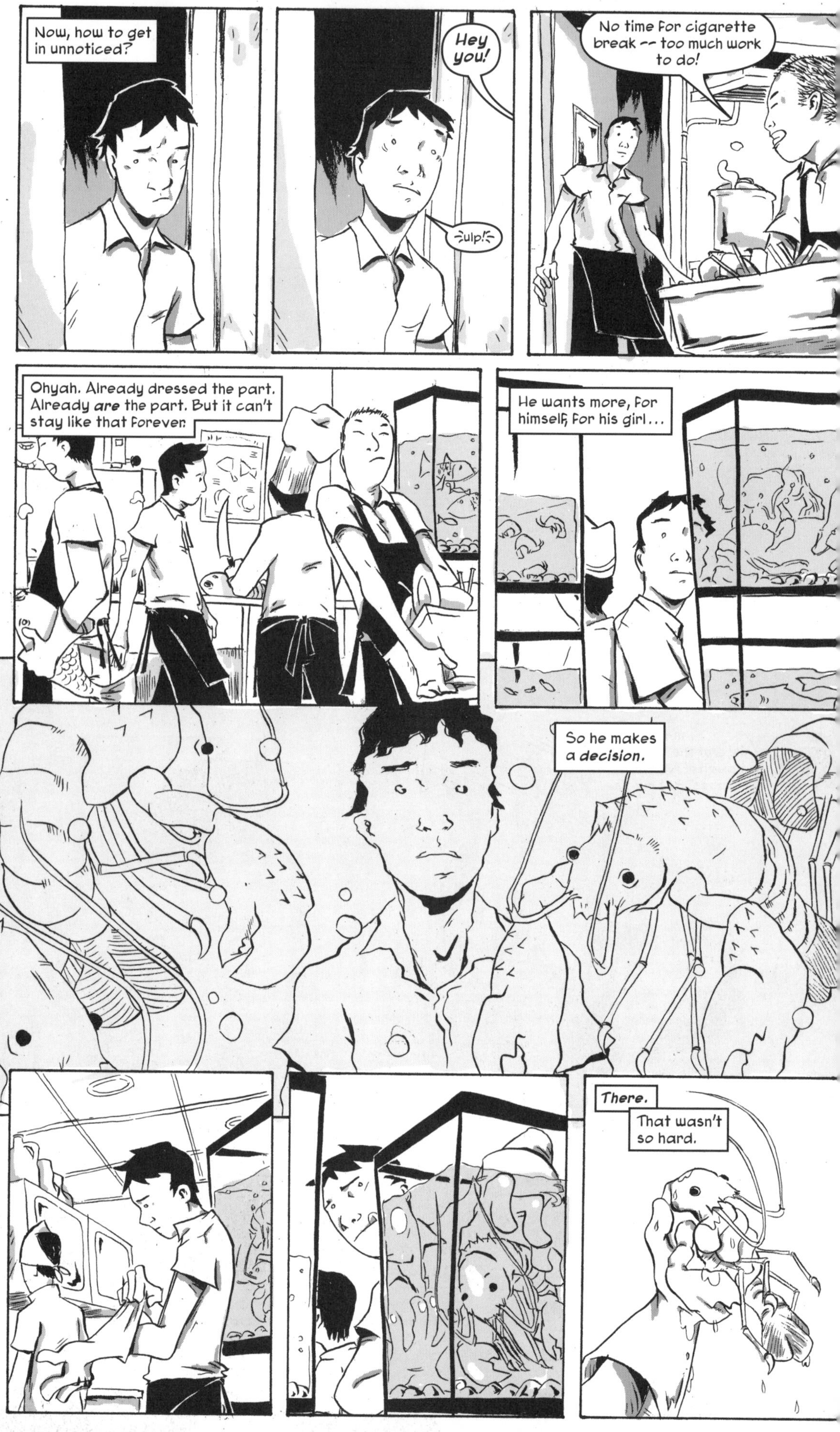

Now, how to get in unnoticed?
Hey you!
-ulp!-
No time for cigarette break -- too much work to do!
Ohyah. Already dressed the part. Already *are* the part. But it can't stay like that forever.
He wants more, for himself, for his girl...
So he makes a *decision.*
There.
That wasn't so hard.

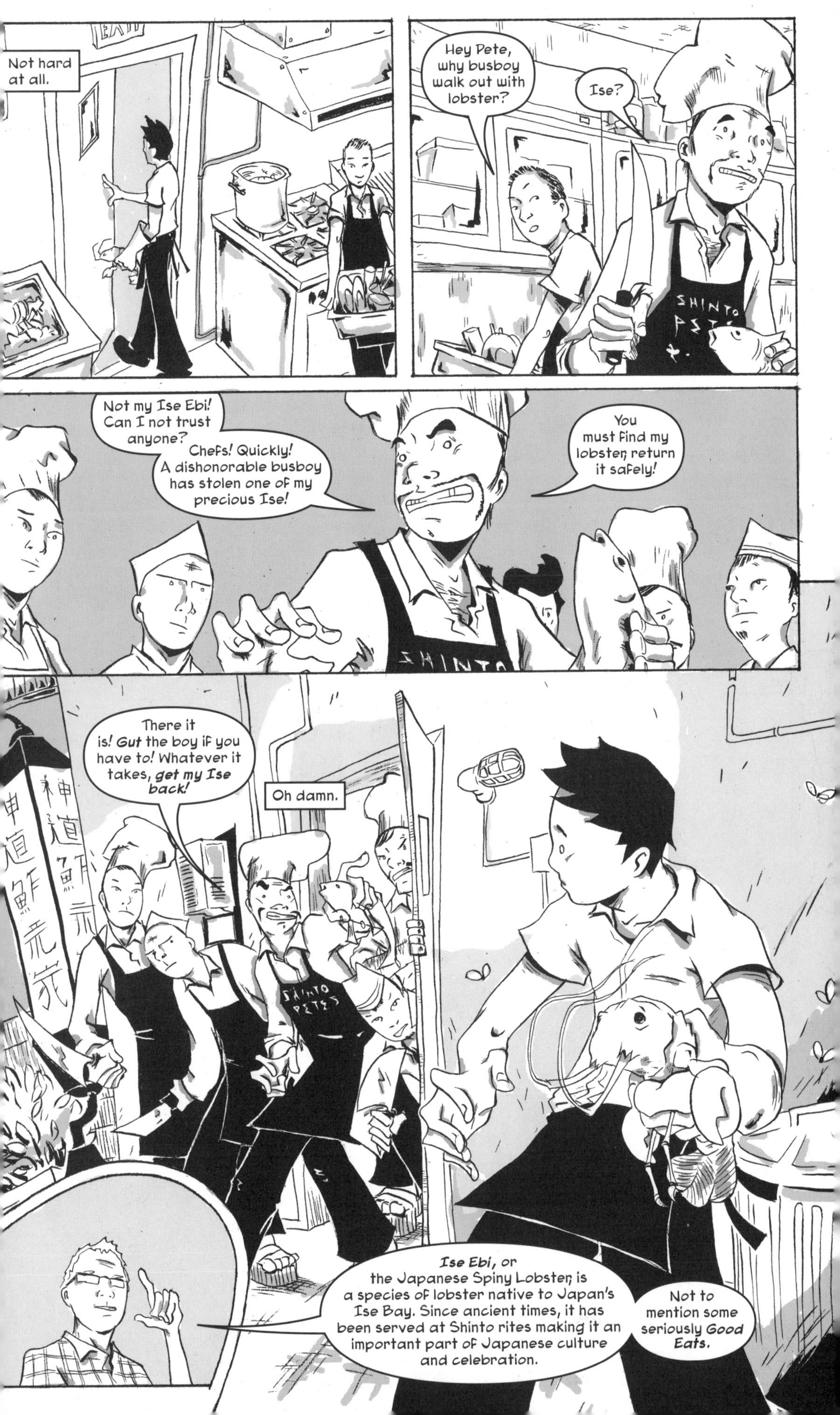
Not hard at all.
Hey Pete, why busboy walk out with lobster?
Ise?
SHINTO PETE'S
Not my Ise Ebi! Can I not trust anyone?
Chefs! Quickly! A dishonorable busboy has stolen one of my precious Ise!
You must find my lobster, return it safely!
There it is! *Gut* the boy if you have to! Whatever it takes, *get my Ise back!*
Oh damn.
SHINTO PETES
Ise Ebi, or the Japanese Spiny Lobster, is a species of lobster native to Japan's Ise Bay. Since ancient times, it has been served at Shinto rites making it an important part of Japanese culture and celebration.
Not to mention some seriously *Good Eats.*

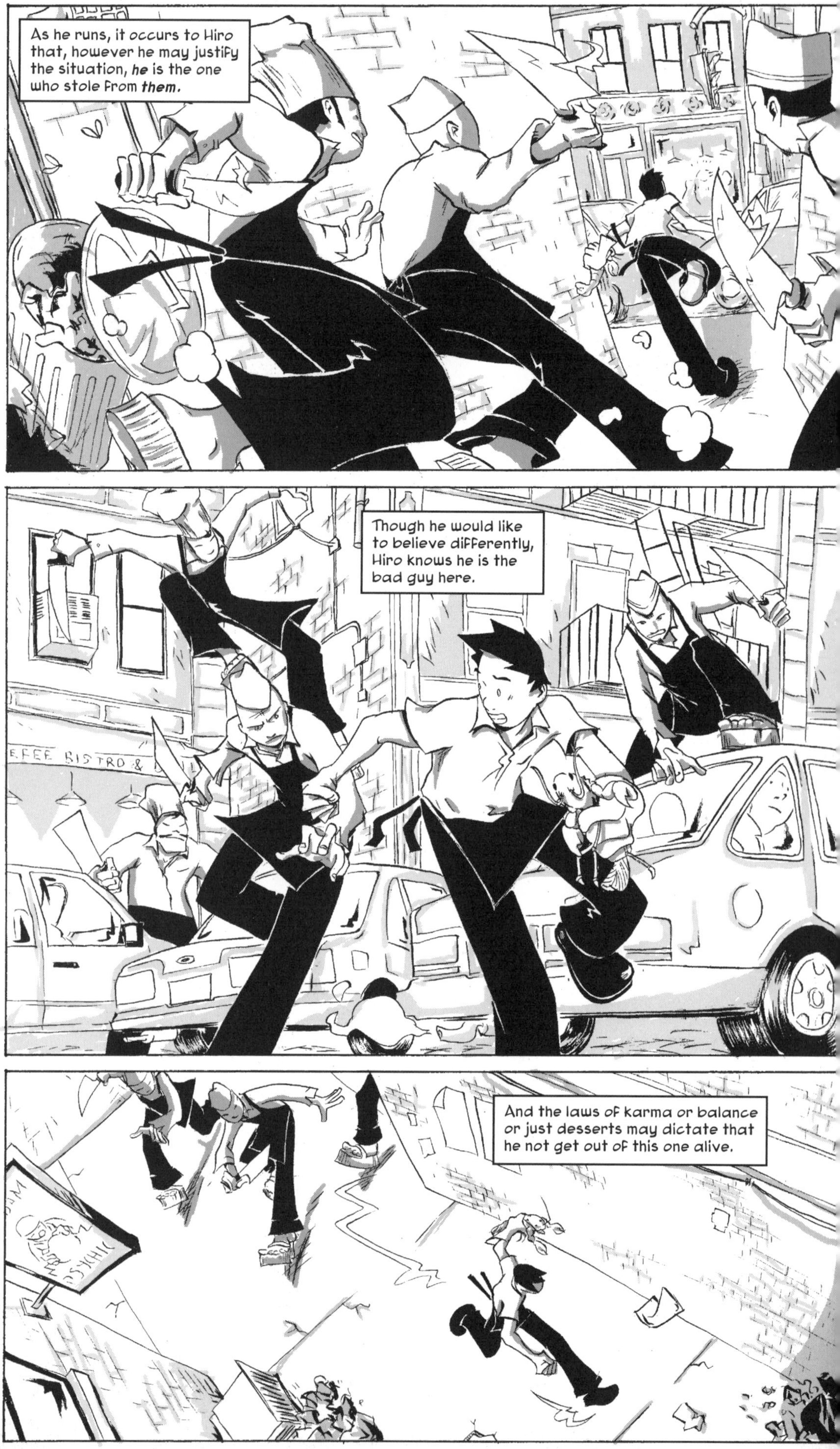
As he runs, it occurs to Hiro that, however he may justify the situation, *he* is the one who stole from *them.*
Though he would like to believe differently, Hiro knows he is the bad guy here.
And the laws of karma or balance or just desserts may dictate that he not get out of this one alive.

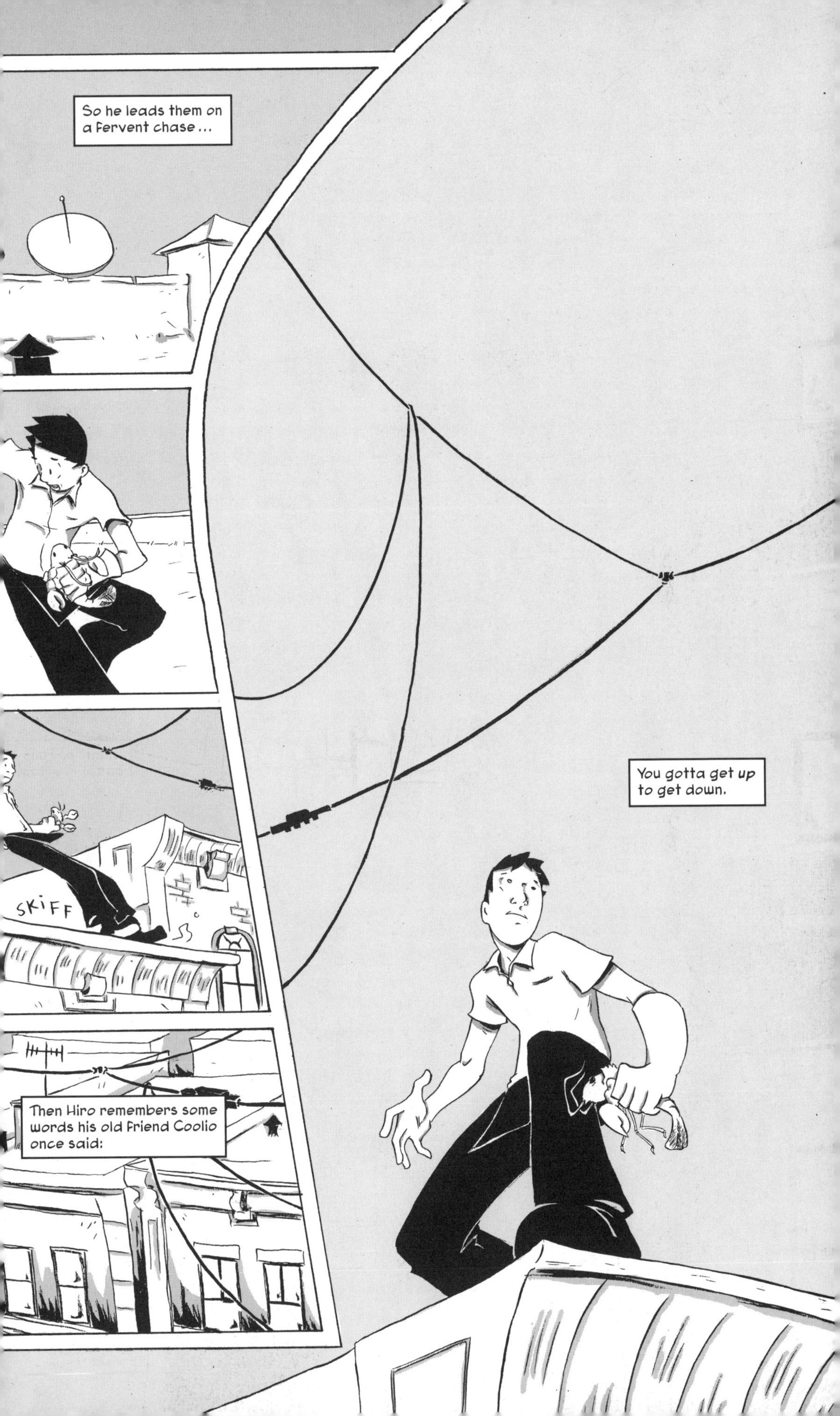

So he leads them on a fervent chase . . .
SKIFF
Then Hiro remembers some words his old friend Coolio once said:
You gotta get up to get down.

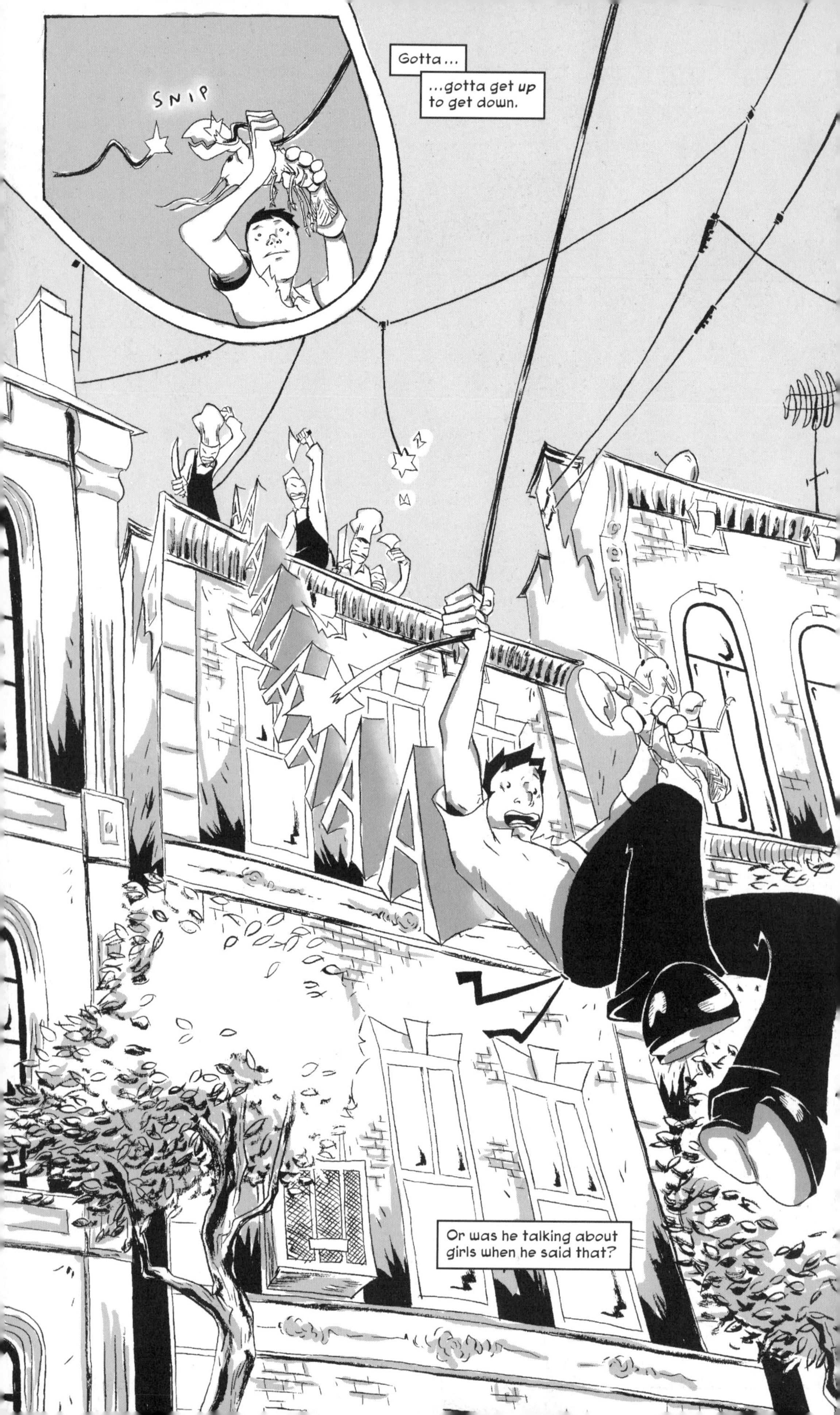
SNIP
Gotta...
...gotta get up to get down.
Or was he talking about girls when he said that?

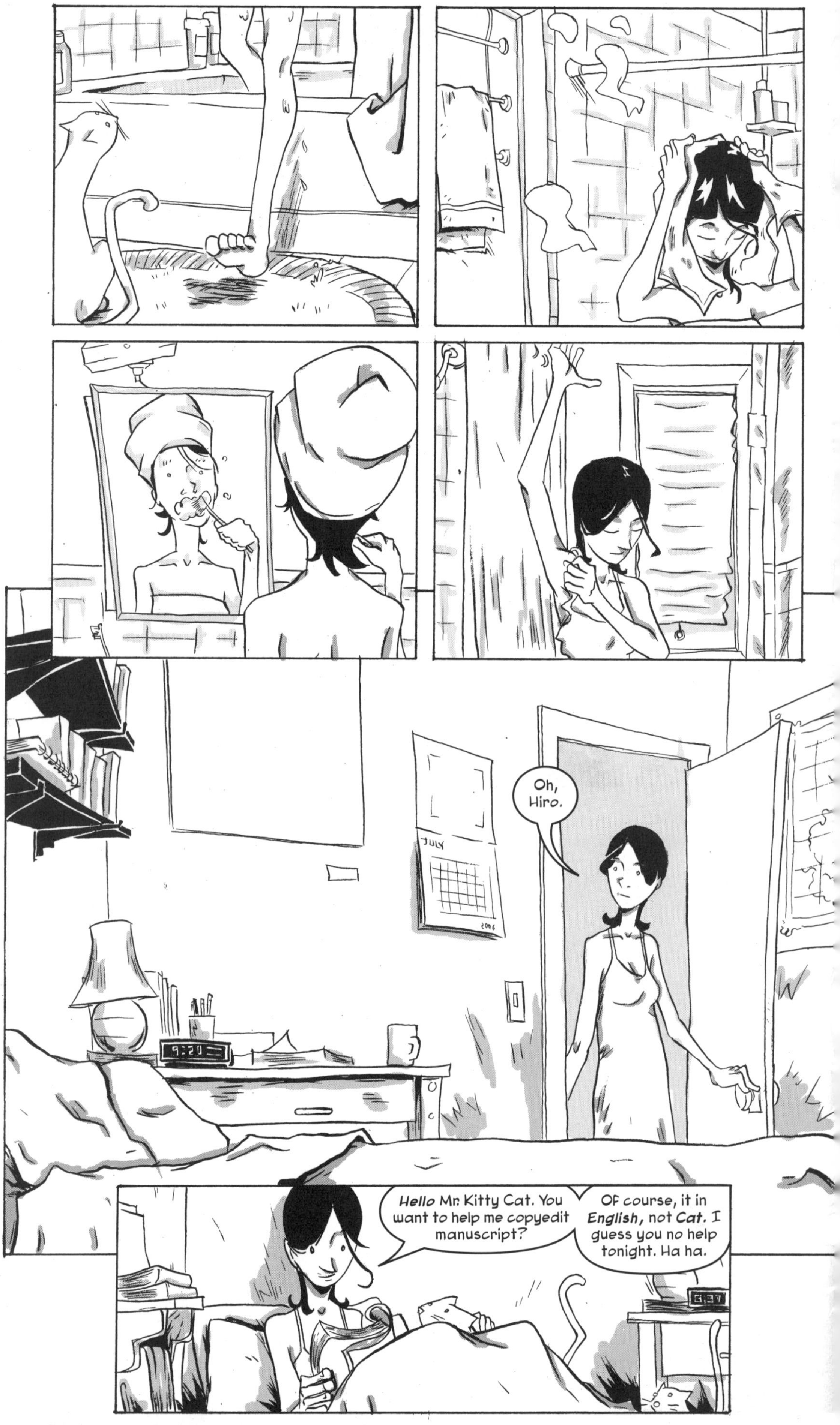

JULY
2006
9:20
Oh, Hiro.
Hello Mr. Kitty Cat. You want to help me copyedit manuscript?
Of course, it in English, not Cat. I guess you no help tonight. Ha ha.

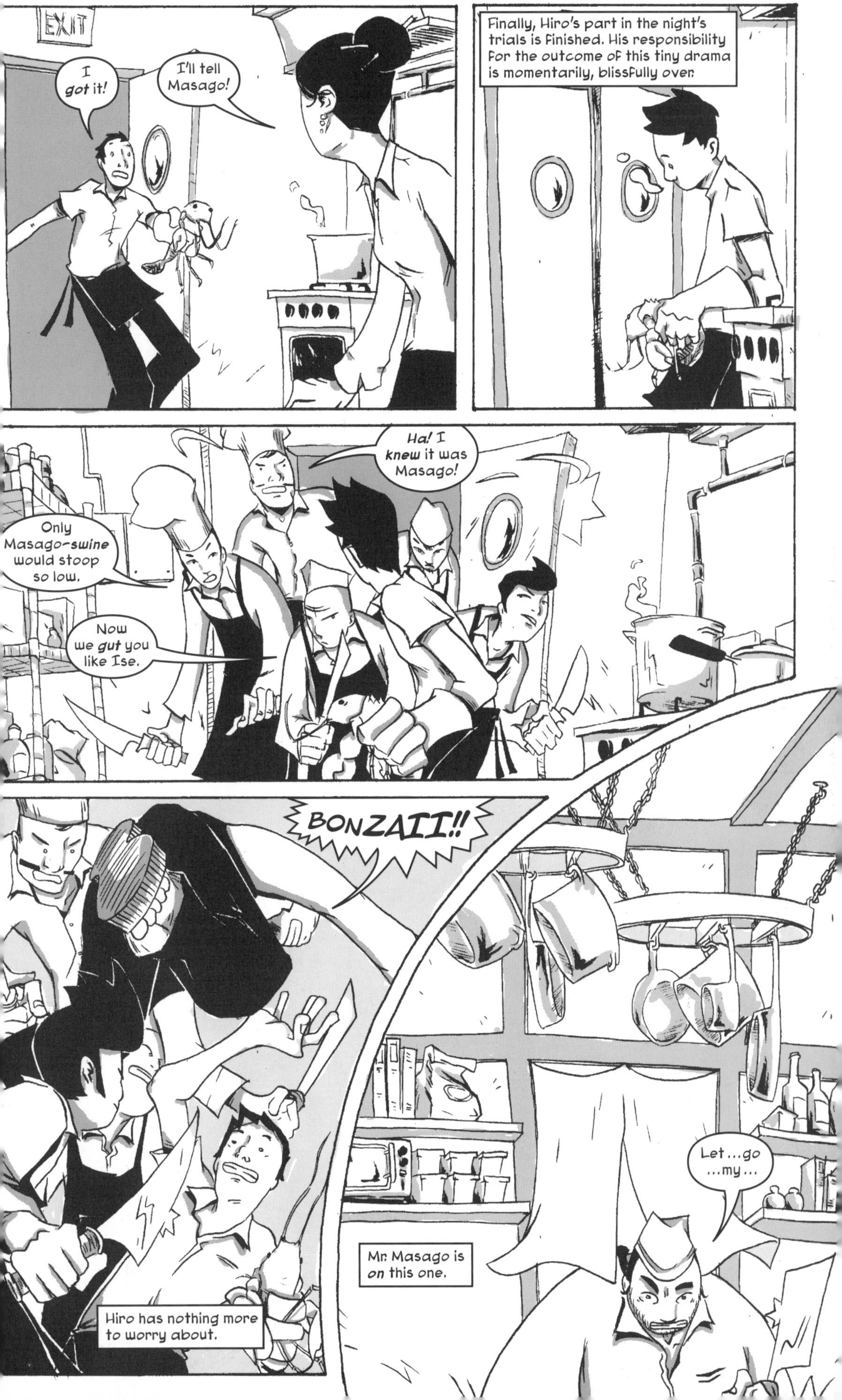
EXIT
I *got* it!
I'll tell Masago!
Finally, Hiro's part in the night's trials is finished. His responsibility for the outcome of this tiny drama is momentarily, blissfully over.
Ha! I *knew* it was Masago!
Only Masago-*swine* would stoop so low.
Now we *gut* you like Ise.
BONZAII!!
Hiro has nothing more to worry about.
Mr. Masago is *on* this one.
Let ... go ... my ...

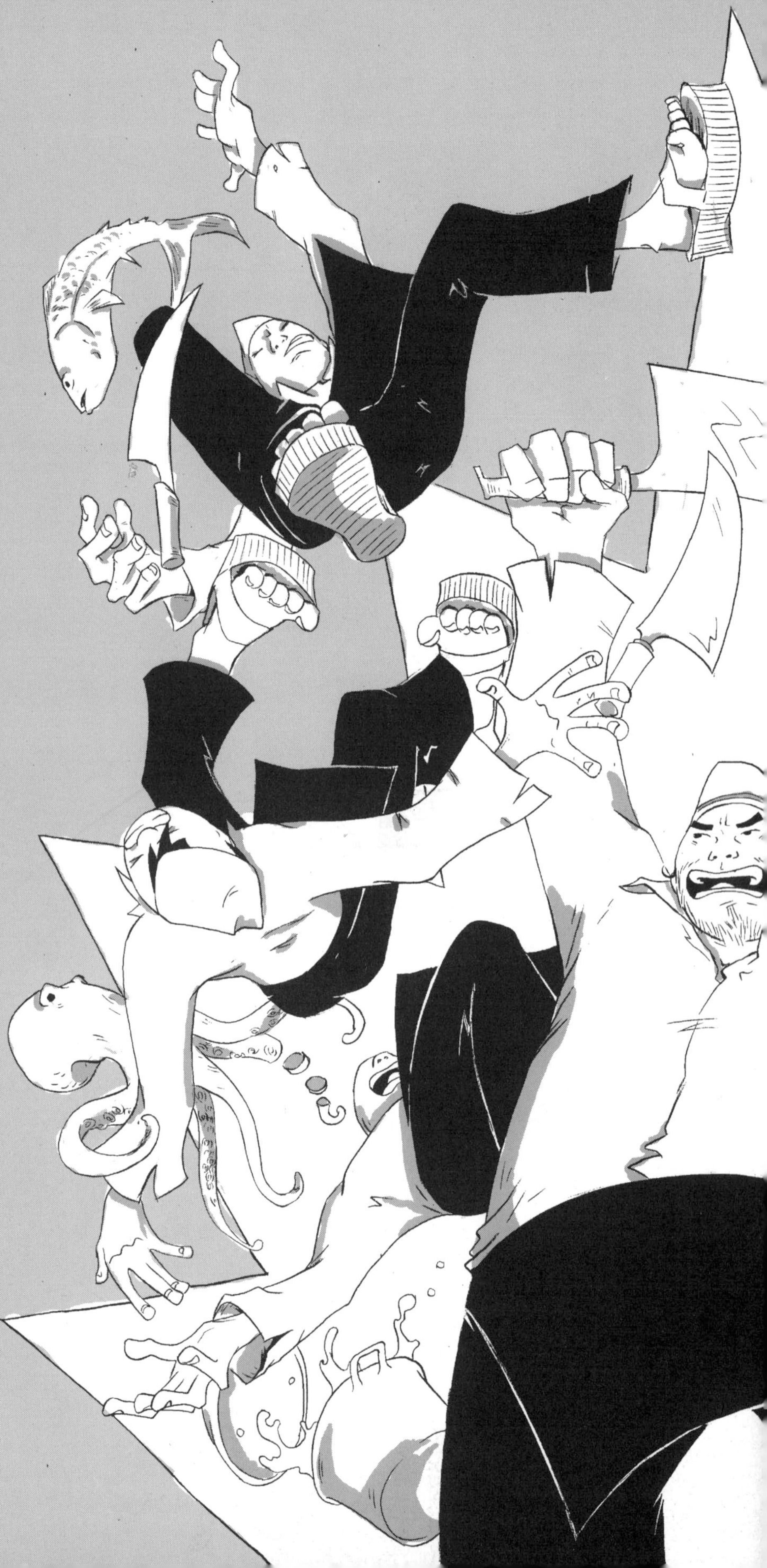

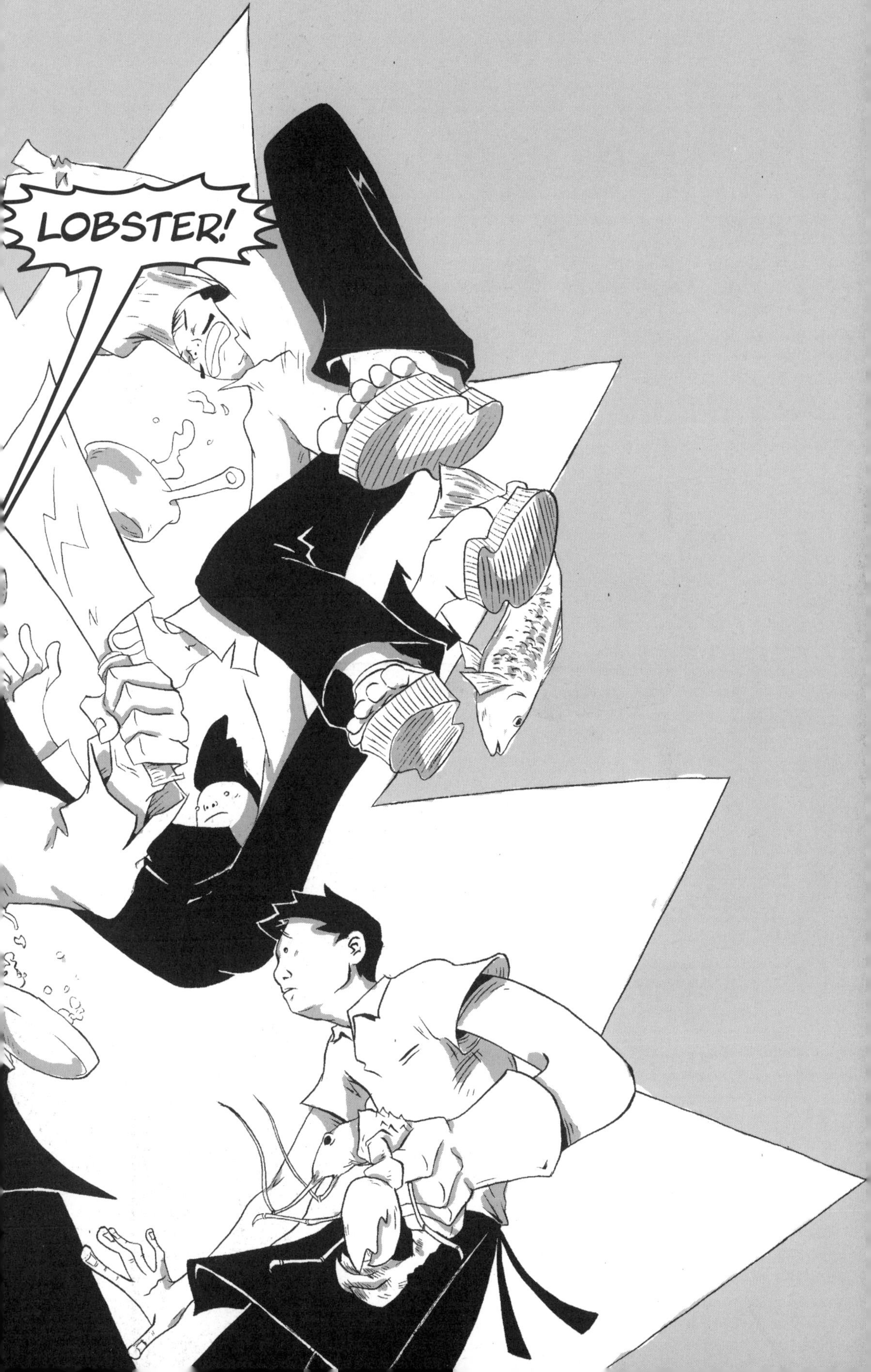
LOBSTER!

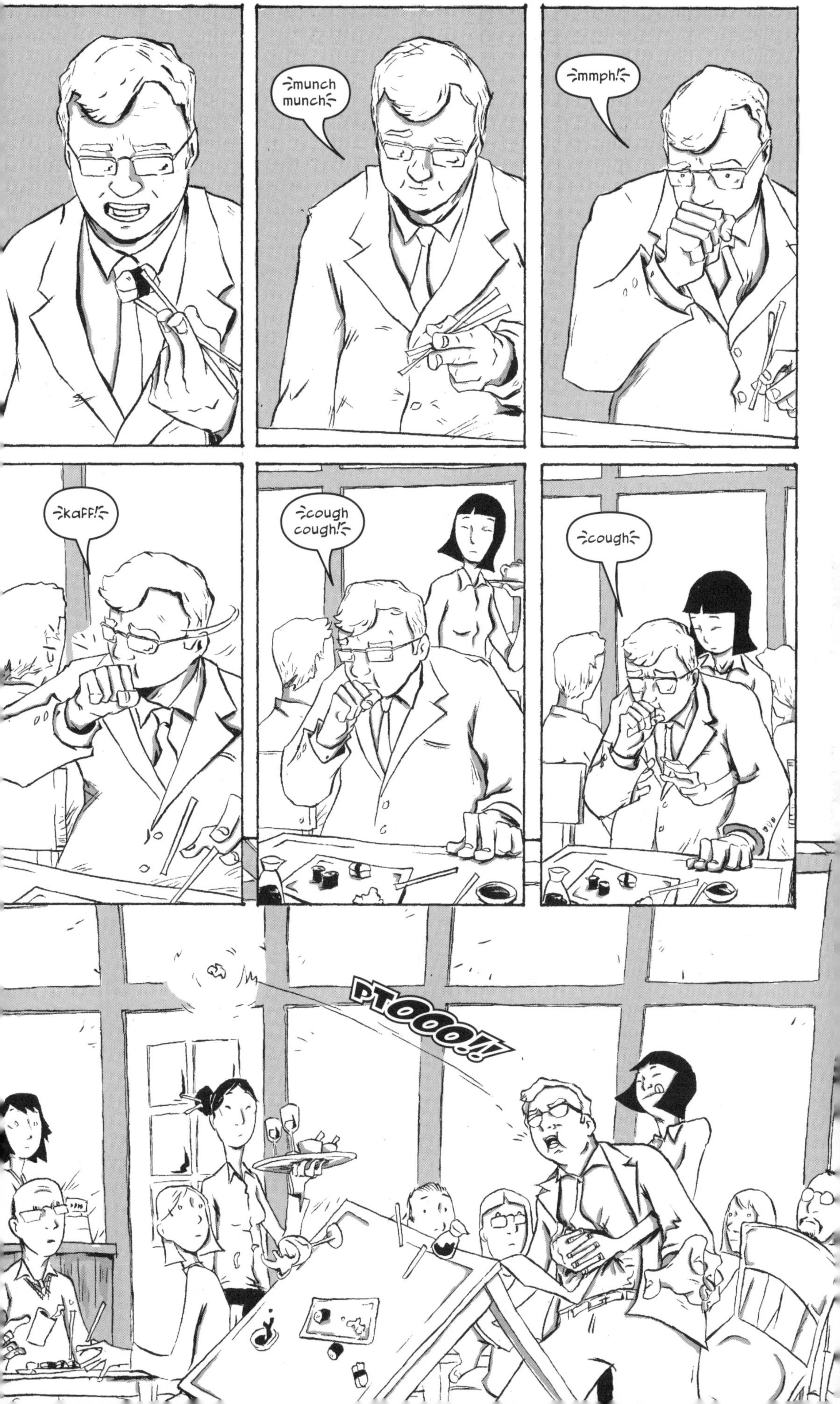
munch munch
mmph!
kaff!
cough cough!
cough
PTOOO!!

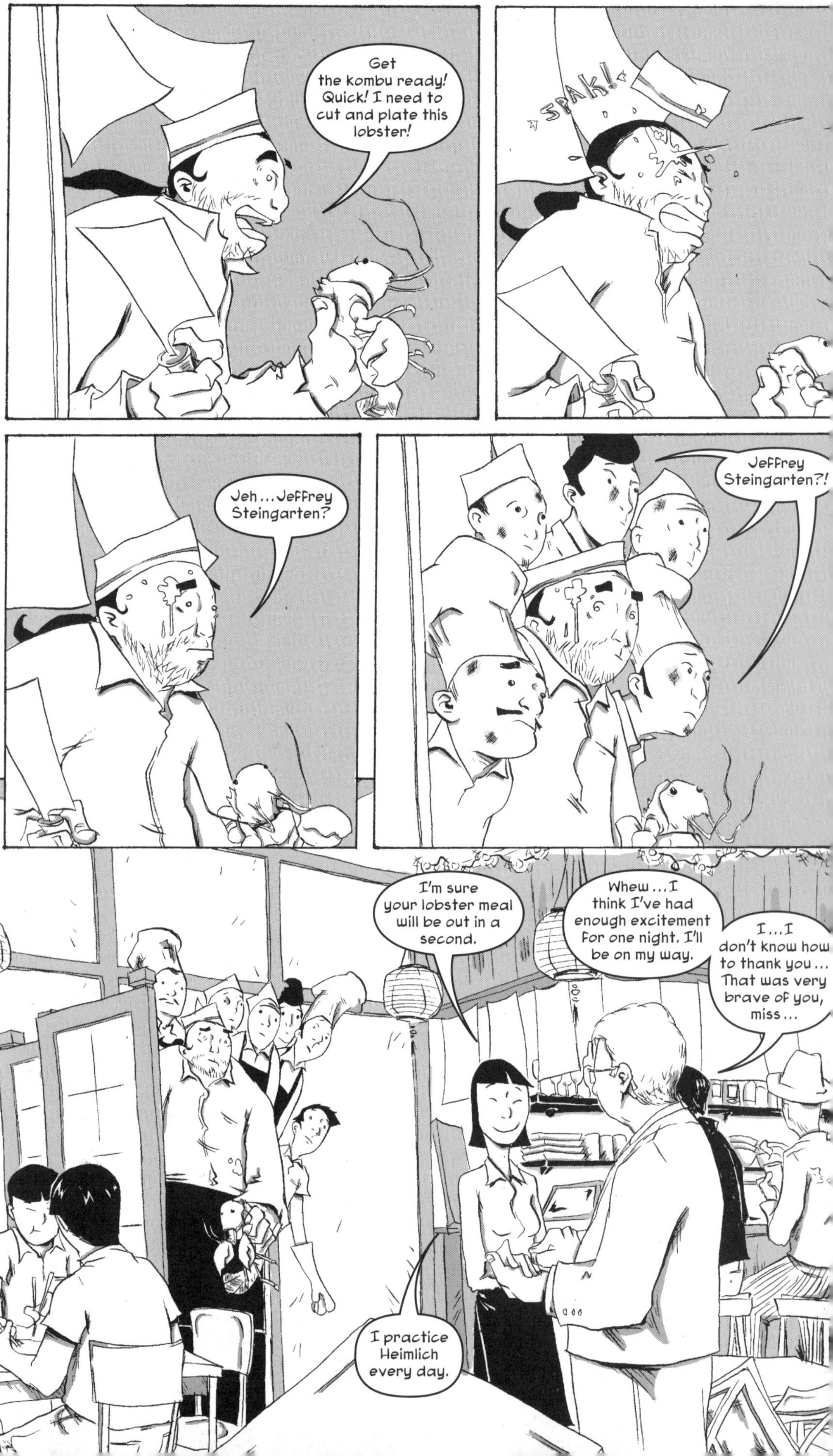
Get the kombu ready! Quick! I need to cut and plate this lobster!
SPAK!
Jeh... Jeffrey Steingarten?
Jeffrey Steingarten?!
I'm sure your lobster meal will be out in a second.
Whew... I think I've had enough excitement for one night. I'll be on my way.
I... I don't know how to thank you... That was very brave of you, miss...
I practice Heimlich every day.

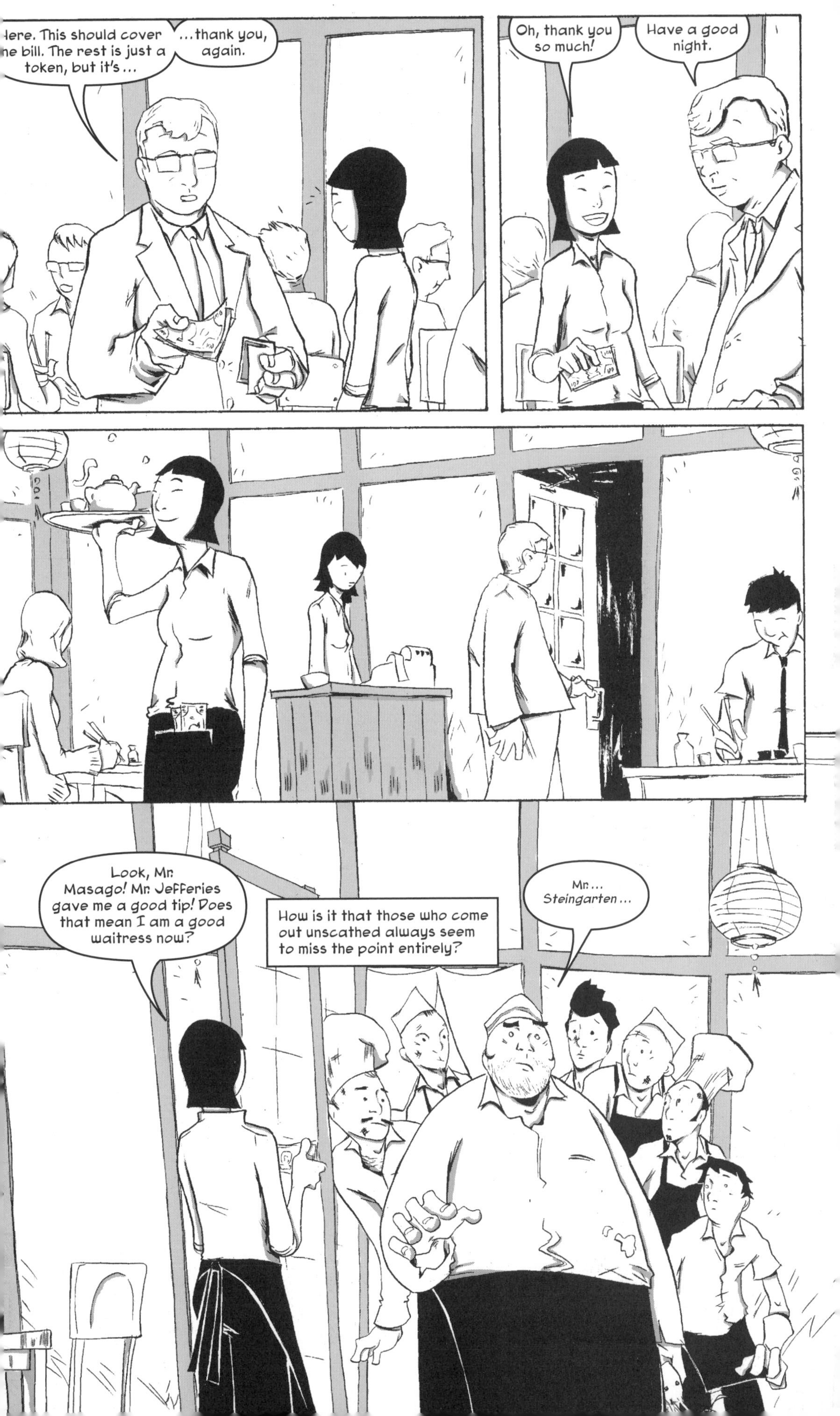
Here. This should cover the bill. The rest is just a token, but it's…
…thank you, again.
Oh, thank you so much!
Have a good night.
Look, Mr. Masago! Mr. Jefferies gave me a good tip! Does that mean I am a good waitress now?
How is it that those who come out unscathed always seem to miss the point entirely?
Mr… Steingarten…

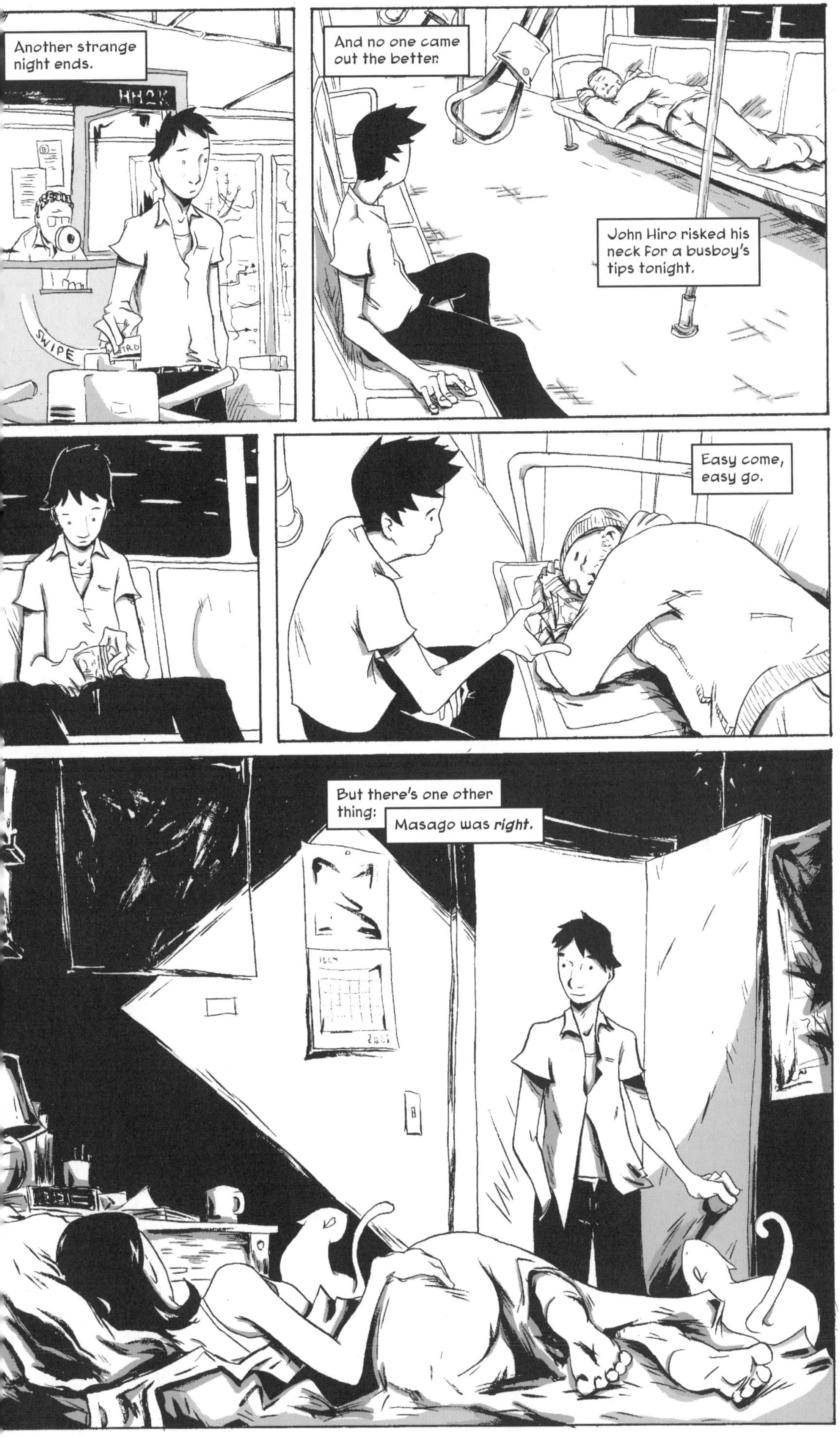

Another strange night ends.
HH2K
SWIPE
METRO
And no one came out the better.
John Hiro risked his neck for a busboy's tips tonight.
Easy come, easy go.
But there's one other thing:
Masago was *right.*

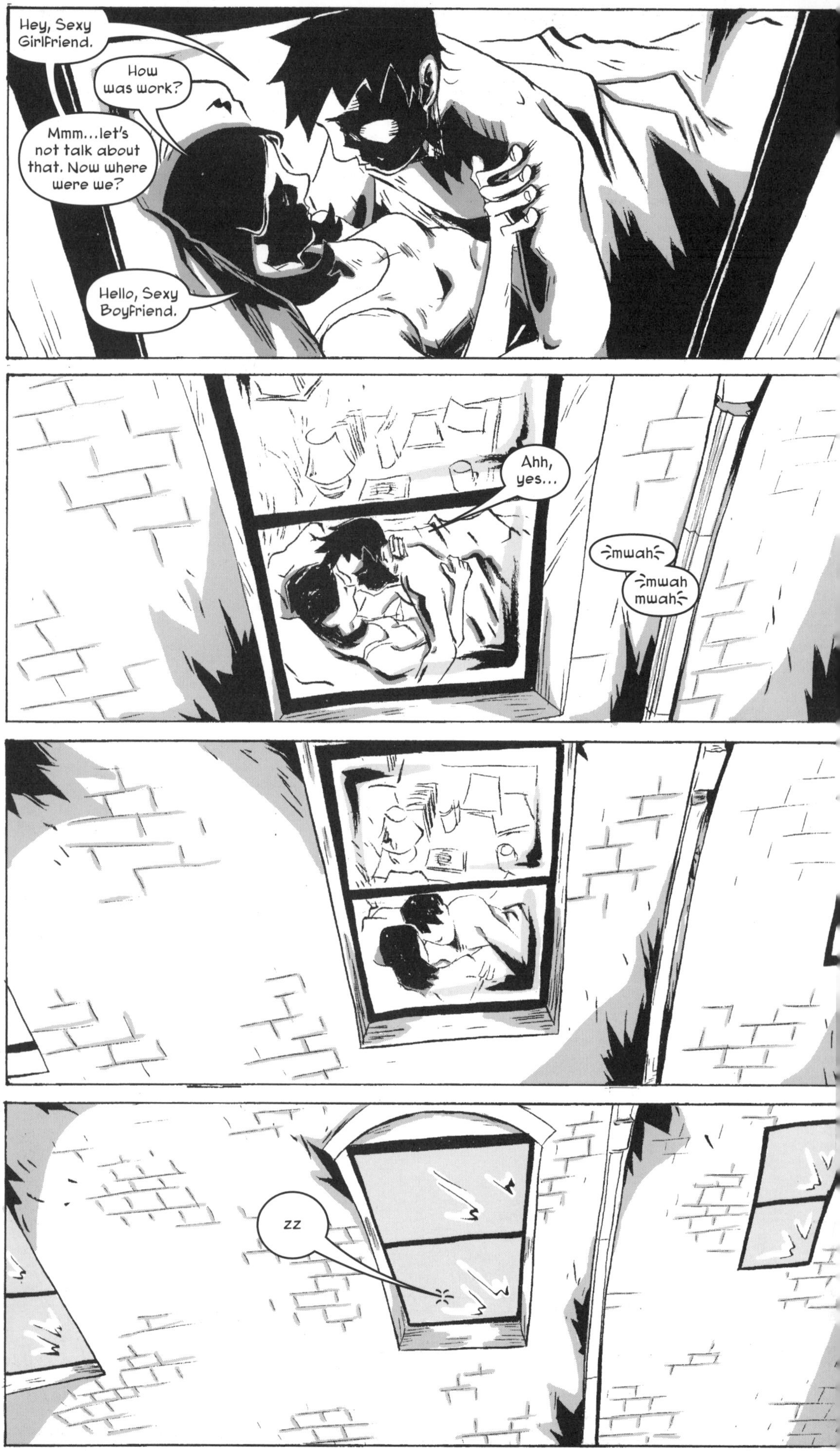
Hey, Sexy Girlfriend.
How was work?
Mmm...let's not talk about that. Now where were we?
Hello, Sexy Boyfriend.
Ahh, yes...
mwah
mwah mwah
zz

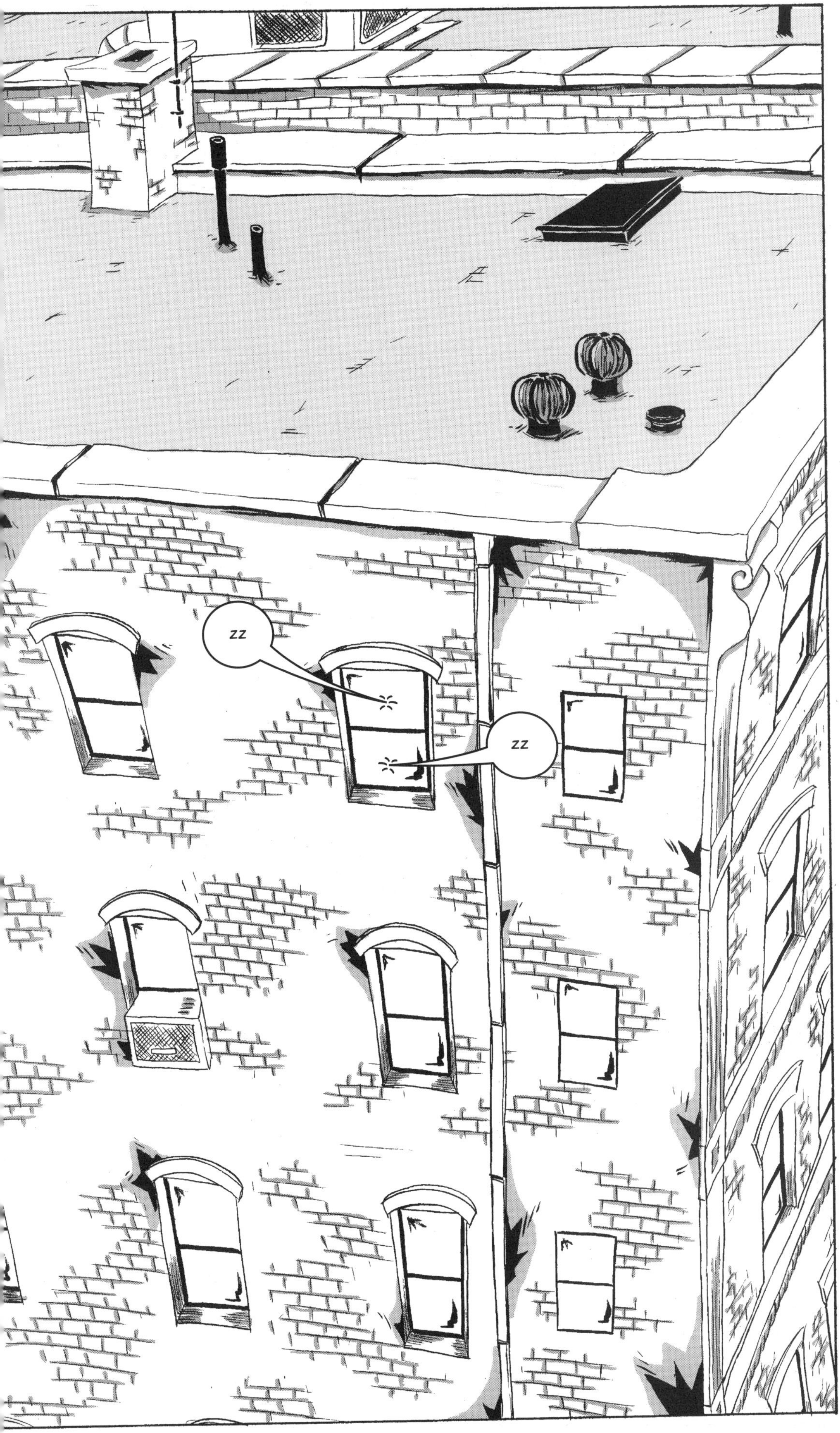
zz
zz

オペラへ行きましょ

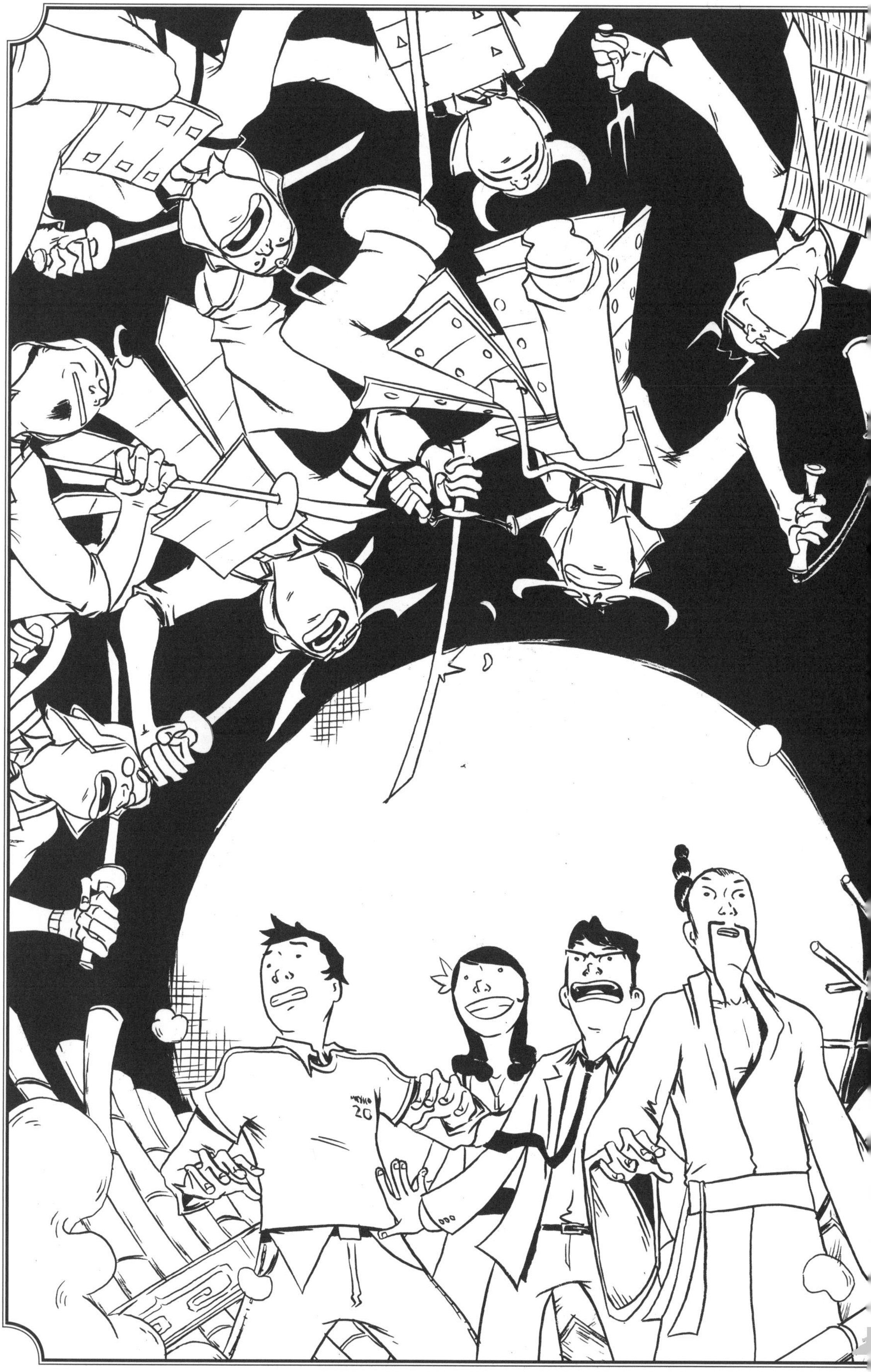
20

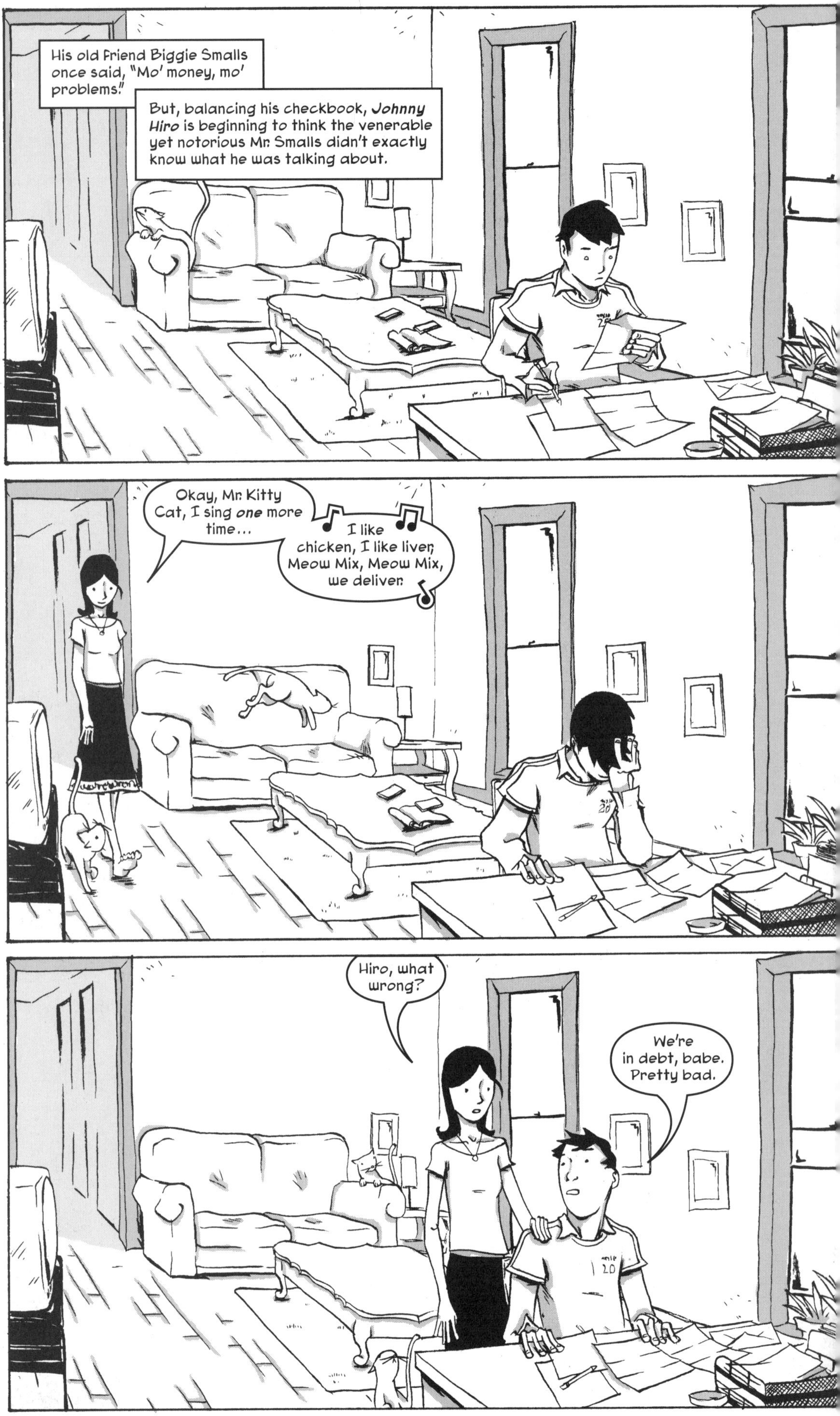
His old friend Biggie Smalls once said, "Mo' money, mo' problems."
But, balancing his checkbook, *Johnny Hiro* is beginning to think the venerable yet notorious Mr. Smalls didn't exactly know what he was talking about.
Okay, Mr. Kitty Cat, I sing *one* more time...
I like chicken, I like liver, Meow Mix, Meow Mix, we deliver.
Hiro, what wrong?
We're in debt, babe. Pretty bad.

*Pogrebin, Robin. "Operas for $20? New Audiences Hear Siren Song." New York Times October 9, 2006

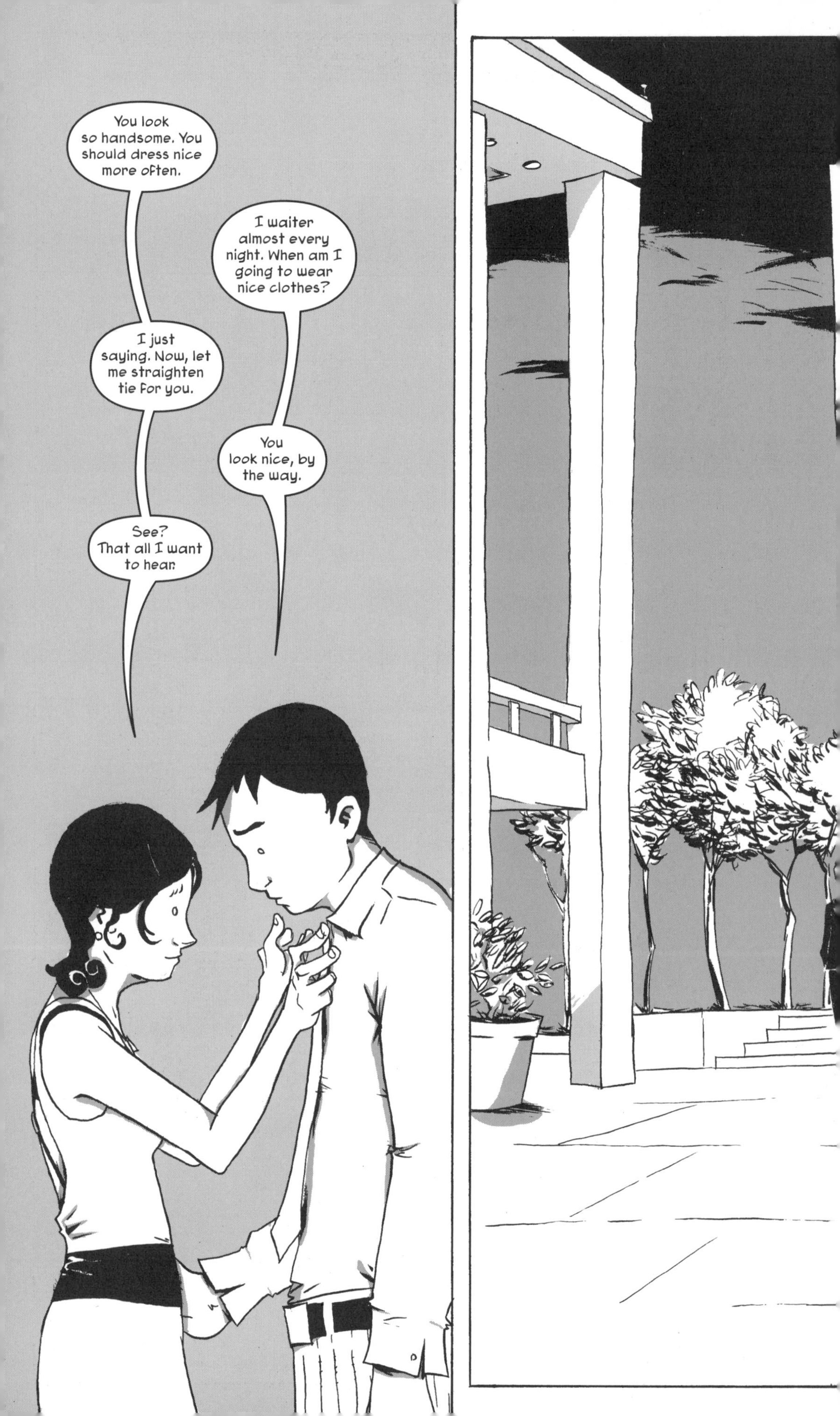
You look so handsome. You should dress nice more often.
I waiter almost every night. When am I going to wear nice clothes?
I just saying. Now, let me straighten tie for you.
You look nice, by the way.
See? That all I want to hear.

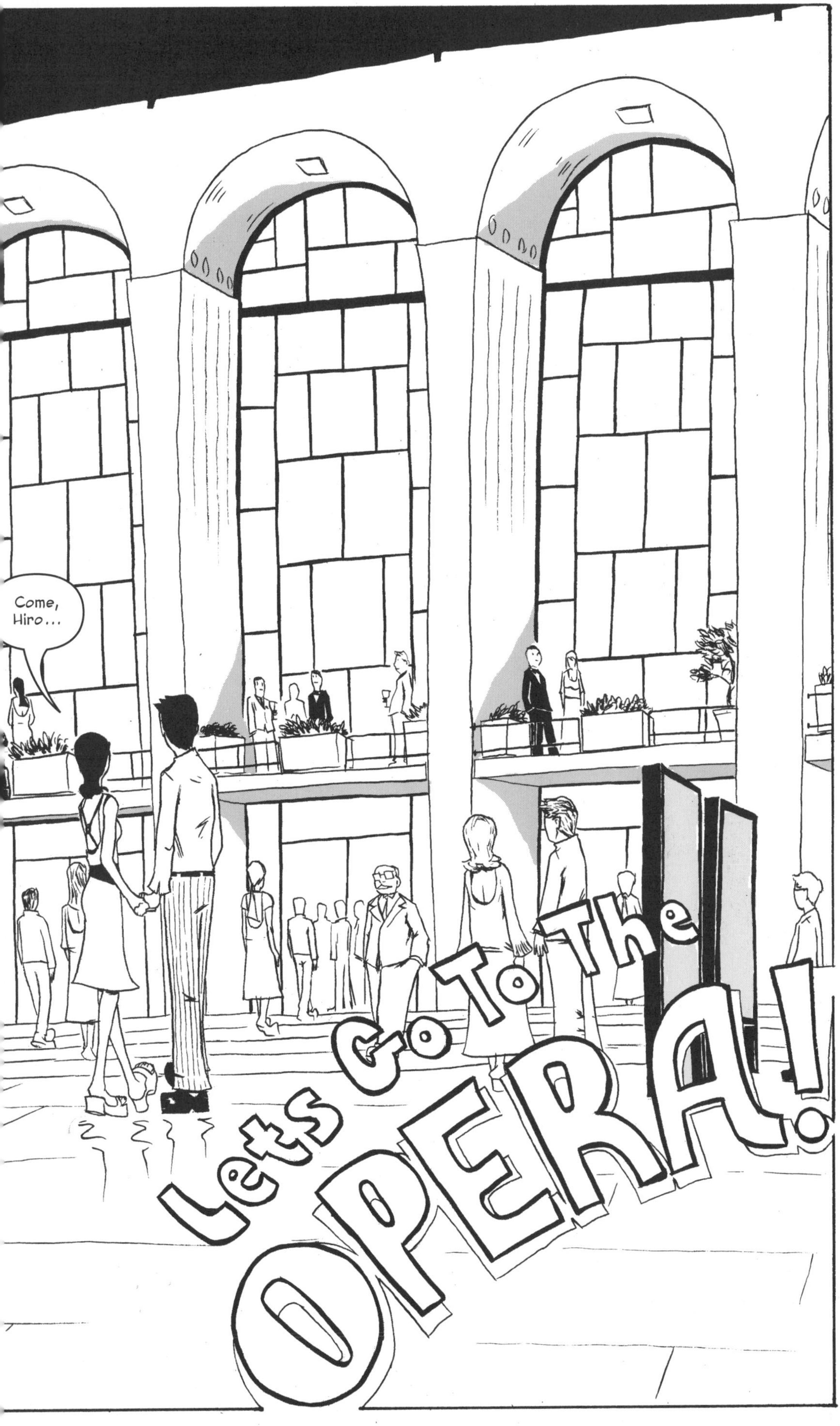
Come, Hiro...
Lets Go To The OPERA!

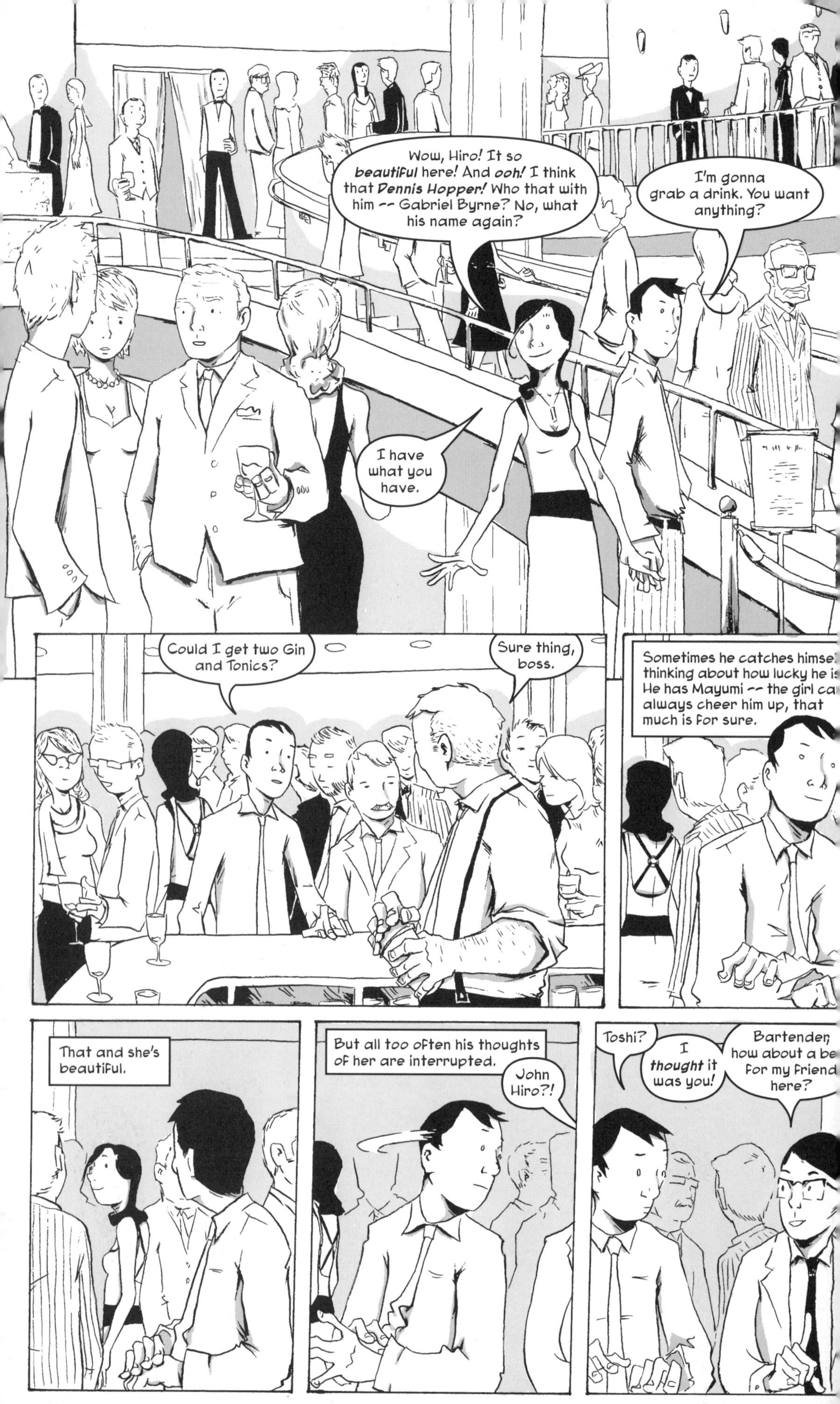
Wow, Hiro! It so *beautiful* here! And *ooh!* I think that *Dennis Hopper!* Who that with him -- Gabriel Byrne? No, what his name again?
I'm gonna grab a drink. You want anything?
I have what you have.
Could I get two Gin and Tonics?
Sure thing, boss.
Sometimes he catches himse thinking about how lucky he is He has Mayumi -- the girl ca always cheer him up, that much is for sure.
That and she's beautiful.
But all too often his thoughts of her are interrupted.
John Hiro?!
Toshi?
I *thought* it was you!
Bartender, how about a be for my friend here?

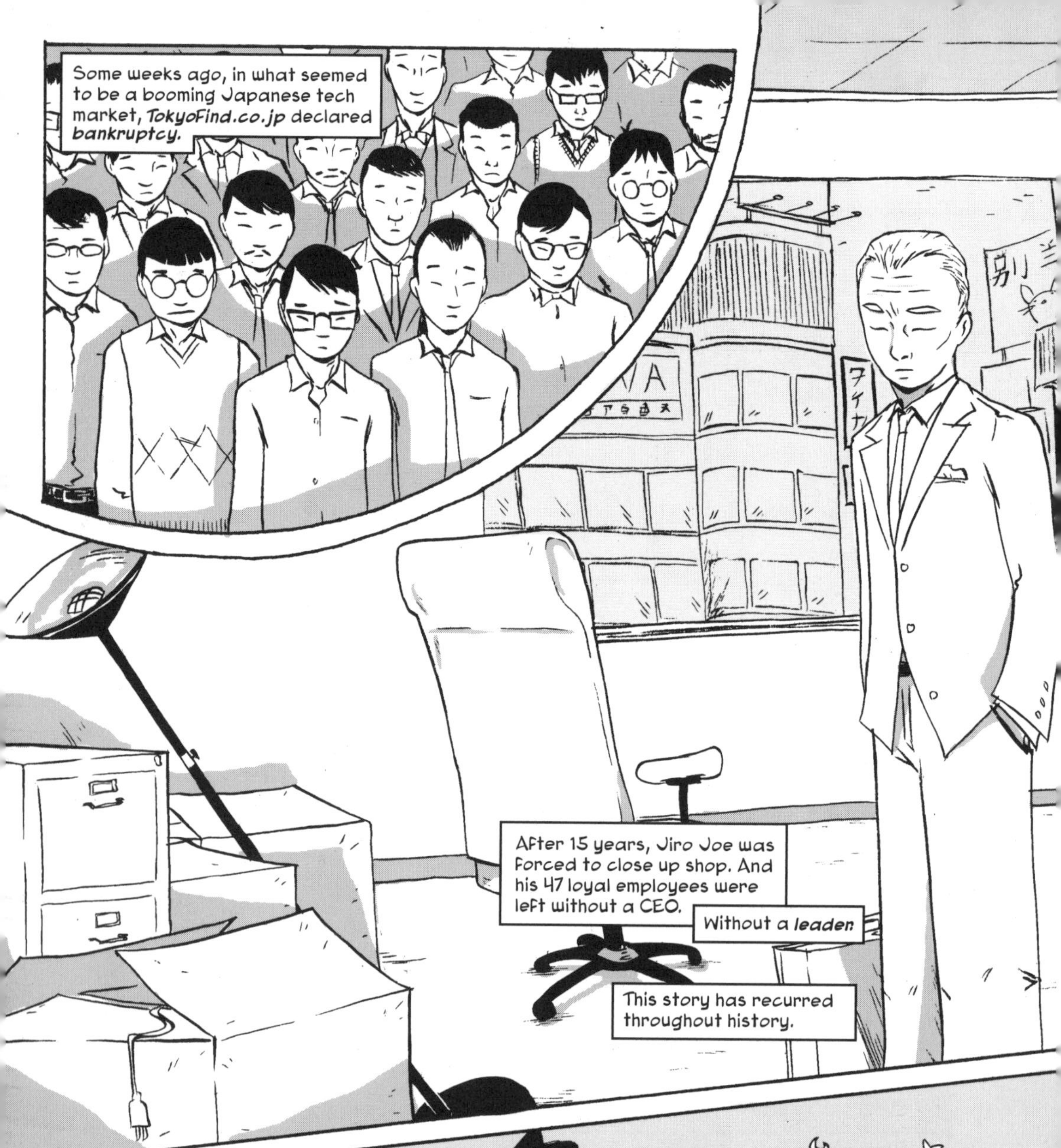

Some weeks ago, in what seemed to be a booming Japanese tech market, TokyoFind.co.jp declared bankruptcy.
After 15 years, Jiro Joe was forced to close up shop. And his 47 loyal employees were left without a CEO.
Without a leader.
This story has recurred throughout history.

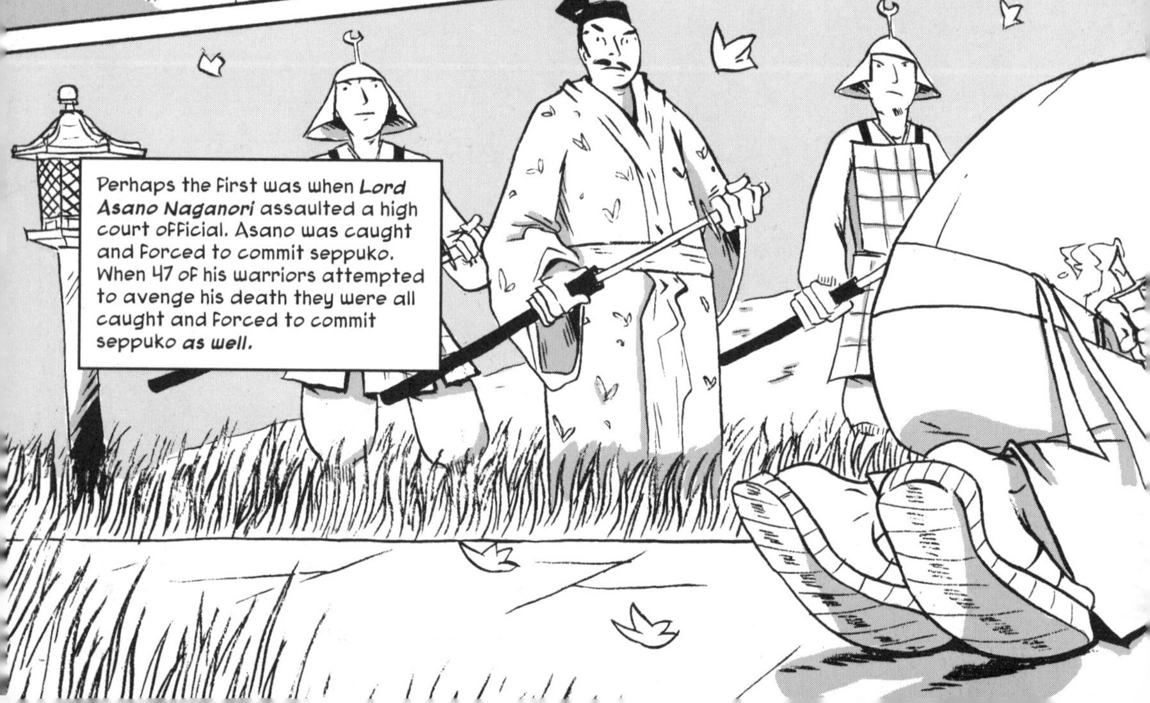

Perhaps the first was when Lord Asano Naganori assaulted a high court official. Asano was caught and forced to commit seppuko. When 47 of his warriors attempted to avenge his death they were all caught and forced to commit seppuko as well.

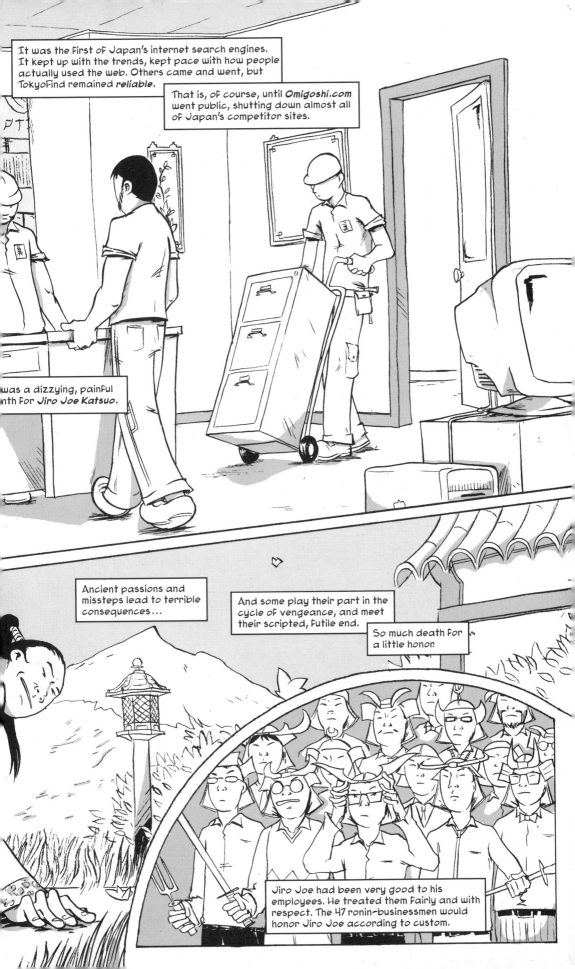

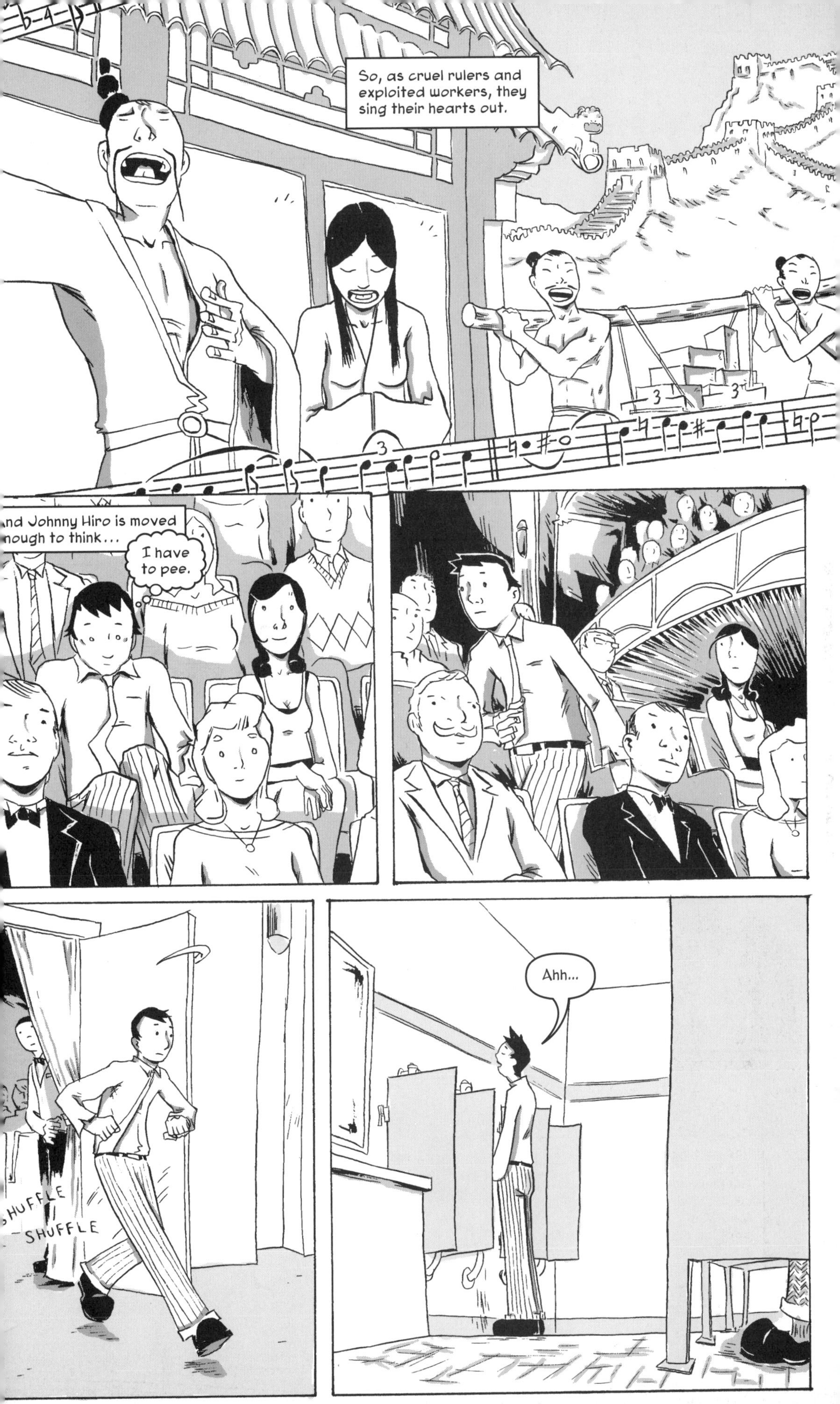
So, as cruel rulers and exploited workers, they sing their hearts out.
3
3
3
nd Johnny Hiro is moved nough to think...
I have to pee.
SHUFFLE
SHUFFLE
Ahh...

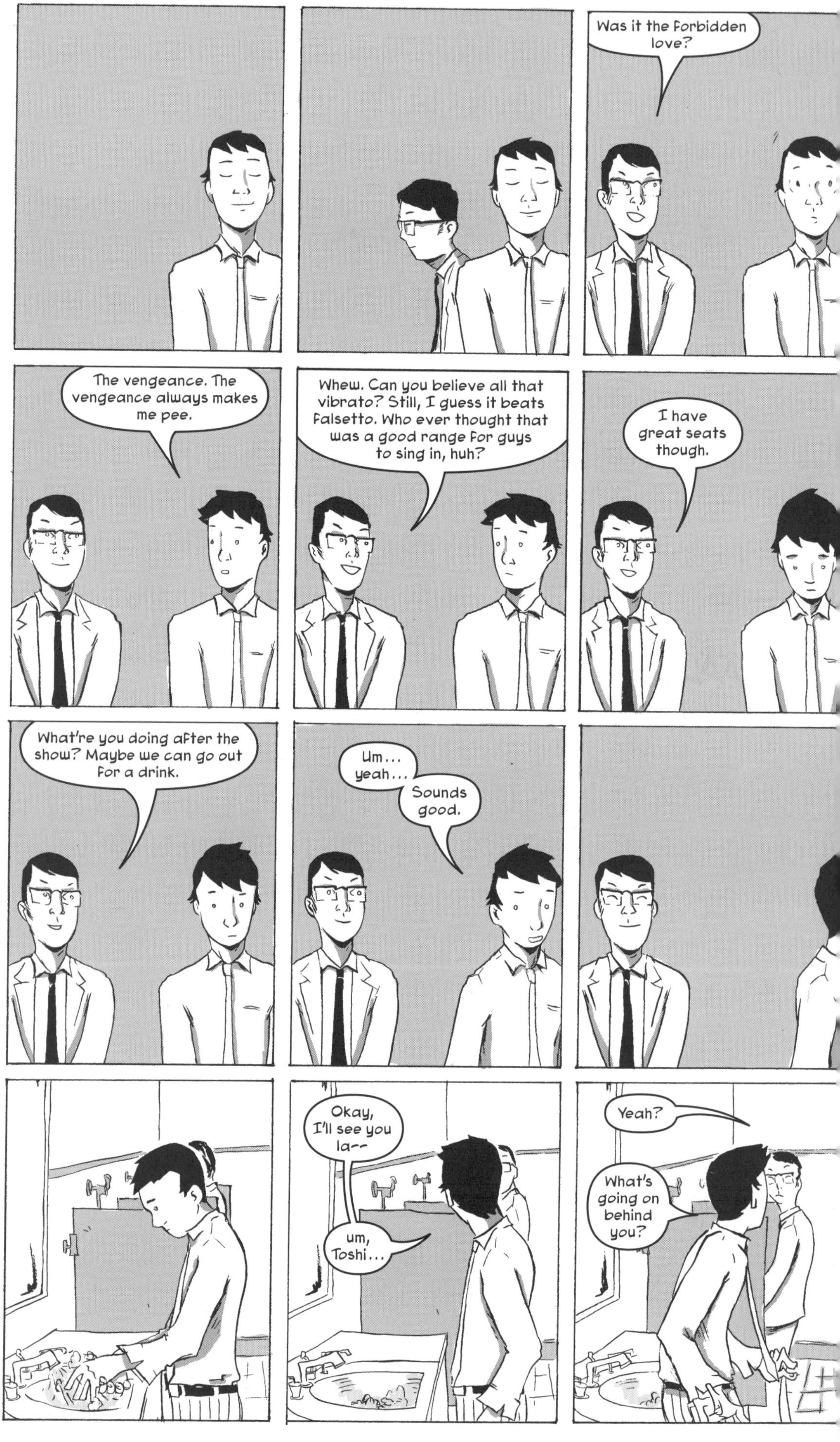
Was it the forbidden love?
The vengeance. The vengeance always makes me pee.
Whew. Can you believe all that vibrato? Still, I guess it beats falsetto. Who ever thought that was a good range for guys to sing in, huh?
I have great seats though.
What're you doing after the show? Maybe we can go out for a drink.
Um... yeah...
Sounds good.
Okay, I'll see you la--
um, Toshi...
Yeah?
What's going on behind you?

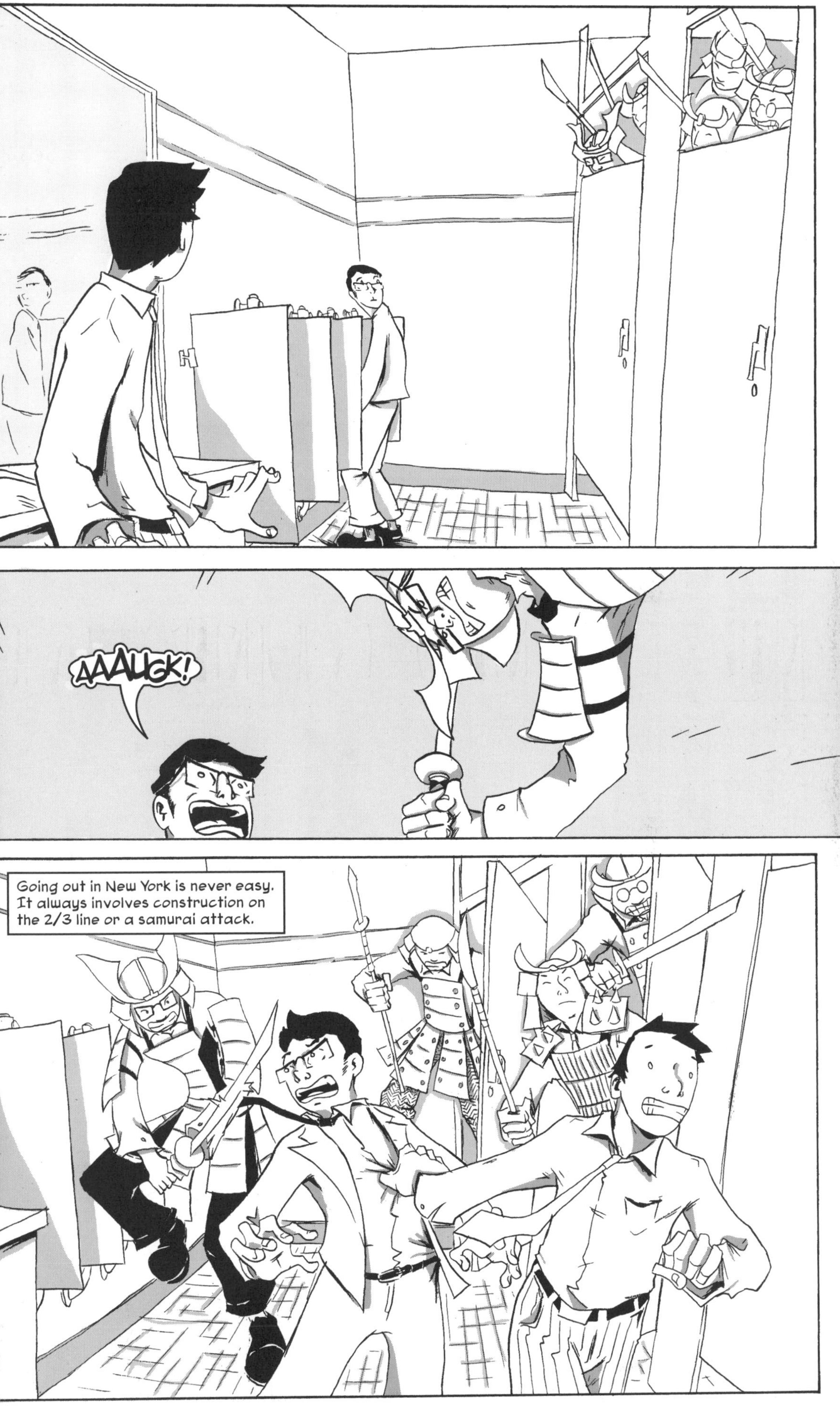
AAAUGK!
Going out in New York is never easy. It always involves construction on the 2/3 line or a samurai attack.

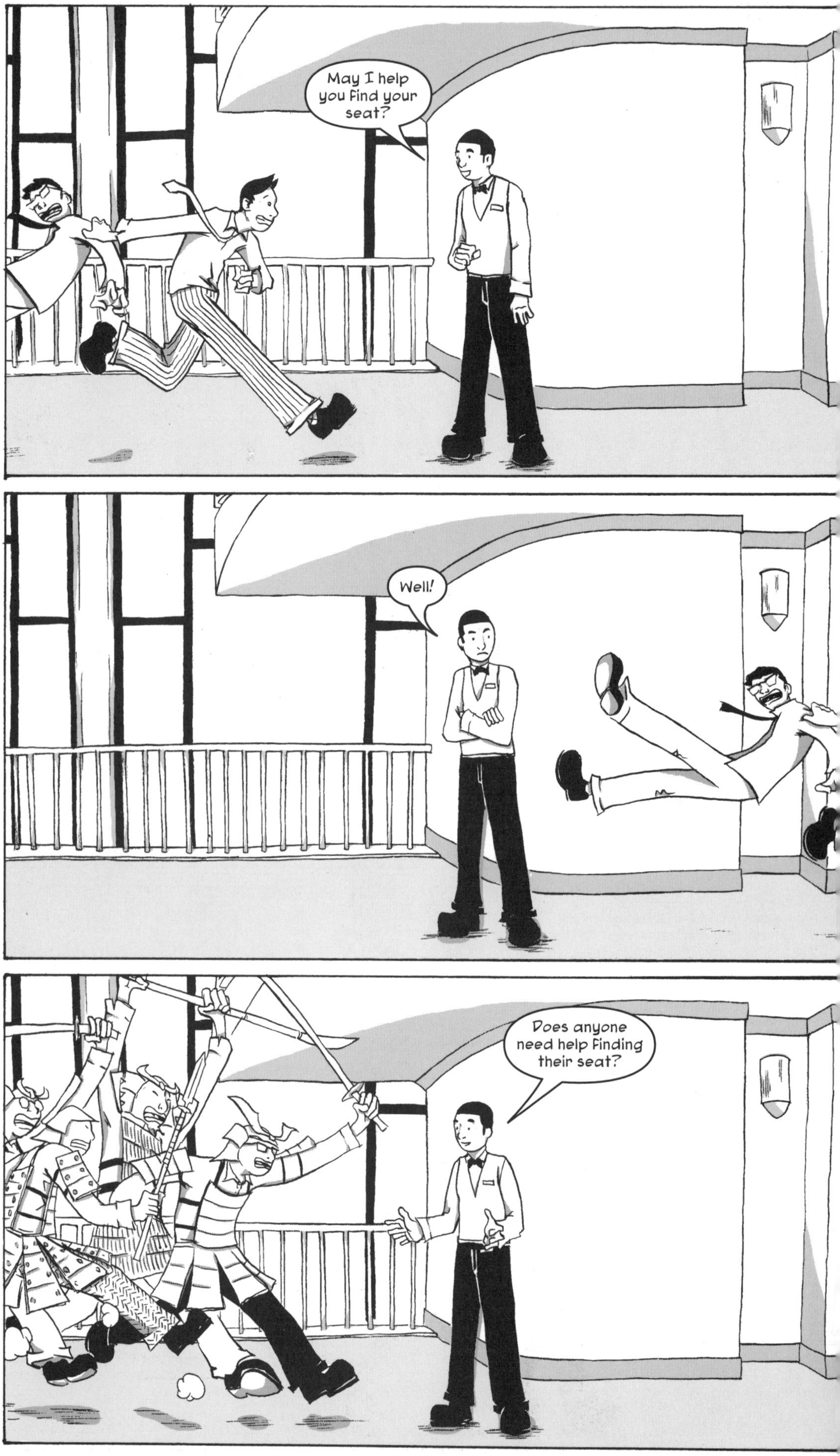
May I help you find your seat?
Well!
Does anyone need help finding their seat?

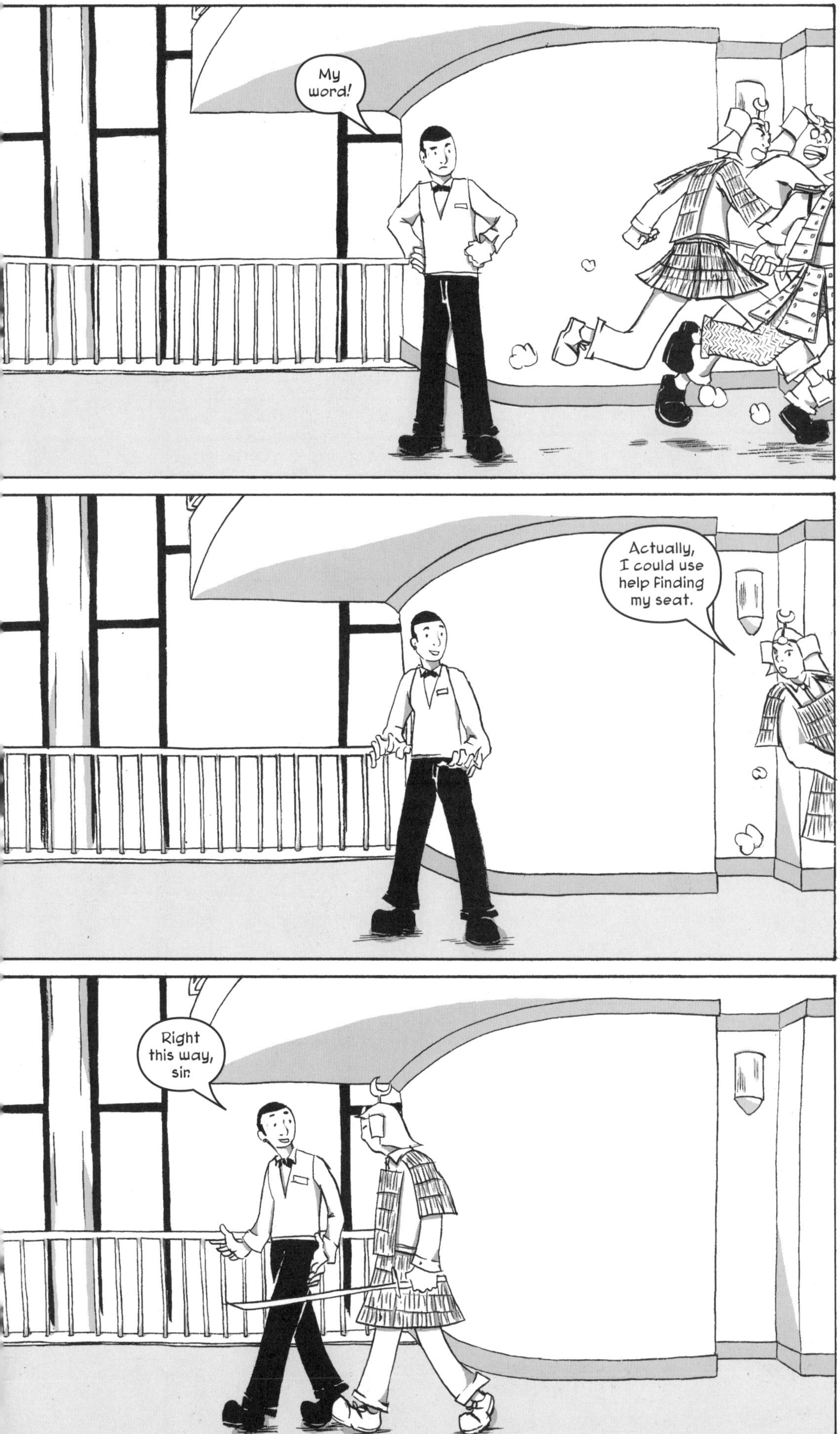
My word!
Actually, I could use help finding my seat.
Right this way, sir.

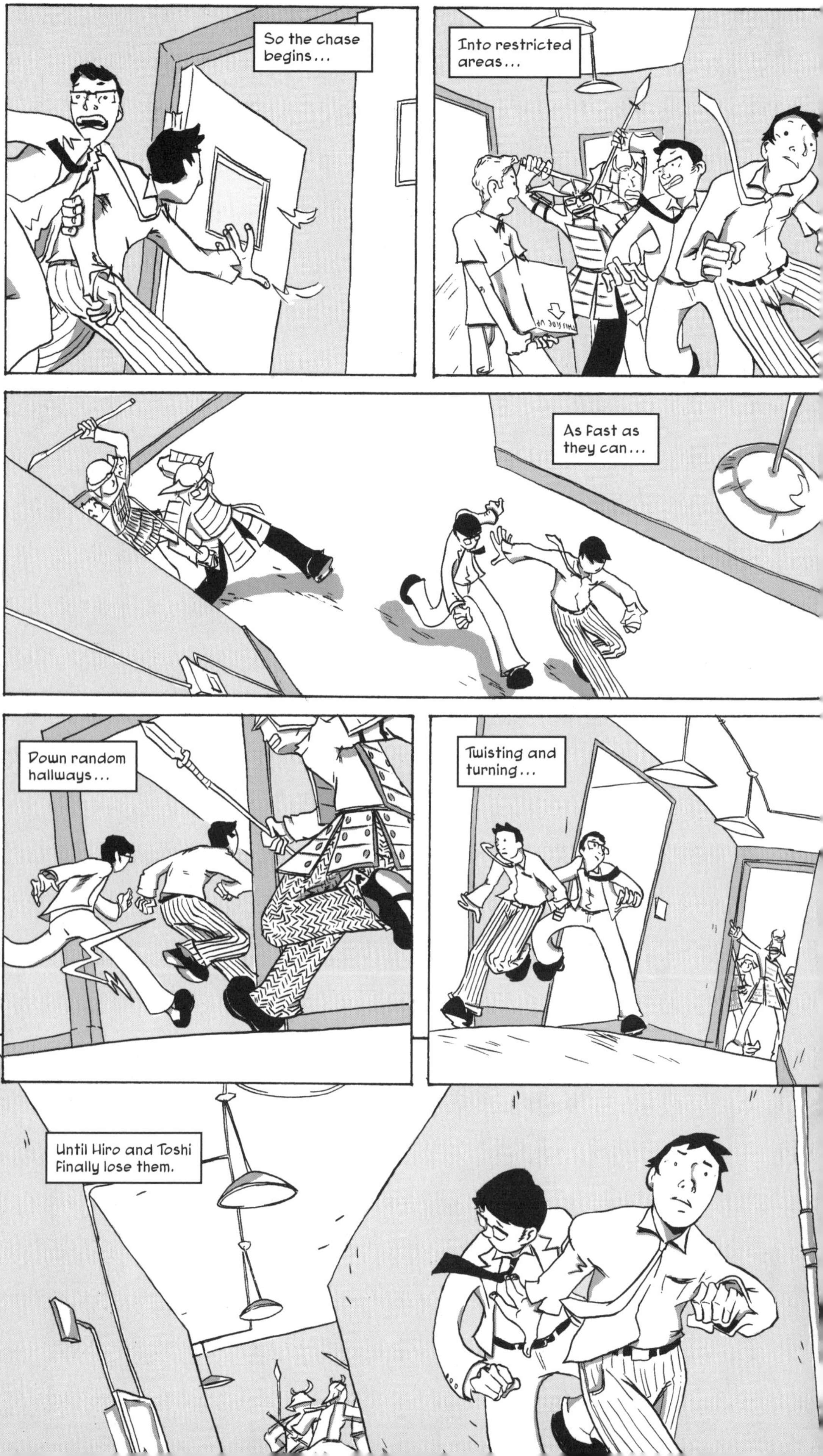
So the chase begins...
Into restricted areas...
THIS SIDE UP
As fast as they can...
Down random hallways...
Twisting and turning...
Until Hiro and Toshi finally lose them.

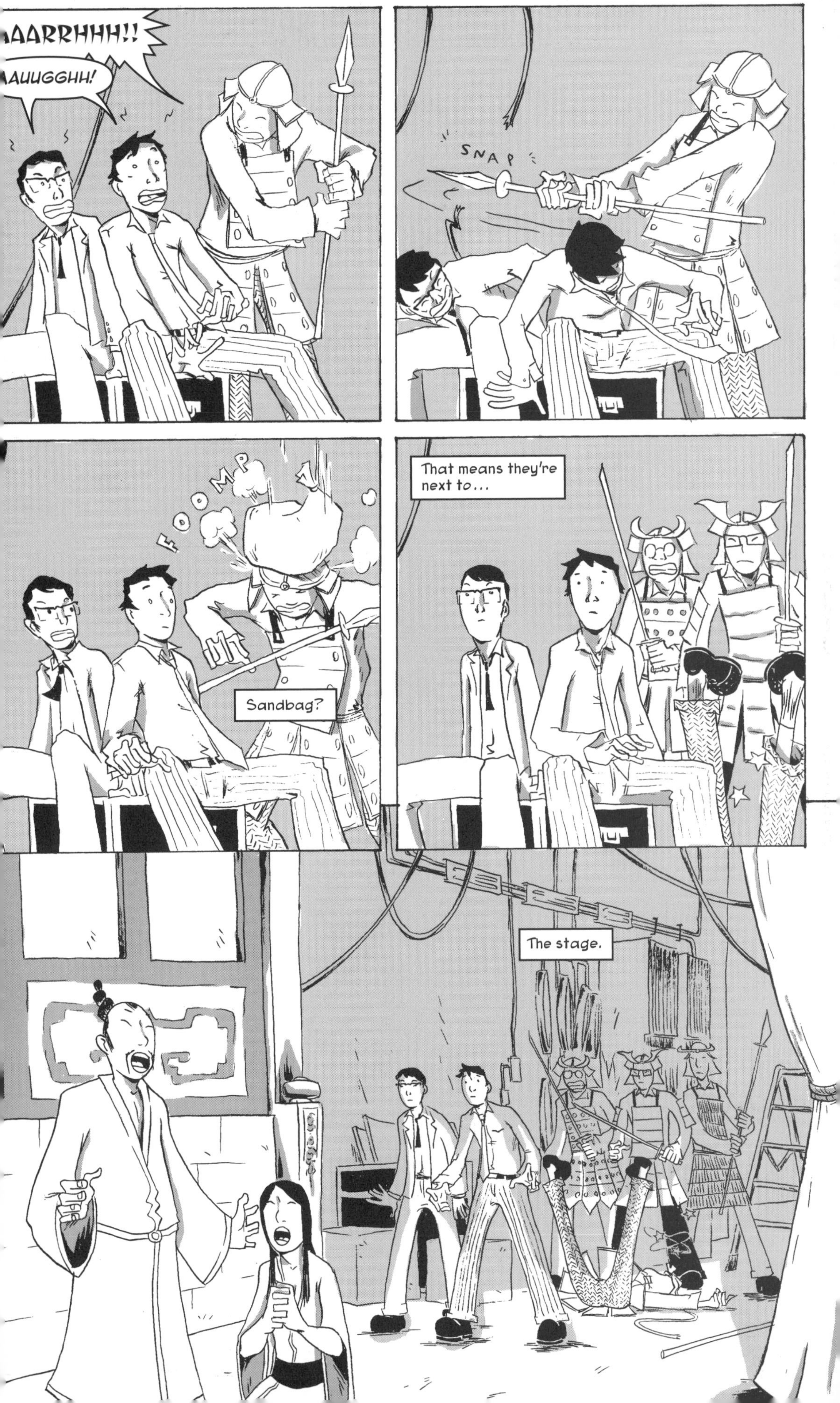
AARRHHH!!
AUUGGHH!
SNAP
FOOMP
Sandbag?
That means they're next to...
The stage.

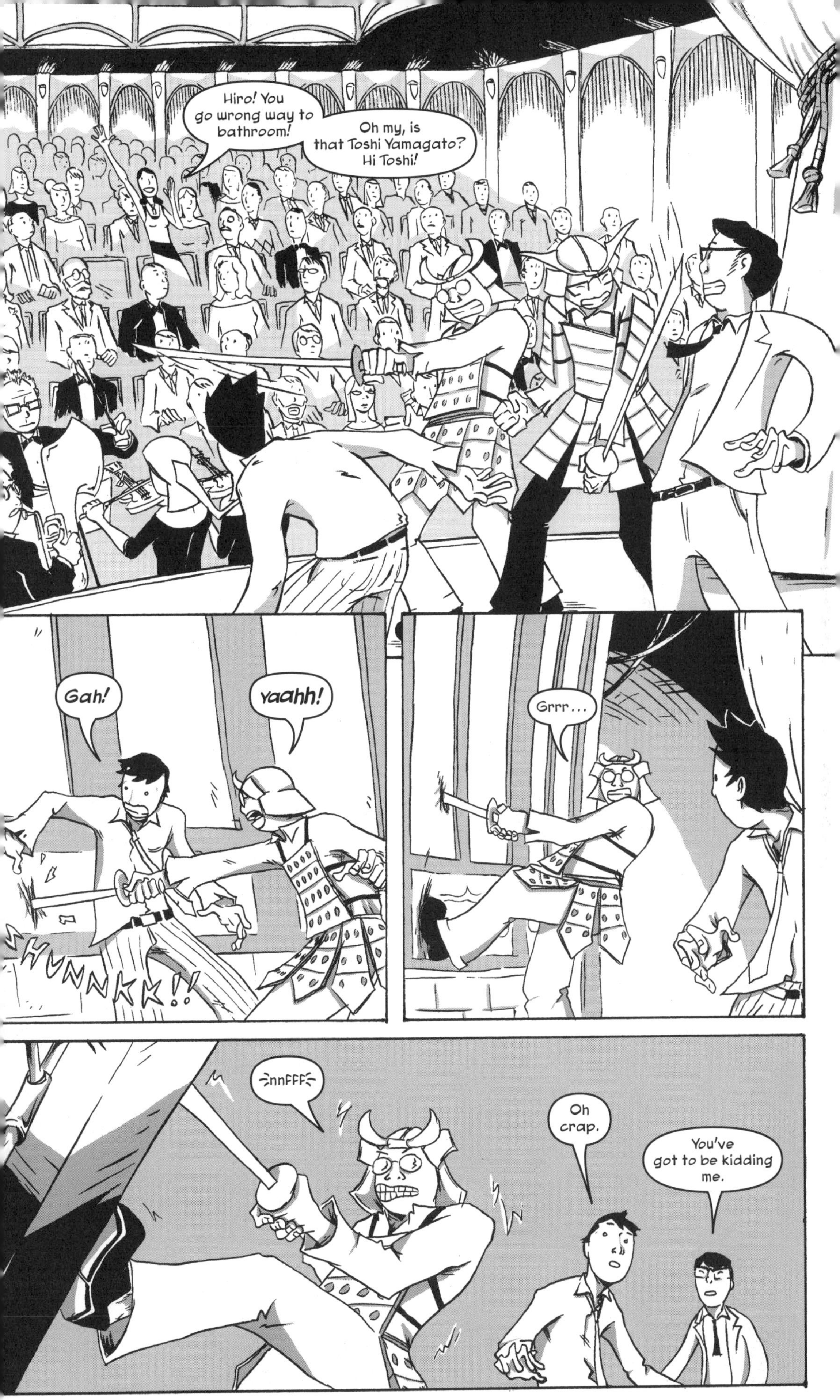
Hiro! You go wrong way to bathroom!
Oh my, is that Toshi Yamagato? Hi Toshi!
Gah!
Yaahh!
SHUNNKK!!
Grrr...
nnFFF
Oh crap.
You've got to be kidding me.

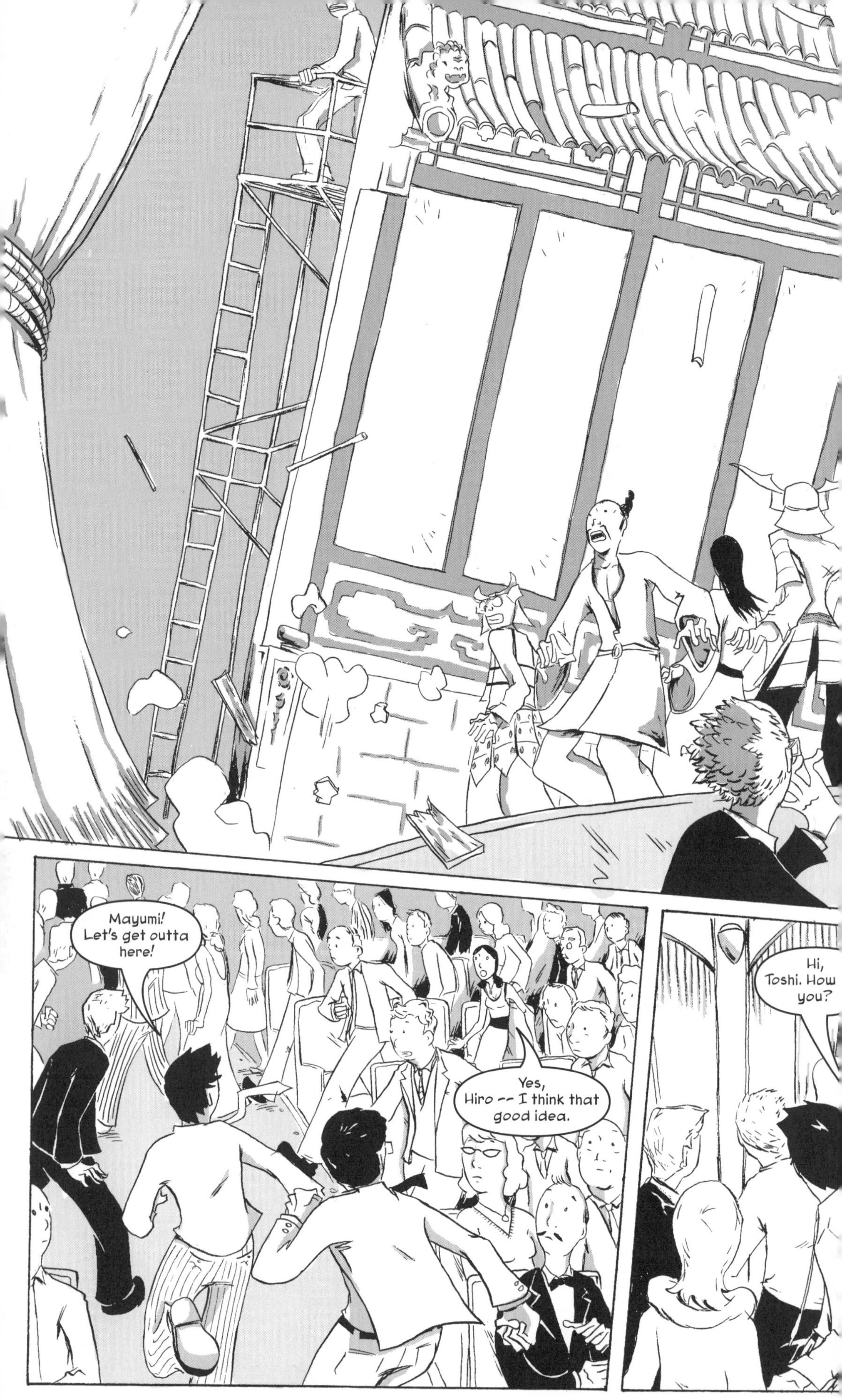
Mayumi! Let's get outta here!
Yes, Hiro -- I think that good idea.
Hi, Toshi. How you?

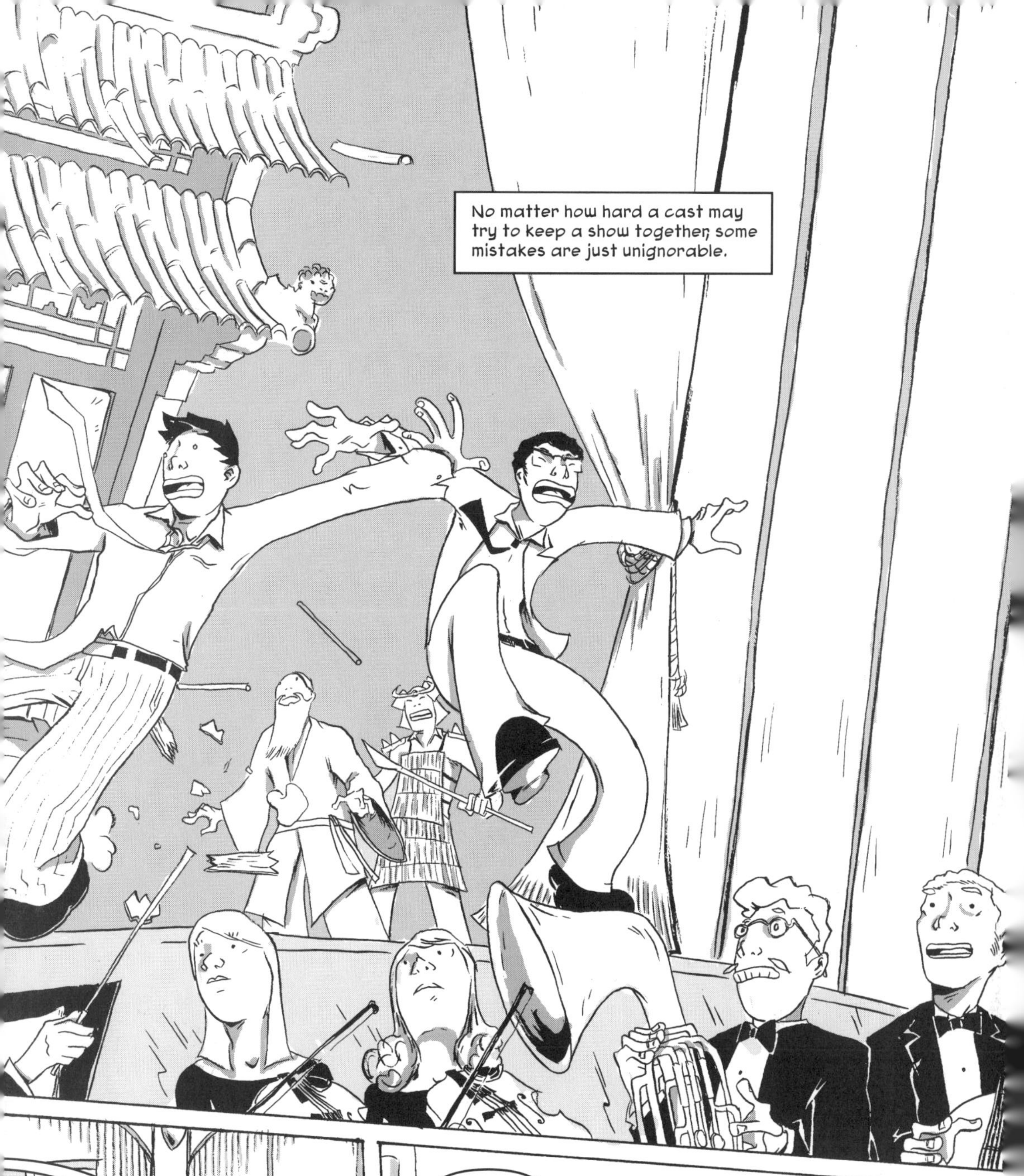
No matter how hard a cast may try to keep a show together, some mistakes are just unignorable.

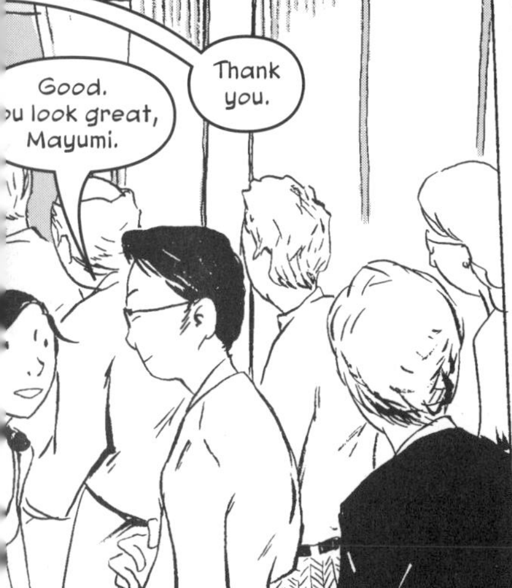
Good. ou look great, Mayumi.
Thank you.

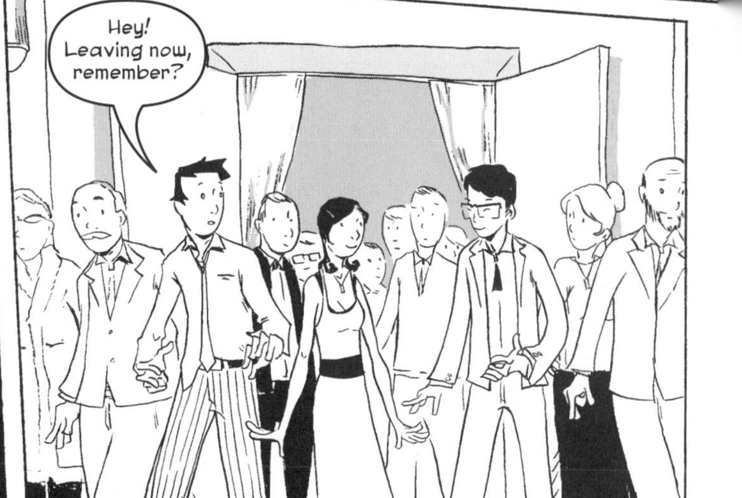
Hey! Leaving now, remember?

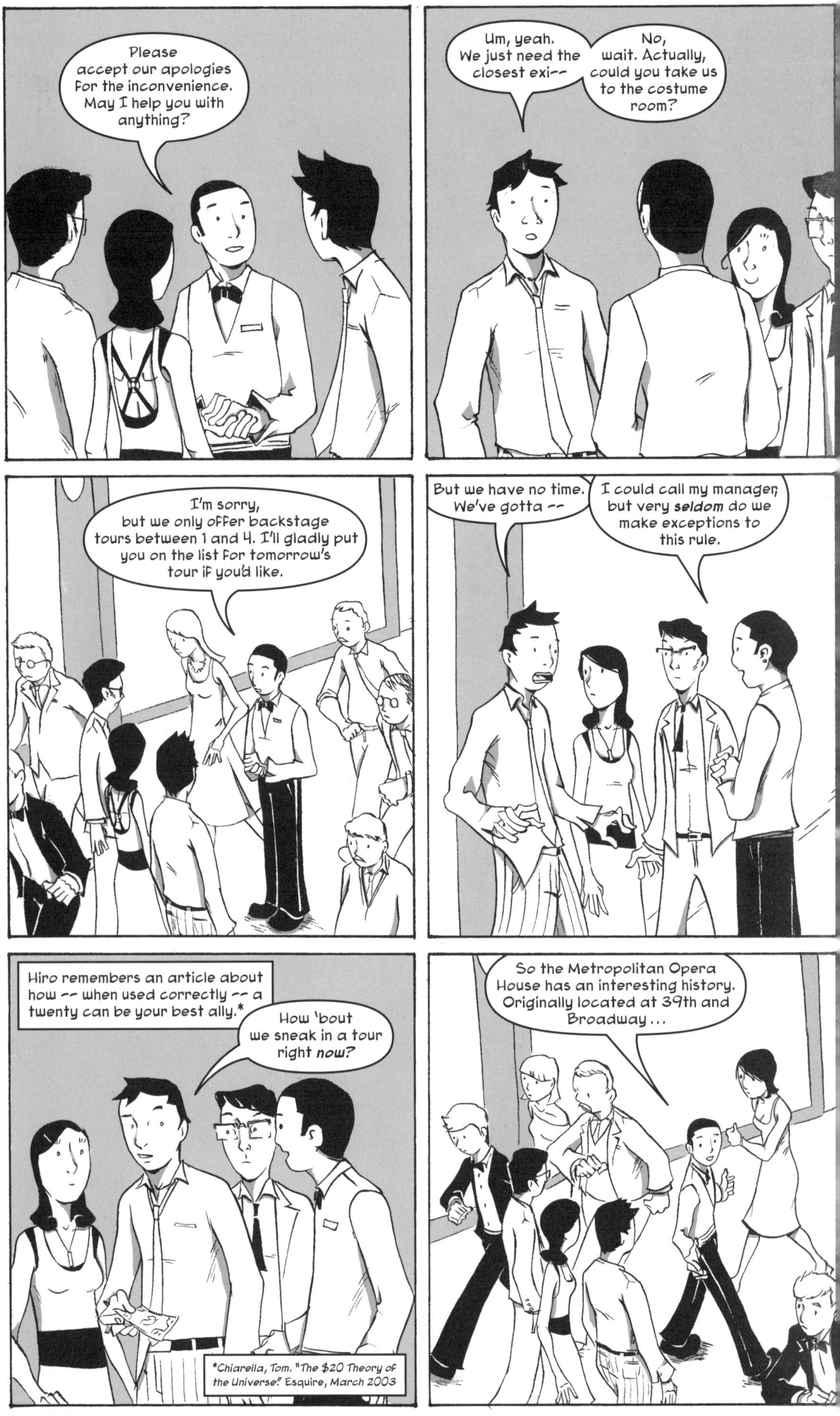

Please accept our apologies for the inconvenience. May I help you with anything?
Um, yeah. We just need the closest exi--
No, wait. Actually, could you take us to the costume room?
I'm sorry, but we only offer backstage tours between 1 and 4. I'll gladly put you on the list for tomorrow's tour if you'd like.
But we have no time. We've gotta --
I could call my manager, but very *seldom* do we make exceptions to this rule.
Hiro remembers an article about how -- when used correctly -- a twenty can be your best ally.*
How 'bout we sneak in a tour right *now?*
*Chiarella, Tom. "The $20 Theory of the Universe." Esquire, March 2003
So the Metropolitan Opera House has an interesting history. Originally located at 39th and Broadway . . .

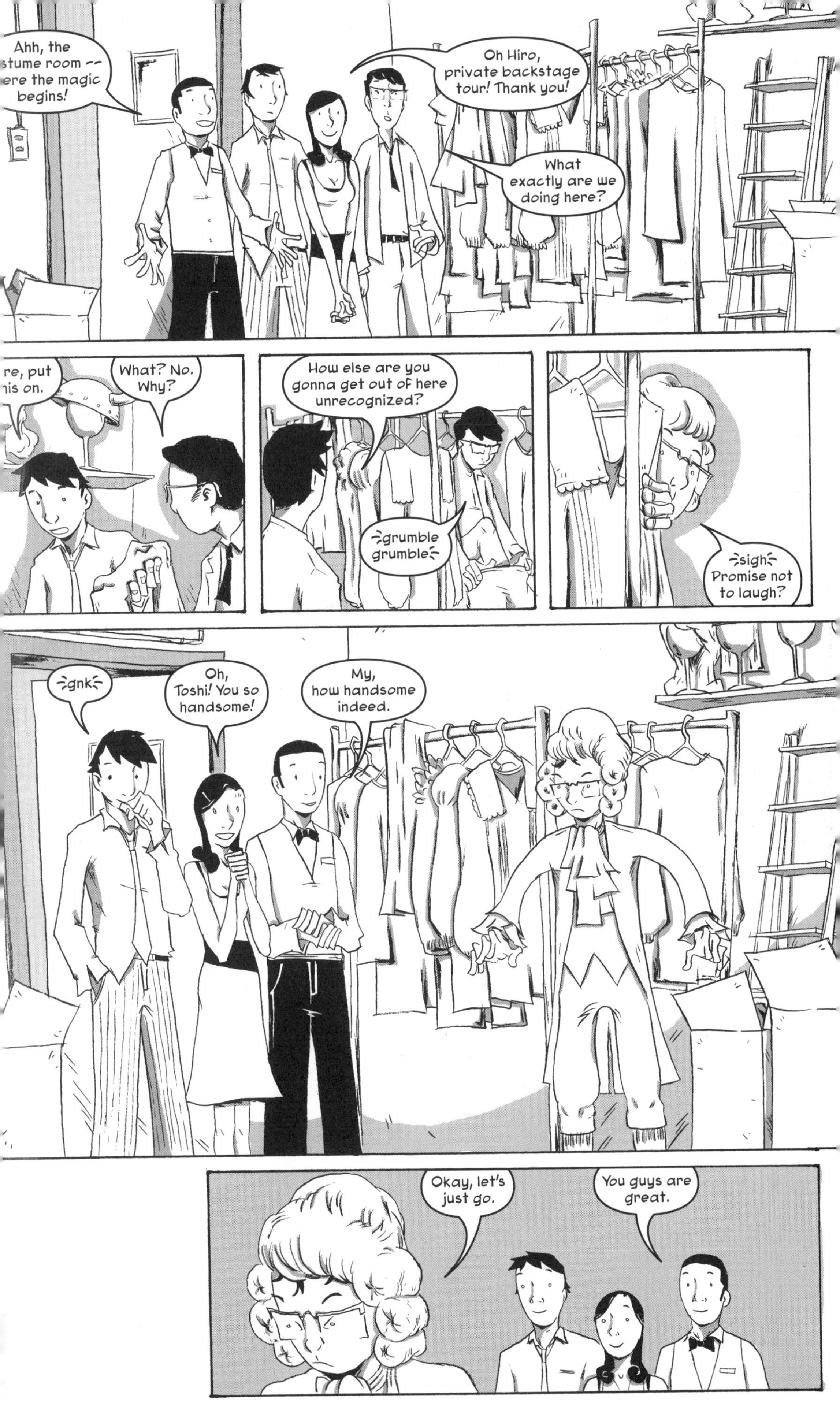
Ahh, the
stume room --
ere the magic
begins!
Oh Hiro,
private backstage
tour! Thank you!
What
exactly are we
doing here?
re, put
his on.
What? No.
Why?
How else are you
gonna get out of here
unrecognized?
grumble
grumble
sigh
Promise not
to laugh?
gnk
Oh,
Toshi! You so
handsome!
My,
how handsome
indeed.
Okay, let's
just go.
You guys are
great.

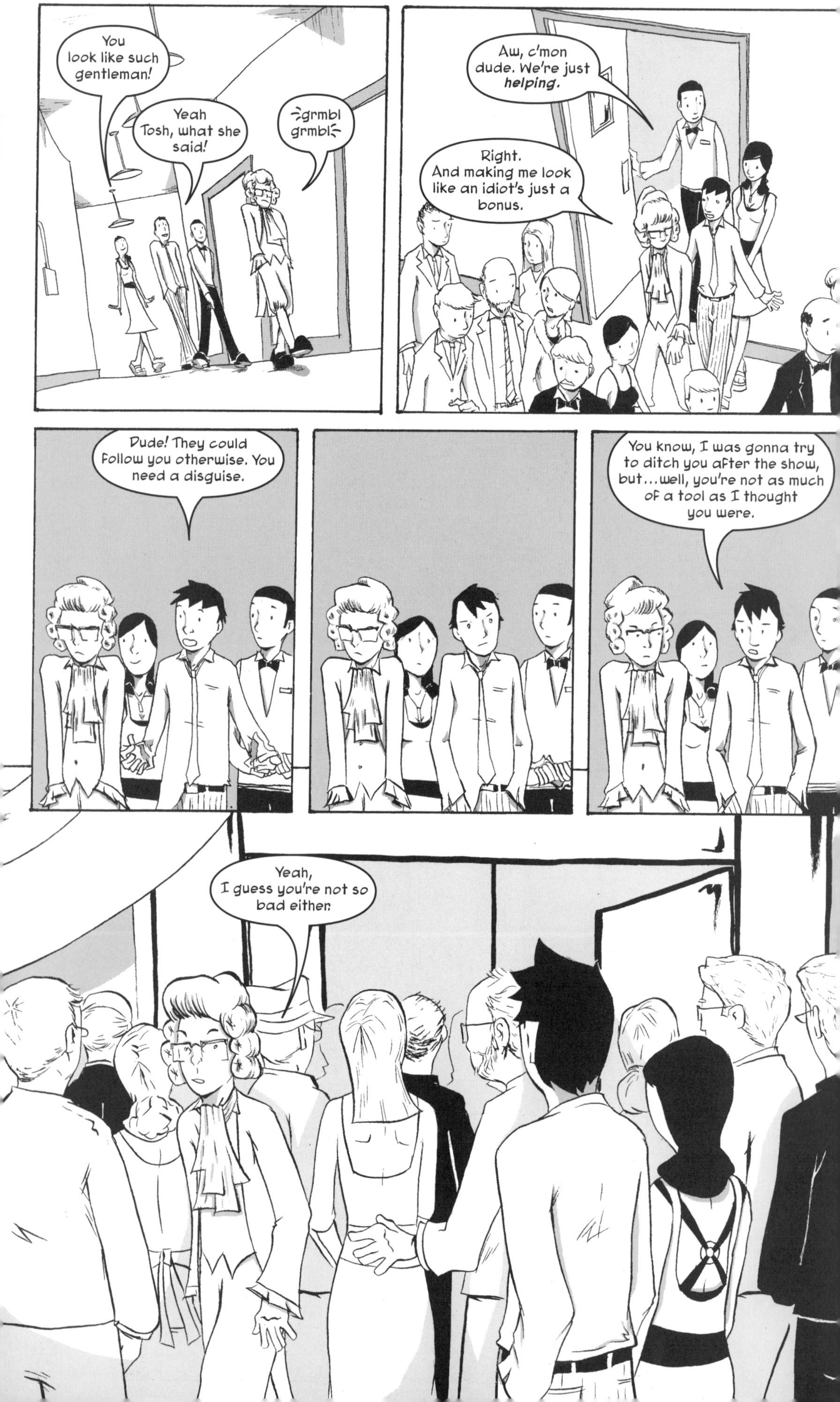
You look like such gentleman!
Yeah Tosh, what she said!
grmbl grmbl
Aw, c'mon dude. We're just ***helping.***
Right. And making me look like an idiot's just a bonus.
Dude! They could follow you otherwise. You need a disguise.
You know, I was gonna try to ditch you after the show, but...well, you're not as much of a tool as I thought you were.
Yeah, I guess you're not so bad either.

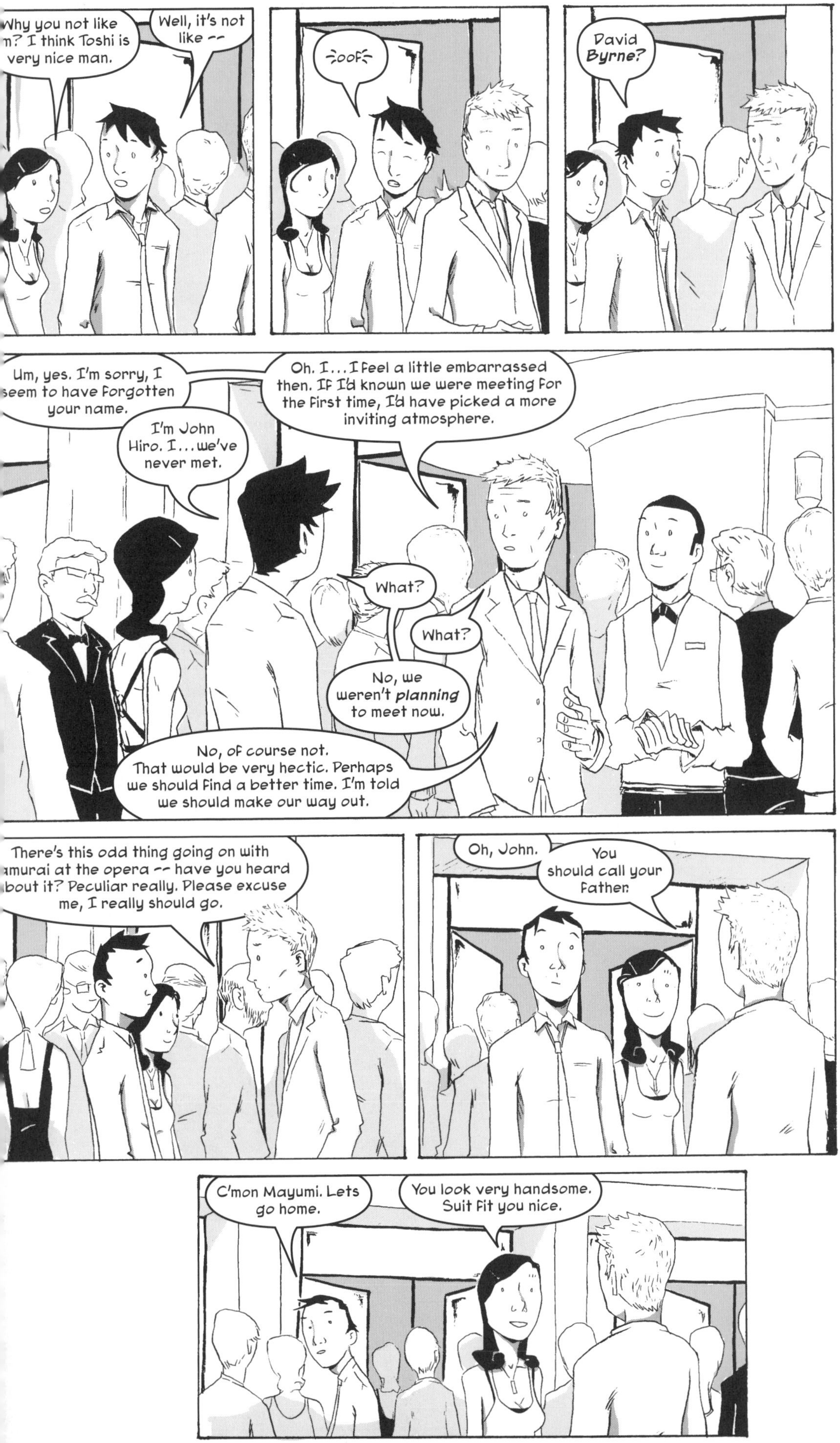
Why you not like
m? I think Toshi is very nice man.
Well, it's not like --
oof
David Byrne?
Um, yes. I'm sorry, I seem to have forgotten your name.
I'm John Hiro. I... we've never met.
Oh. I... I feel a little embarrassed then. If I'd known we were meeting for the first time, I'd have picked a more inviting atmosphere.
What?
What?
No, we weren't planning to meet now.
No, of course not. That would be very hectic. Perhaps we should find a better time. I'm told we should make our way out.
There's this odd thing going on with
amurai at the opera -- have you heard
bout it? Peculiar really. Please excuse me, I really should go.
Oh, John.
You should call your father.
C'mon Mayumi. Lets go home.
You look very handsome. Suit fit you nice.

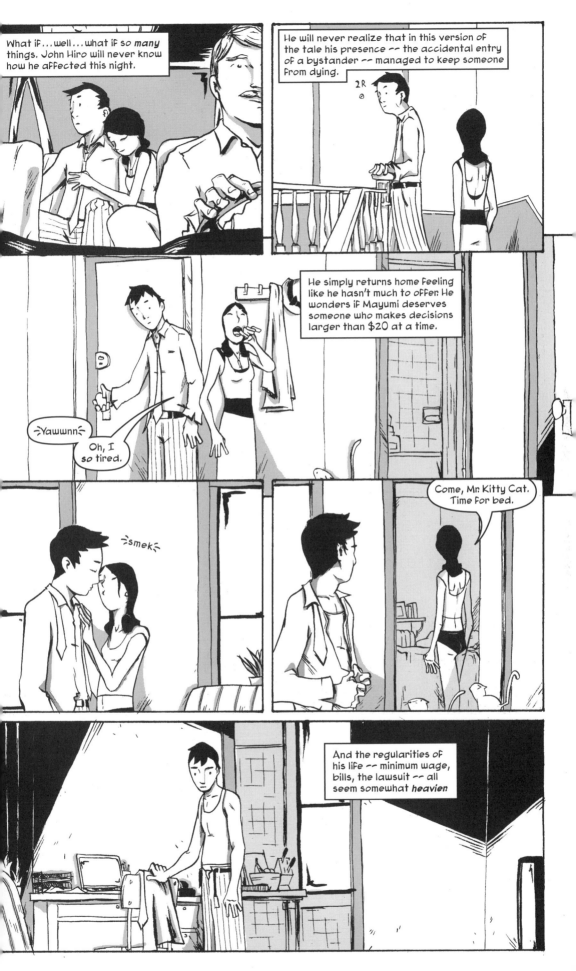

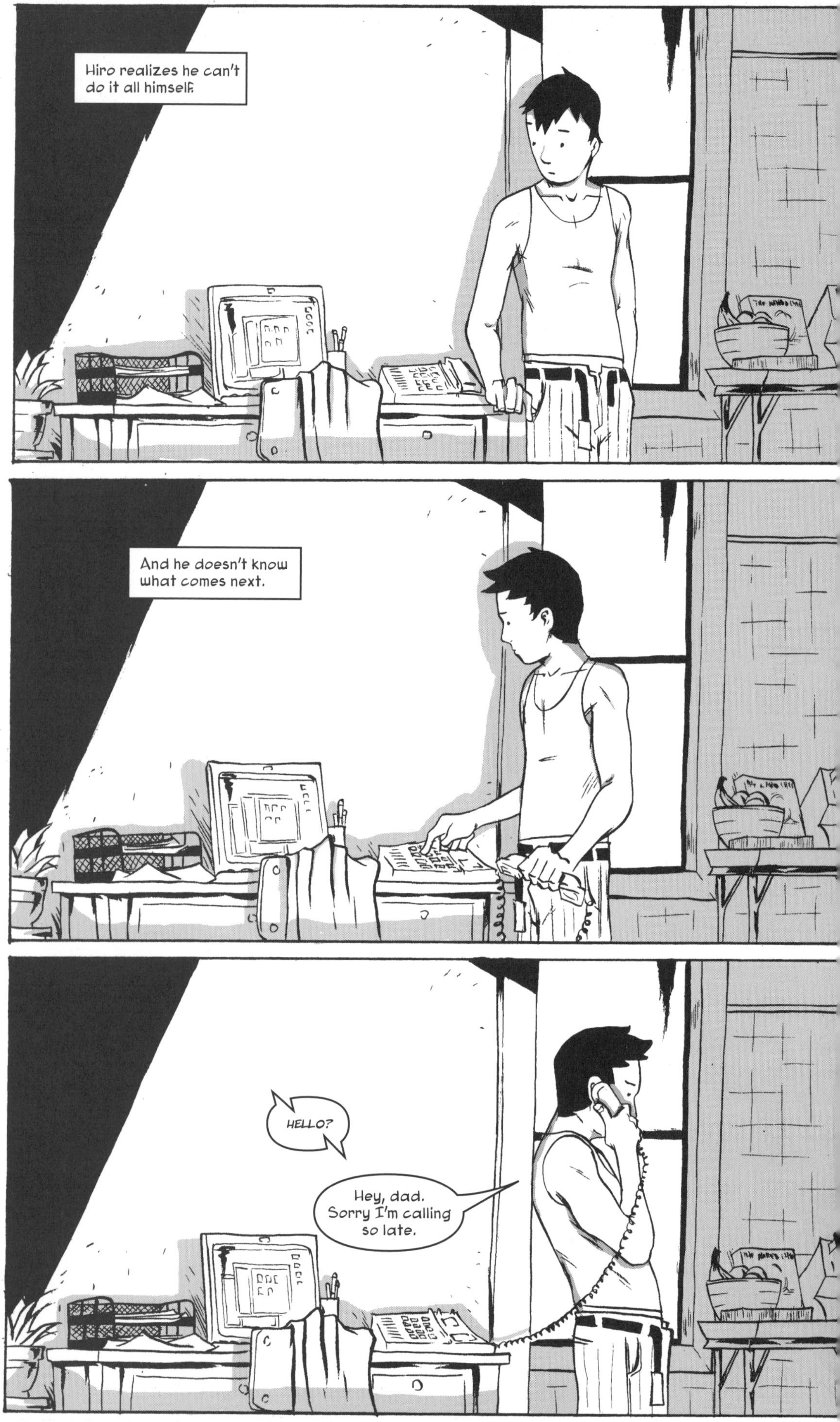
Hiro realizes he can't do it all himself.
And he doesn't know what comes next.
HELLO?
Hey, dad. Sorry I'm calling so late.

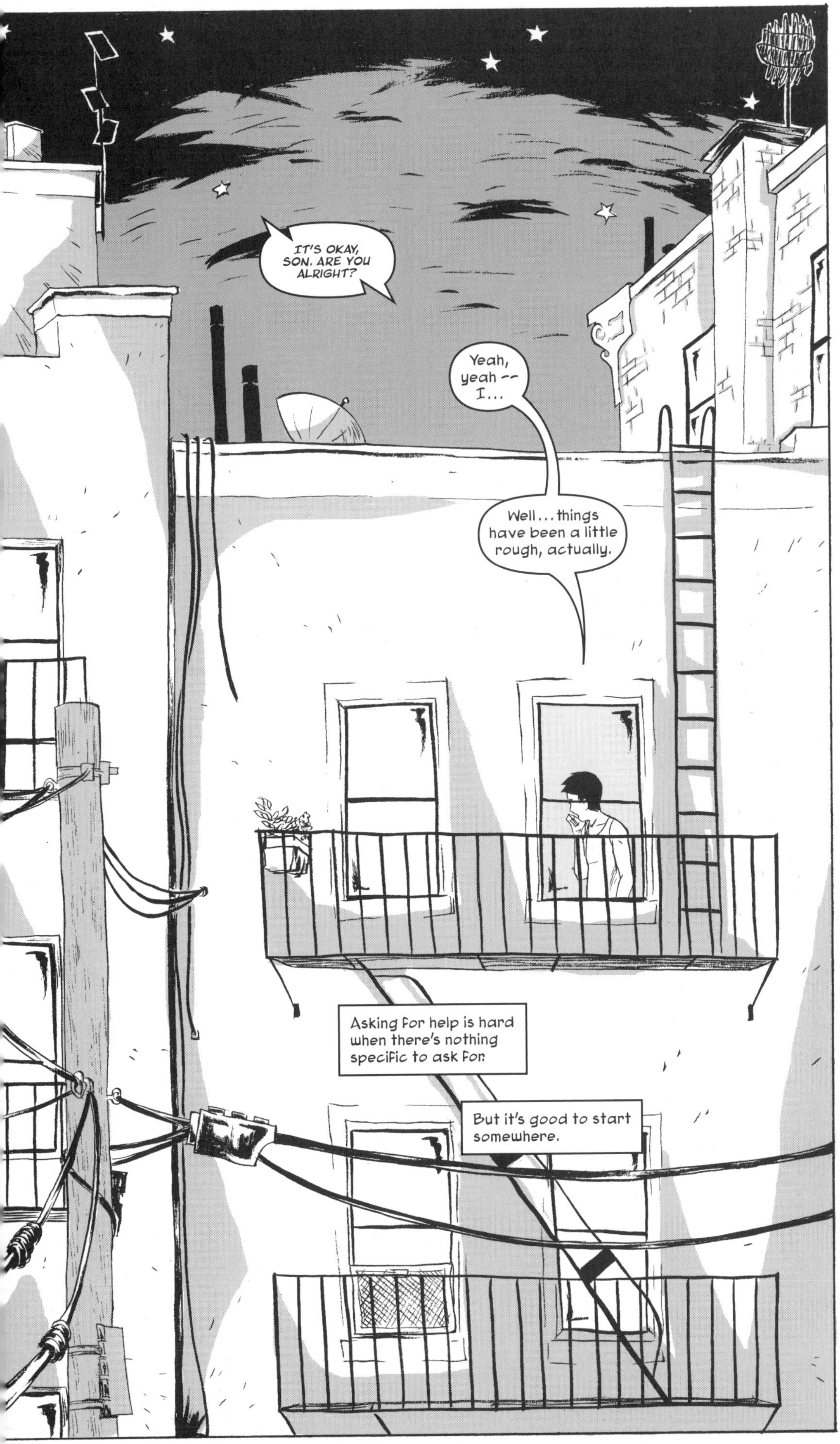
IT'S OKAY, SON. ARE YOU ALRIGHT?
Yeah, yeah -- I...
Well... things have been a little rough, actually.
Asking for help is hard when there's nothing specific to ask for.
But it's good to start somewhere.

僕の魚を平手で叩い

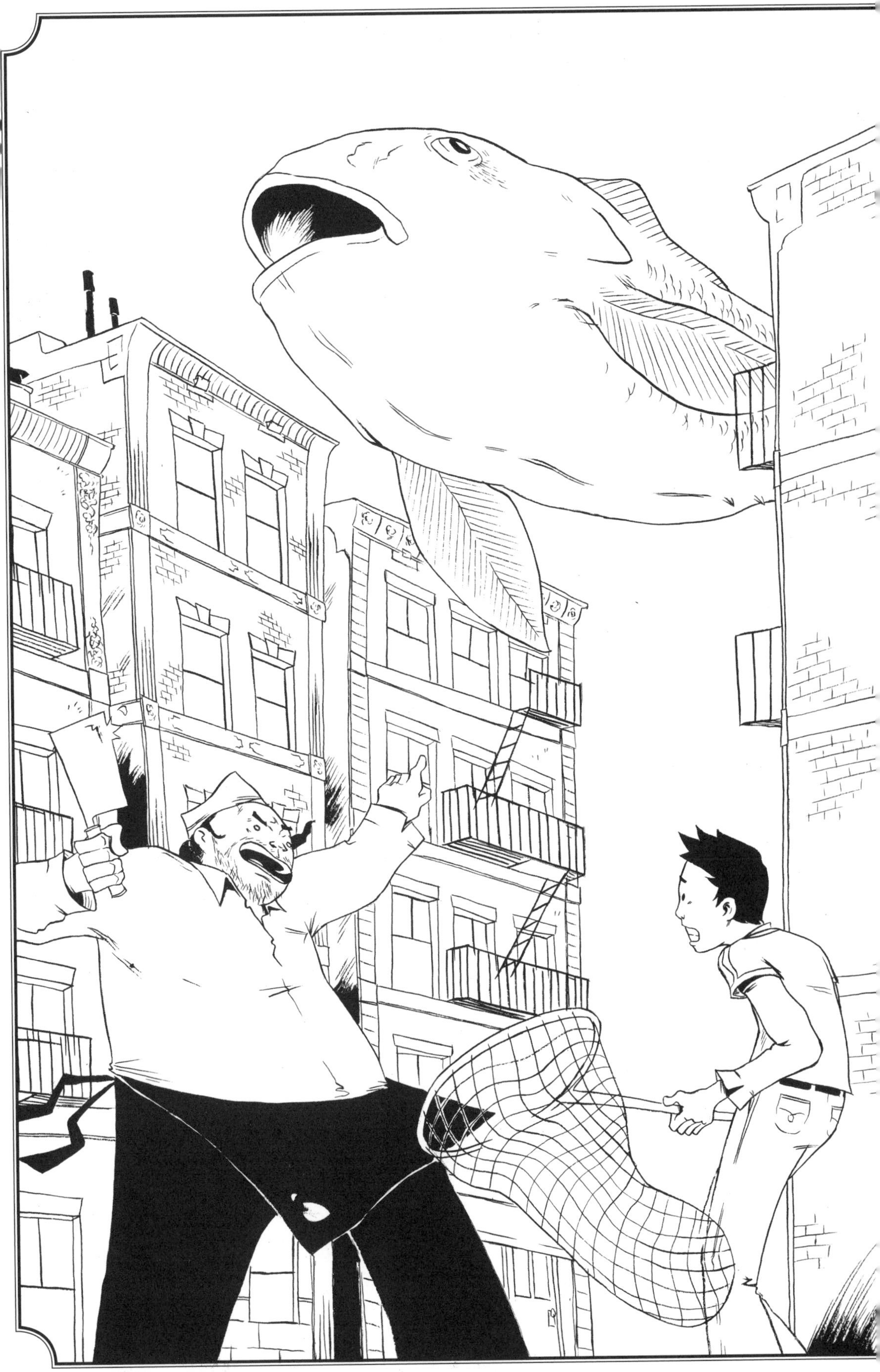

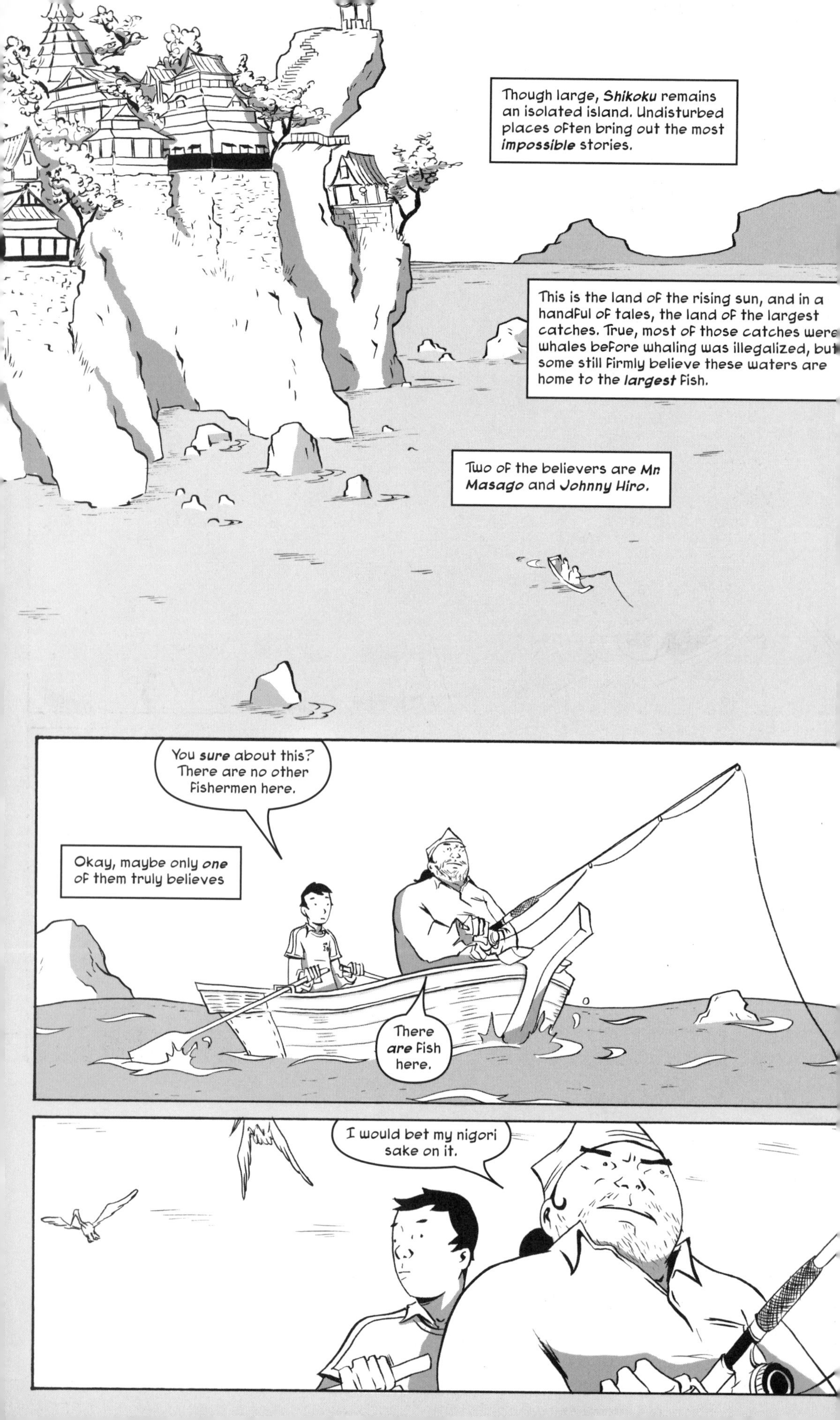
Though large, Shikoku remains an isolated island. Undisturbed places often bring out the most impossible stories.
This is the land of the rising sun, and in a handful of tales, the land of the largest catches. True, most of those catches were whales before whaling was illegalized, but some still firmly believe these waters are home to the largest fish.
Two of the believers are Mr. Masago and Johnny Hiro.
You sure about this? There are no other fishermen here.
Okay, maybe only one of them truly believes
There are fish here.
I would bet my nigori sake on it.

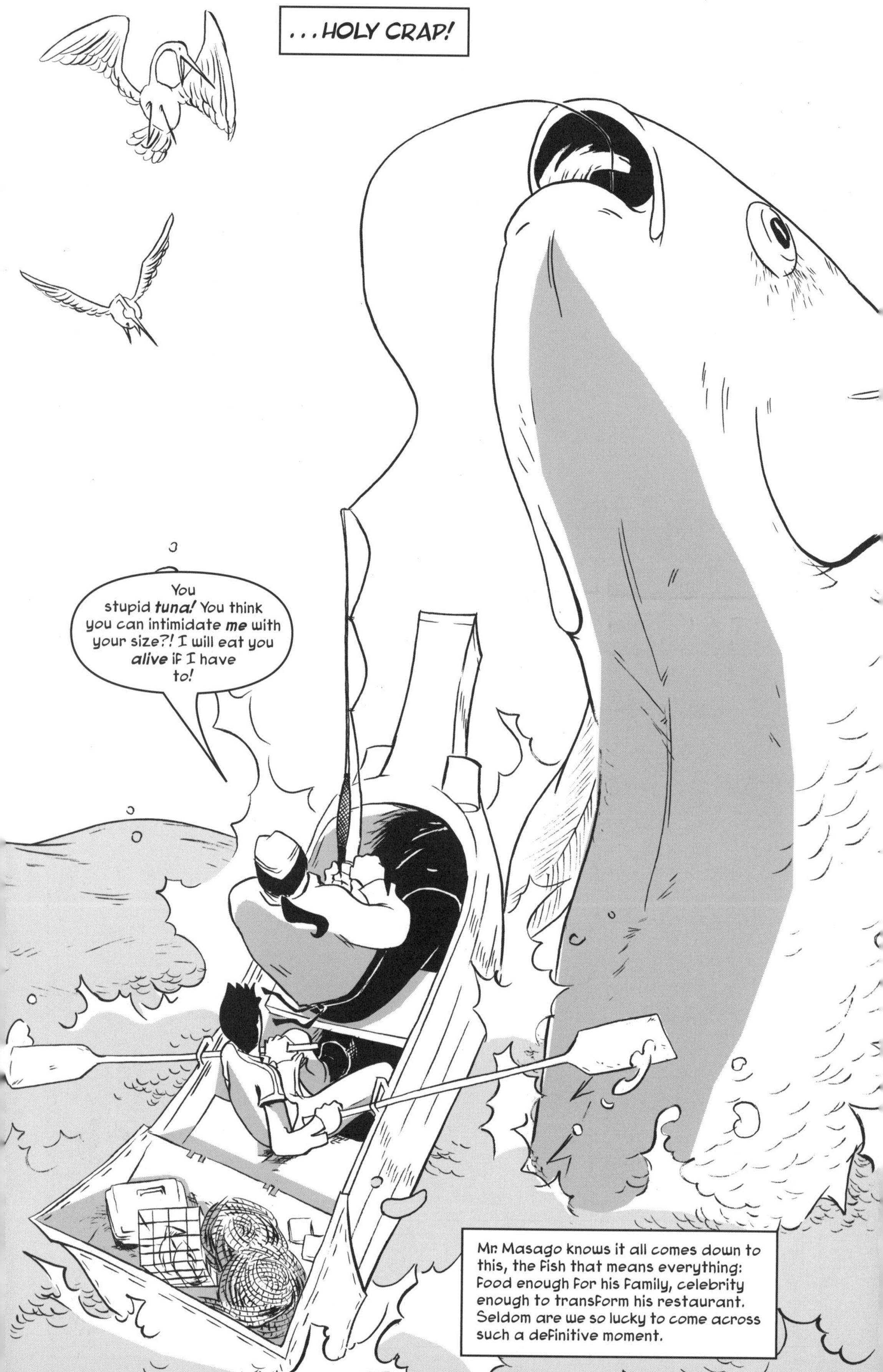

...HOLY CRAP!
You stupid *tuna!* You think you can intimidate *me* with your size?! I will eat you *alive* if I have to!
Mr. Masago knows it all comes down to this, the fish that means everything: food enough for his family, celebrity enough to transform his restaurant. Seldom are we so lucky to come across such a definitive moment.

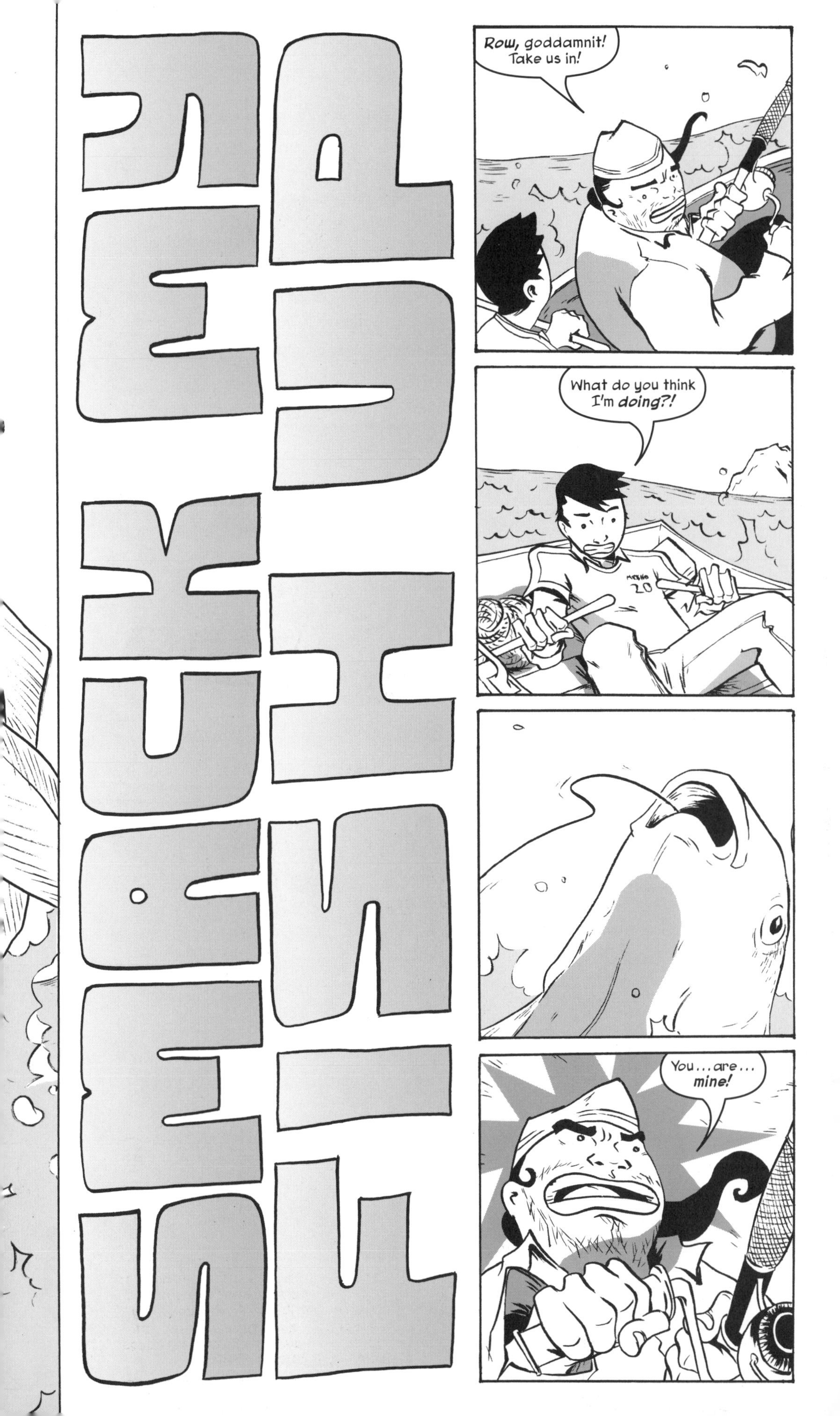

Row, goddamnit! Take us in!
What do you think I'm doing?!
You... are... mine!

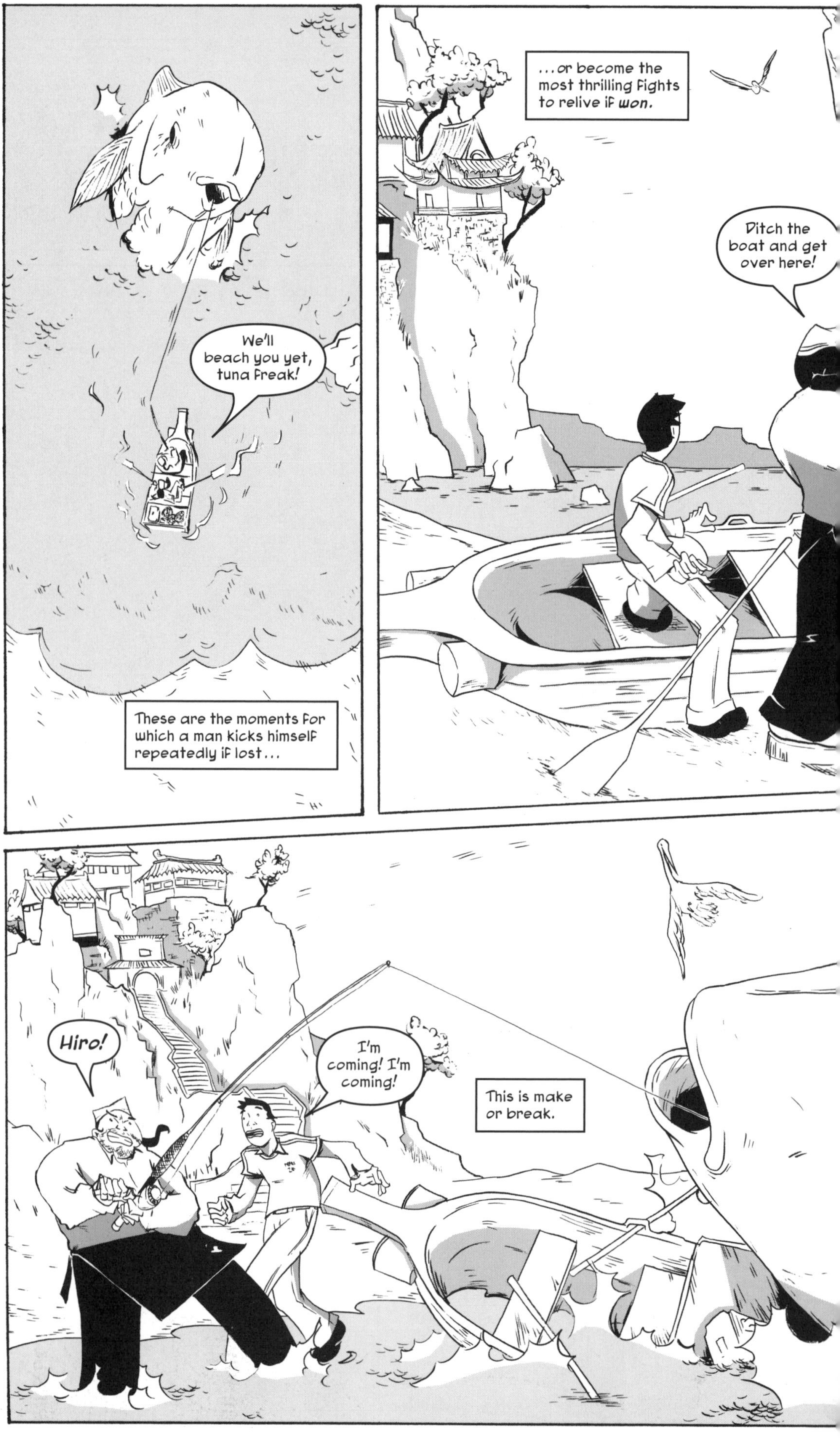
We'll beach you yet, tuna freak!
These are the moments for which a man kicks himself repeatedly if lost...
...or become the most thrilling fights to relive if *won*.
Ditch the boat and get over here!
Hiro!
I'm coming! I'm coming!
This is make or break.

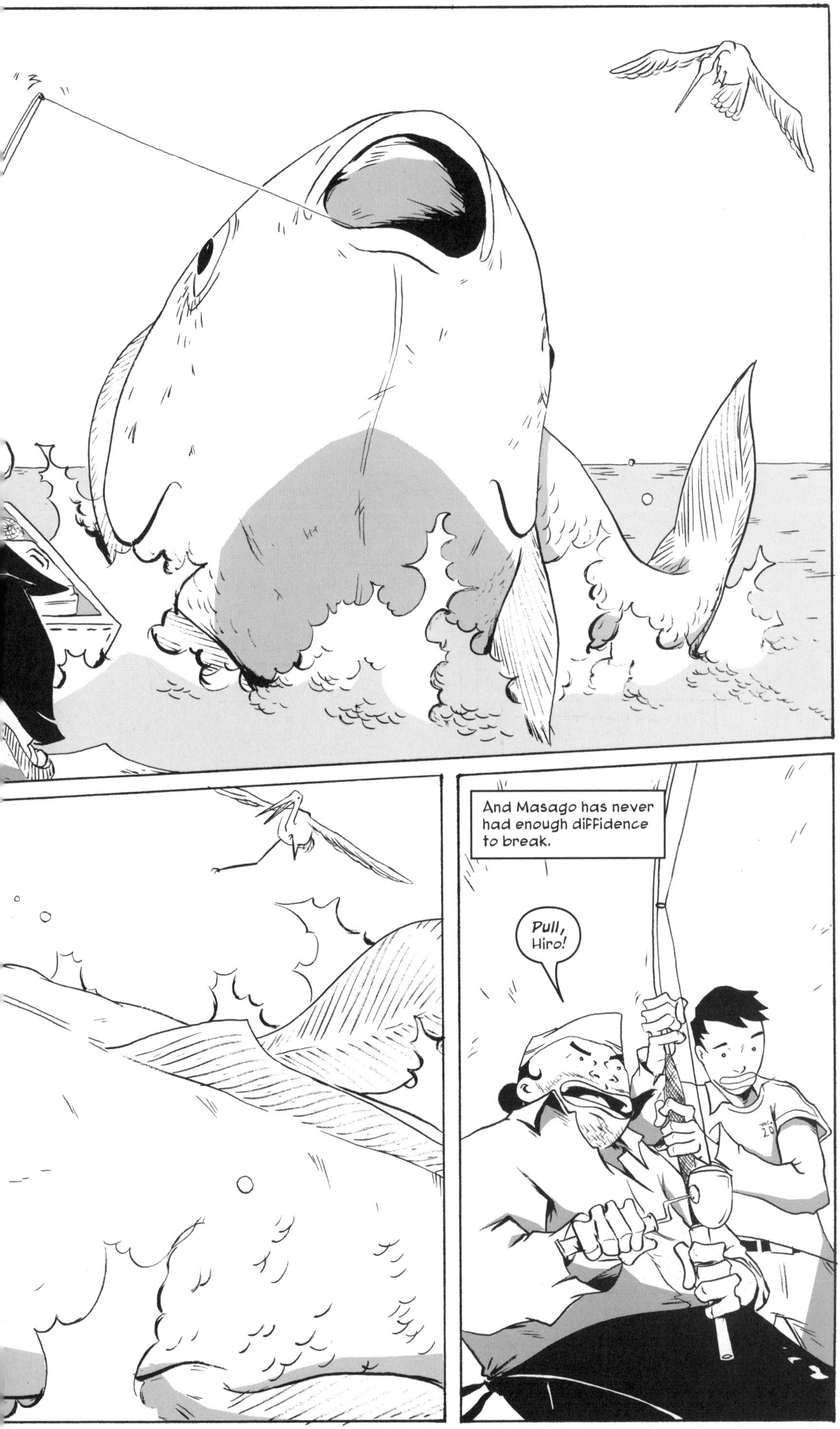
And Masago has never had enough diffidence to break.
Pull, Hiro!

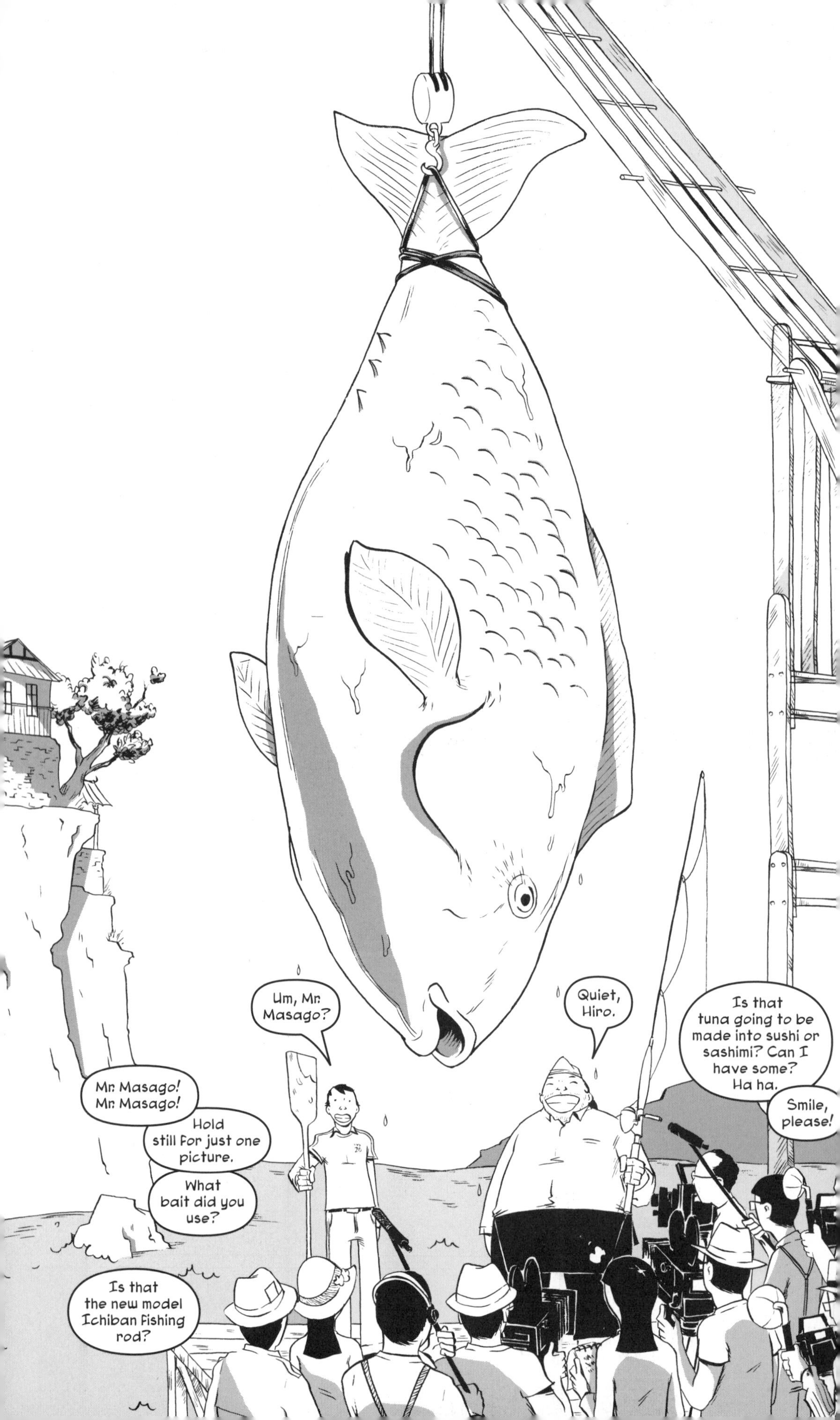
Um, Mr. Masago?
Quiet, Hiro.
Is that tuna going to be made into sushi or sashimi? Can I have some? Ha ha.
Smile, please!
Mr. Masago! Mr. Masago!
Hold still for just one picture.
What bait did you use?
Is that the new model Ichiban fishing rod?

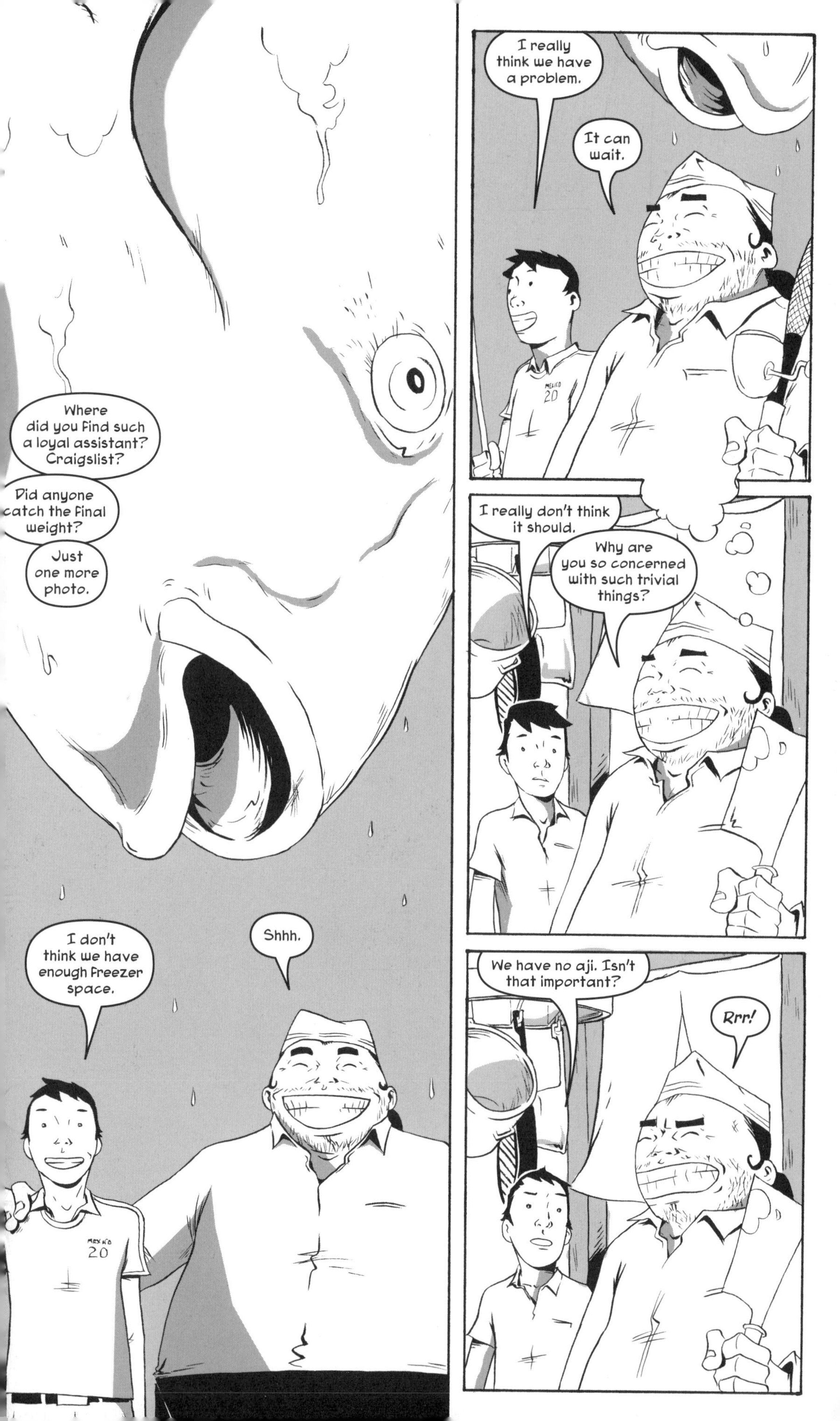
Where did you find such a loyal assistant? Craigslist?
Did anyone catch the final weight?
Just one more photo.
I don't think we have enough freezer space.
Shhh.
MEXICO 20
I really think we have a problem.
It can wait.
MEXICO 20
I really don't think it should.
Why are you so concerned with such trivial things?
We have no aji. Isn't that important?
Rrr!

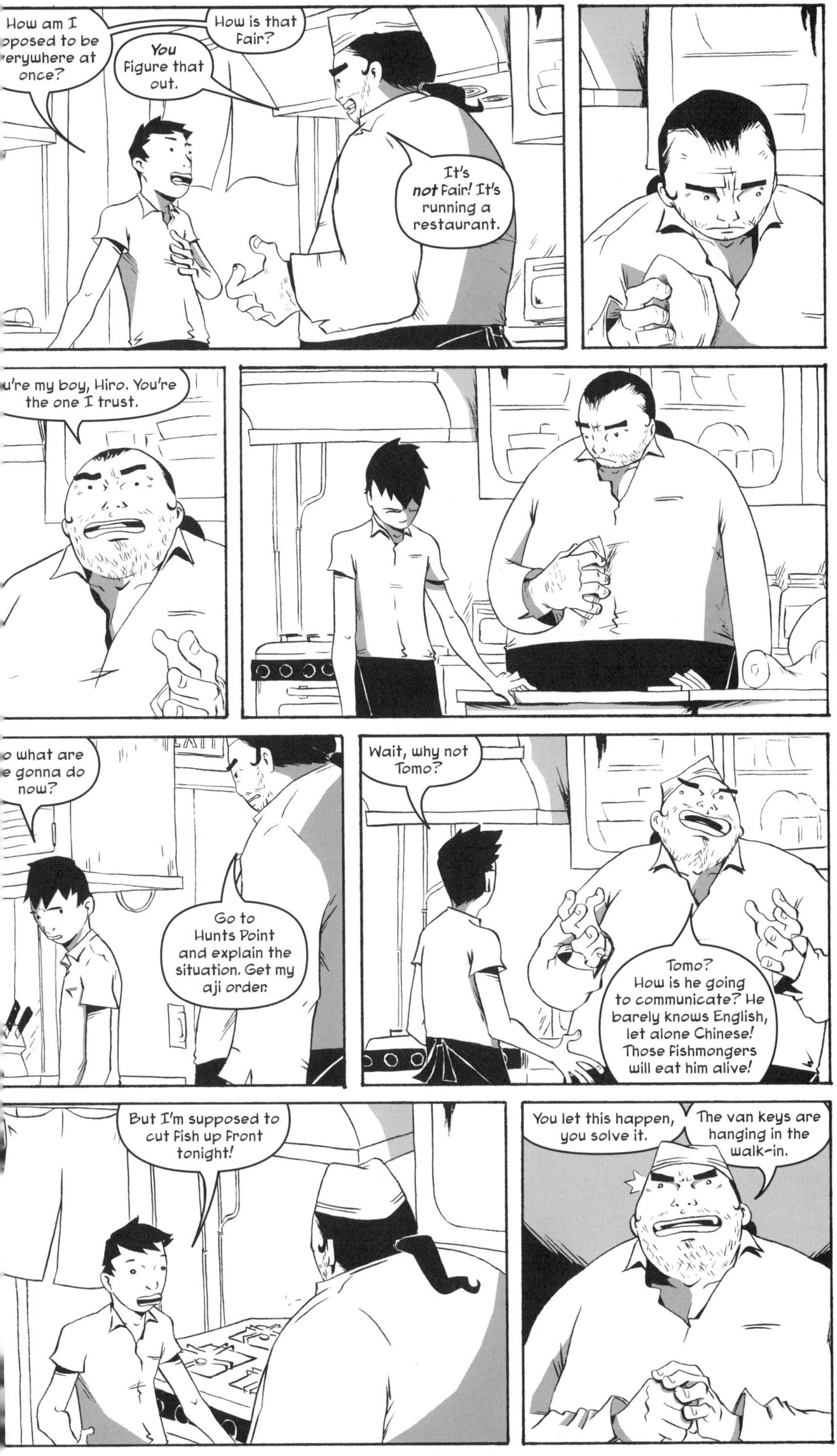
How am I
pposed to be
erywhere at
once?
How is that
fair?
You
figure that
out.
It's
not fair! It's
running a
restaurant.
u're my boy, Hiro. You're
the one I trust.
o what are
e gonna do
now?
Go to
Hunts Point
and explain the
situation. Get my
aji order.
Wait, why not
Tomo?
Tomo?
How is he going
to communicate? He
barely knows English,
let alone Chinese!
Those fishmongers
will eat him alive!
But I'm supposed to
cut fish up front
tonight!
You let this happen,
you solve it.
The van keys are
hanging in the
walk-in.

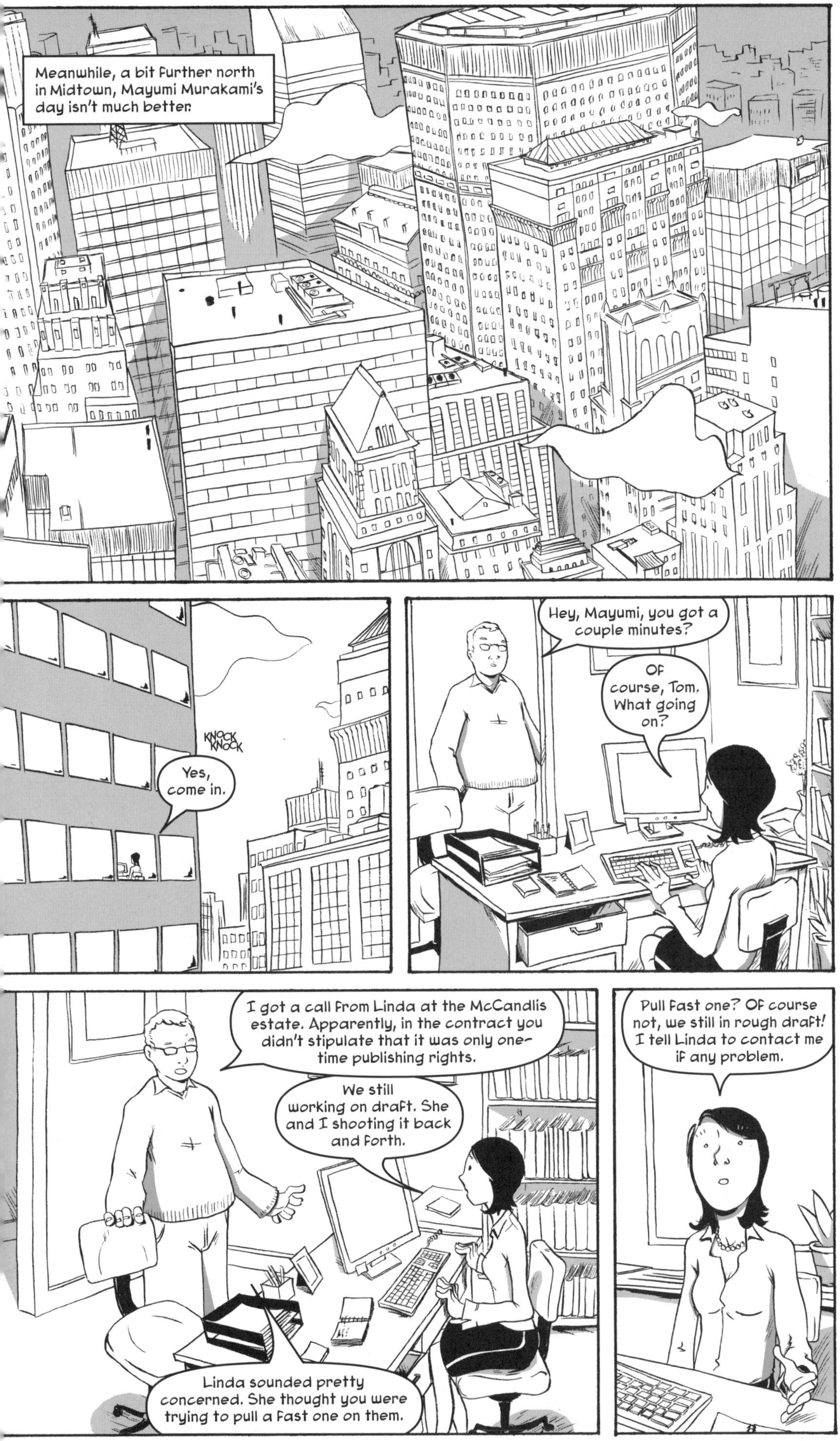
Meanwhile, a bit further north in Midtown, Mayumi Murakami's day isn't much better.
KNOCK KNOCK
Yes, come in.
Hey, Mayumi, you got a couple minutes?
Of course, Tom. What going on?
I got a call from Linda at the McCandlis estate. Apparently, in the contract you didn't stipulate that it was only one-time publishing rights.
We still working on draft. She and I shooting it back and forth.
Linda sounded pretty concerned. She thought you were trying to pull a fast one on them.
Pull fast one? Of course not, we still in rough draft! I tell Linda to contact me if any problem.

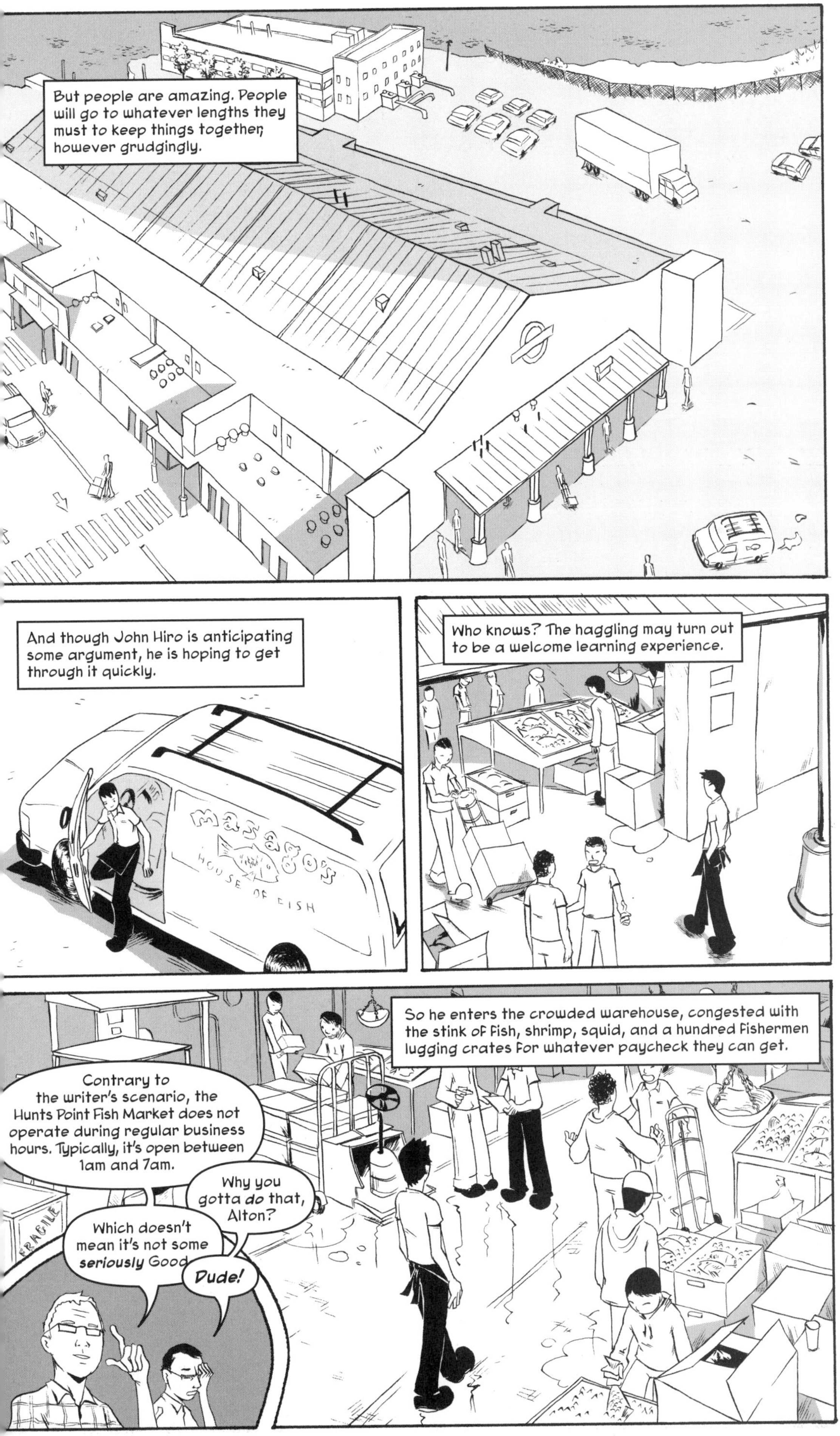
But people are amazing. People will go to whatever lengths they must to keep things together, however grudgingly.
And though John Hiro is anticipating some argument, he is hoping to get through it quickly.
HOUSE OF FISH
Who knows? The haggling may turn out to be a welcome learning experience.
So he enters the crowded warehouse, congested with the stink of fish, shrimp, squid, and a hundred fishermen lugging crates for whatever paycheck they can get.
Contrary to the writer's scenario, the Hunts Point Fish Market does not operate during regular business hours. Typically, it's open between 1am and 7am.
Why you gotta *do* that, Alton?
Which doesn't mean it's not some *seriously* Good
Dude!
FRAGILE

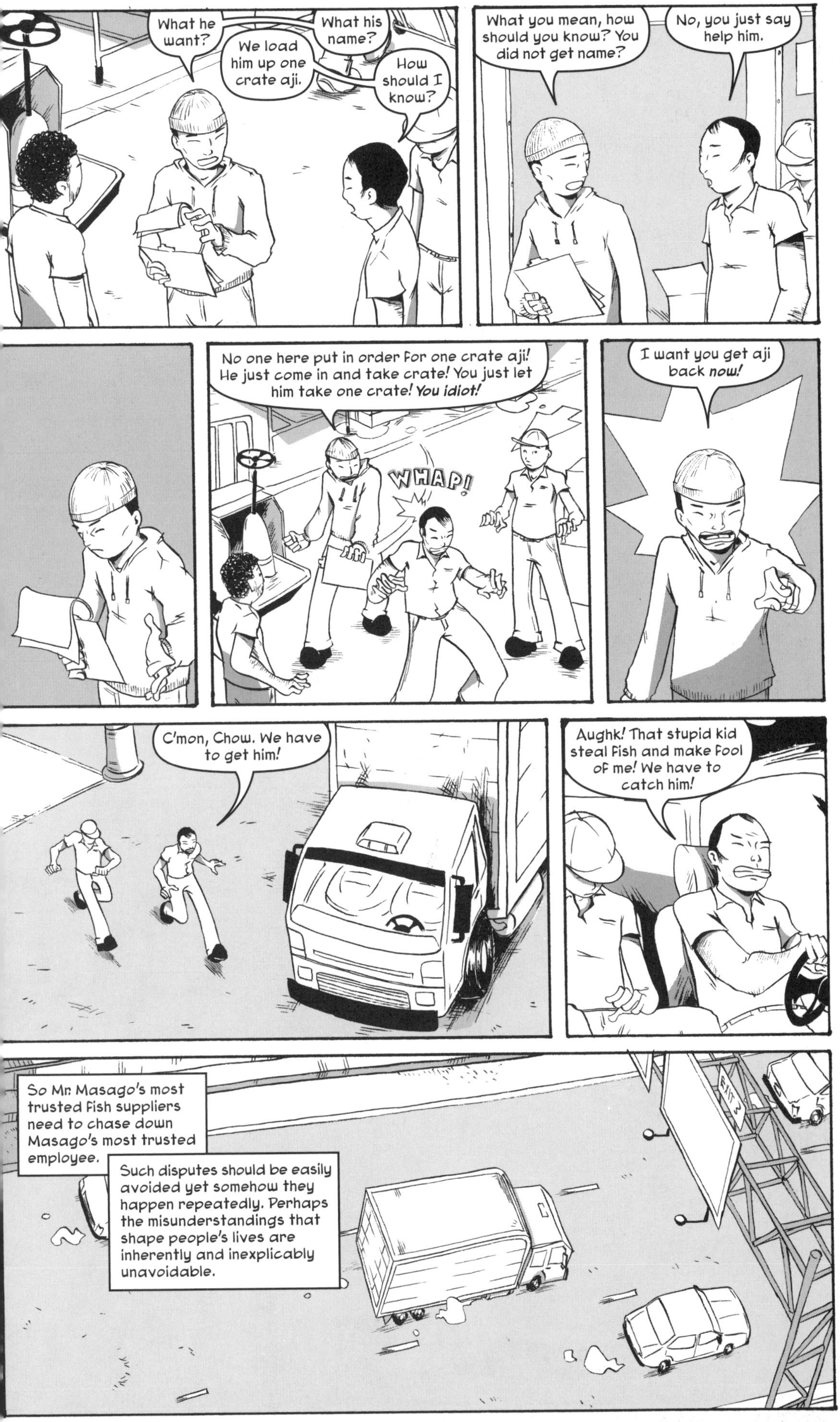
What he want?
What his name?
We load him up one crate aji.
How should I know?
What you mean, how should you know? You did not get name?
No, you just say help him.
No one here put in order for one crate aji! He just come in and take crate! You just let him take one crate! *You idiot!*
WHAP!
I want you get aji back *now!*
C'mon, Chow. We have to get him!
Aughk! That stupid kid steal fish and make fool of me! We have to catch him!
So Mr. Masago's most trusted fish suppliers need to chase down Masago's most trusted employee.
Such disputes should be easily avoided yet somehow they happen repeatedly. Perhaps the misunderstandings that shape people's lives are inherently and inexplicably unavoidable.
EXIT 3

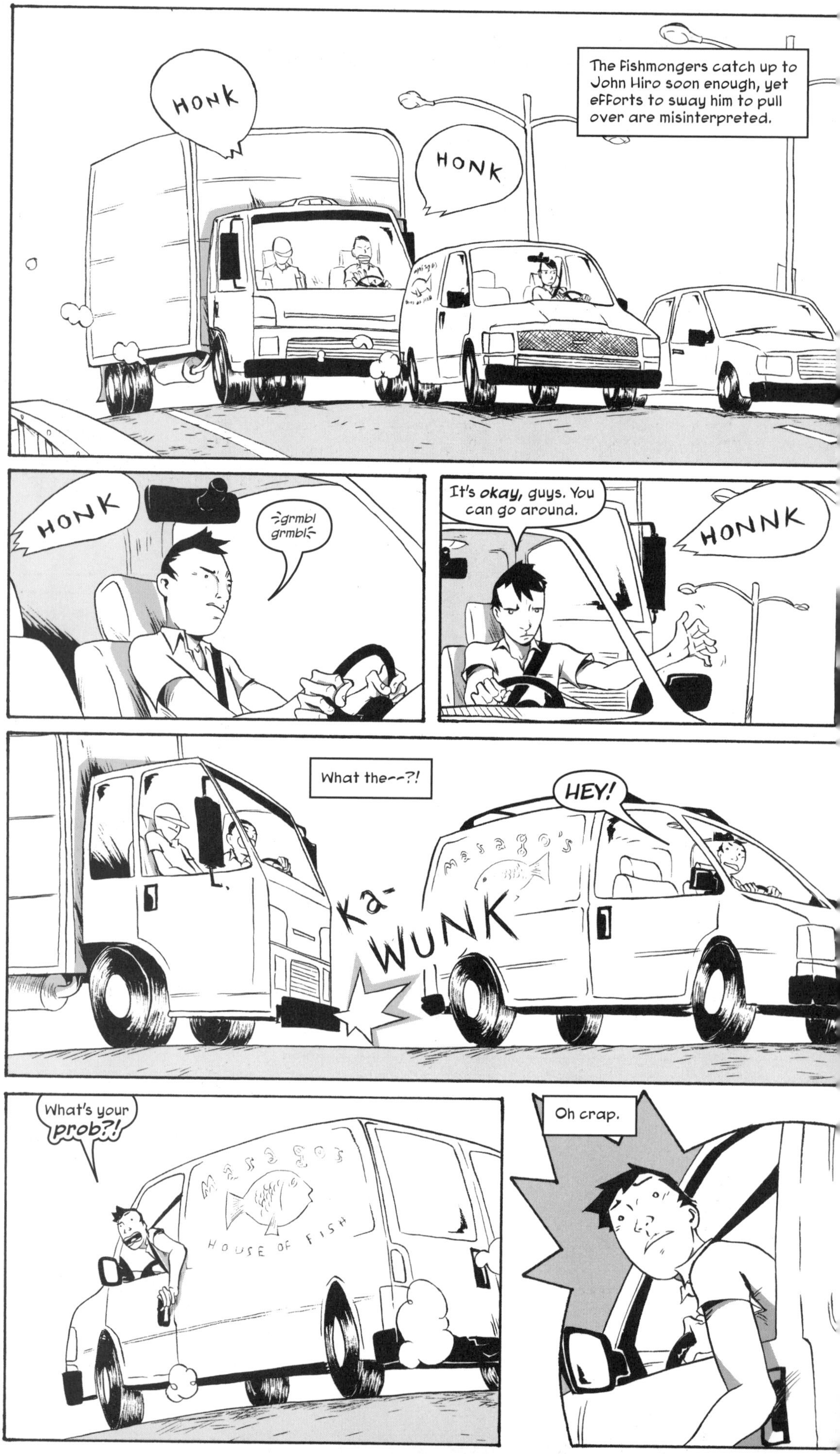
The fishmongers catch up to John Hiro soon enough, yet efforts to sway him to pull over are misinterpreted.
HONK
HONK
HONK
grmbl grmbl
It's *okay,* guys. You can go around.
HONNK
What the--?!
HEY!
KA-WUNK
What's your *prob?!*
Oh crap.

Perhaps John Hiro is settling in to his own racism. It seems that in the past few months, every time he comes across other Asians, they're out for his balls.

Fine. If it's time to play rough, he'll show them how it's done.

The chase begins.

Are his actions based on some kind of pride? A swill of fear and escape instincts? Either way, it's a stupid reason to weave recklessly through New York City traffic.

Finally.

This is where he'd lose them...

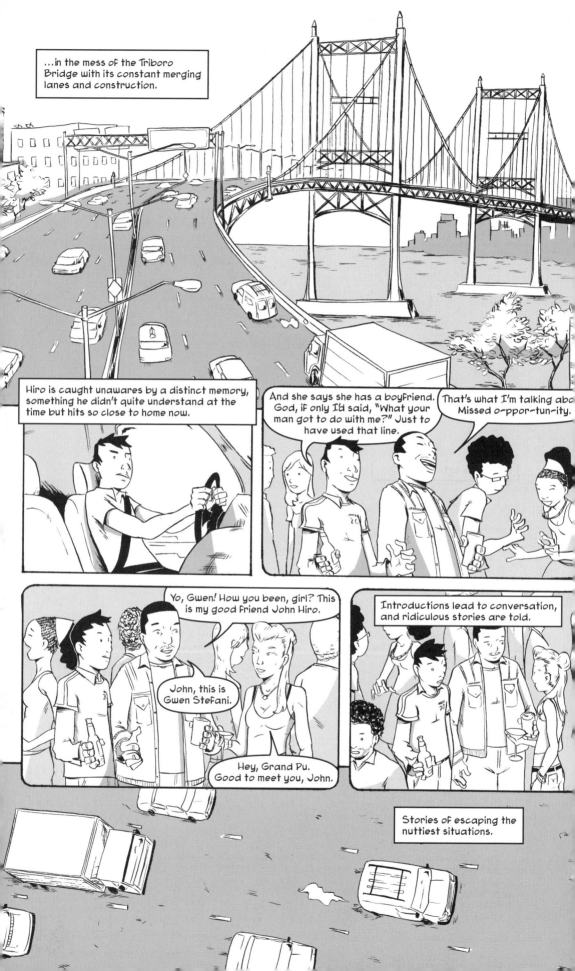

I thought I could be happy with him, I mean *really* happy. Well, one night when he's not around, I meet this other guy. This guy's hot and says all the right things. So I'm like, whatever, my boyfriend will never know.

Of course I feel guilty and tell him that I'd been bad. He doesn't forgive me. I tell him that it won't happen again, that we can make it better. But because I'm me...I do it again.

"He walks out on me. I think about him a lot."

POCK

"Thing is, I didn't mean for him to get hurt. It was never about him. It was -- well, let's just say I'd give almost anything to be his favorite girl again."

KKRRRSSHHH

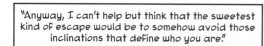

"Anyway, I can't help but think that the sweetest kind of escape would be to somehow avoid those inclinations that define who you are."

KFMP

That's when Akon, drunk, came around screaming:

Woo-hoo!

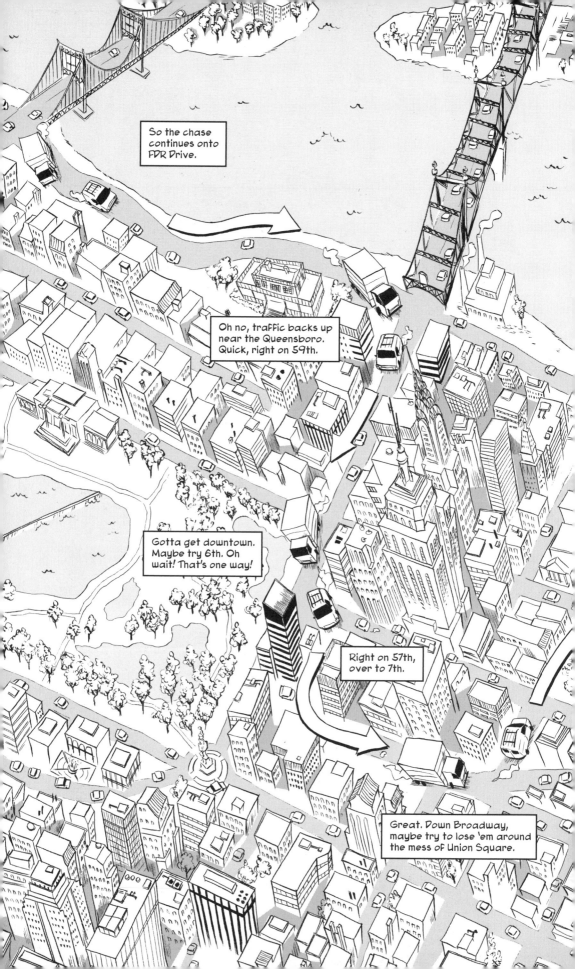

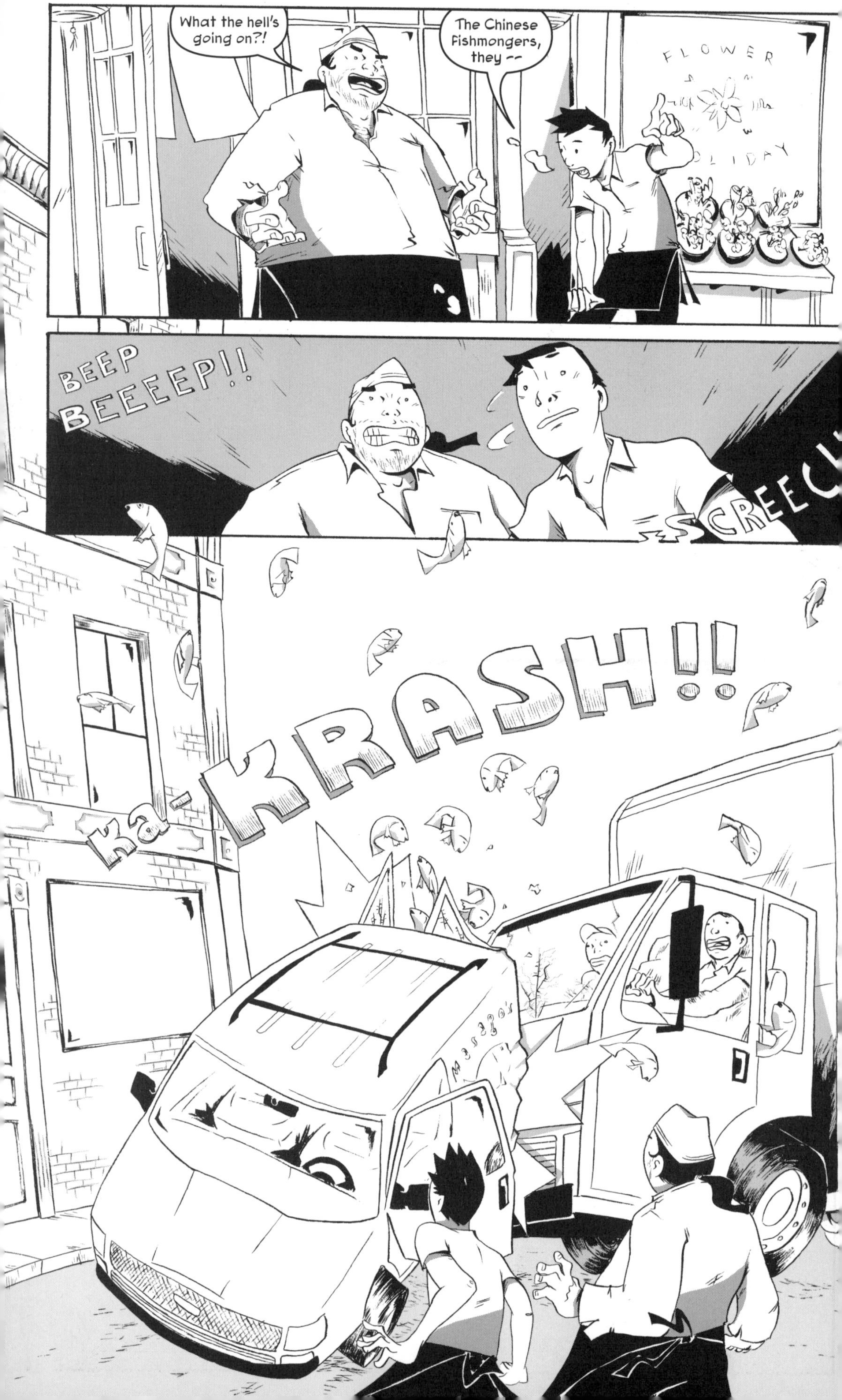

What the hell's going on?!
The Chinese fishmongers, they --
FLOWER
OLIDAY
BEEP
BEEEEP!!
SCREECH
Ka-KRASH!!

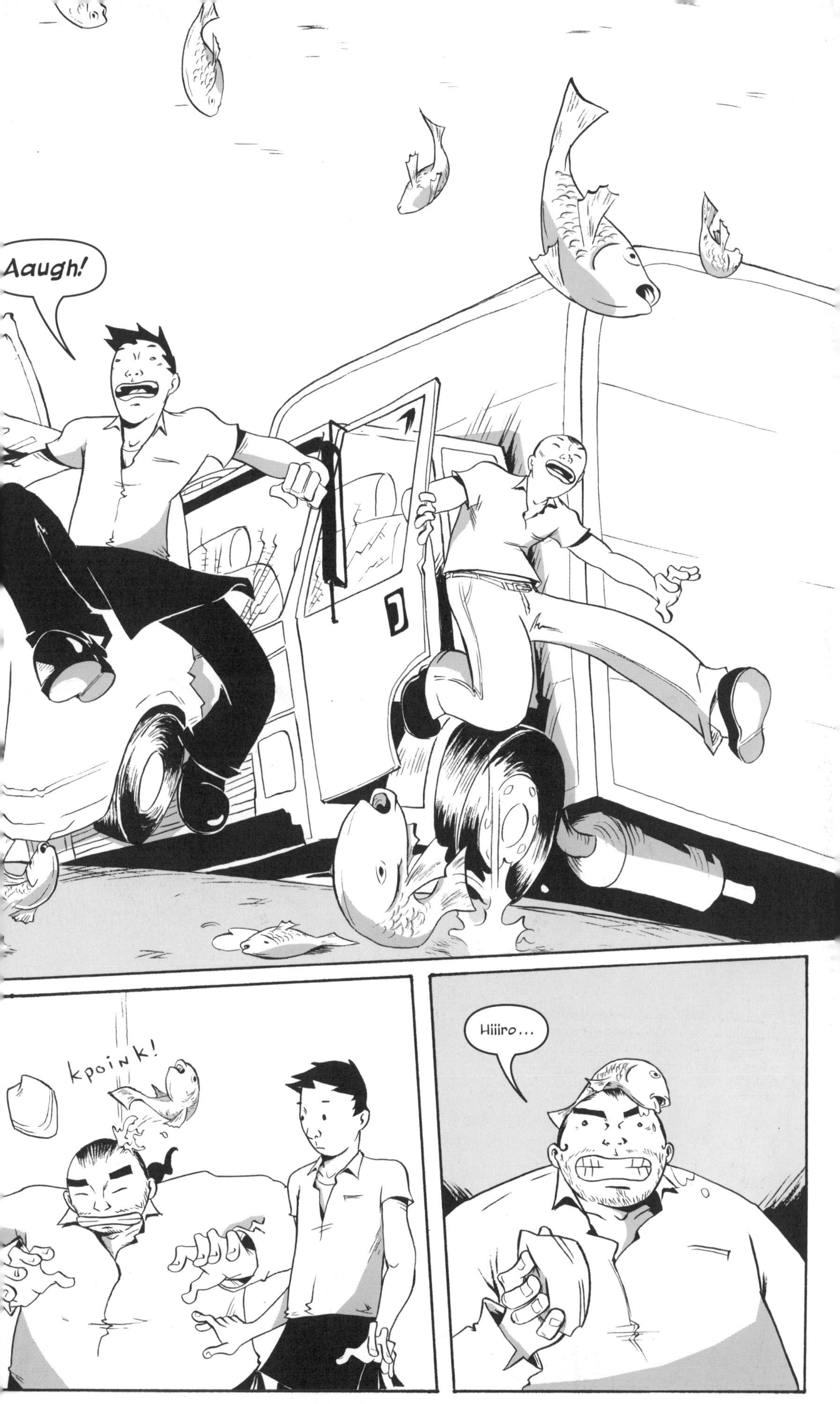
Aaugh!
kpoink!
Hiiiro...

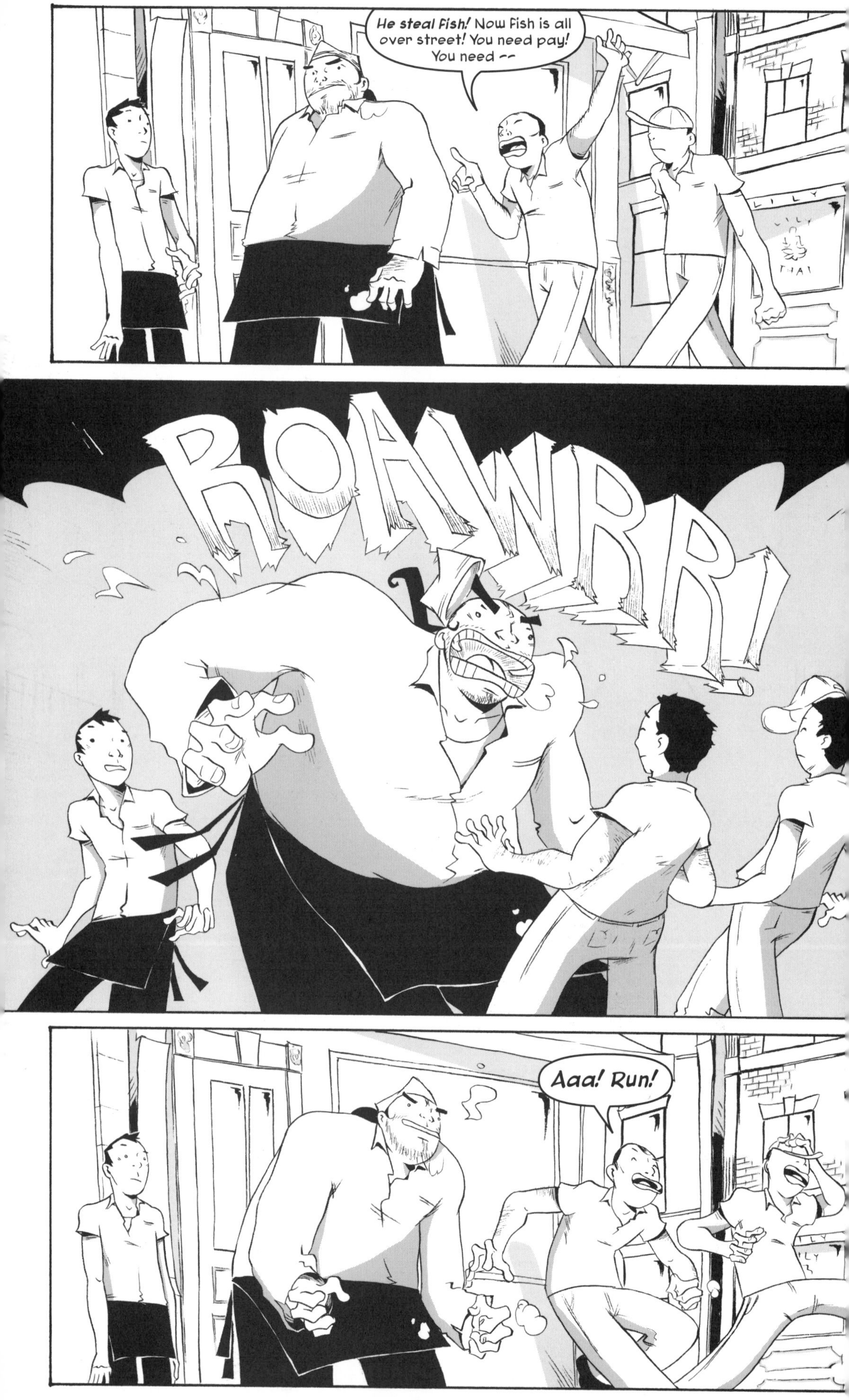
He steal fish! Now fish is all over street! You need pay! You need --
ROAWRR!
Aaa! Run!

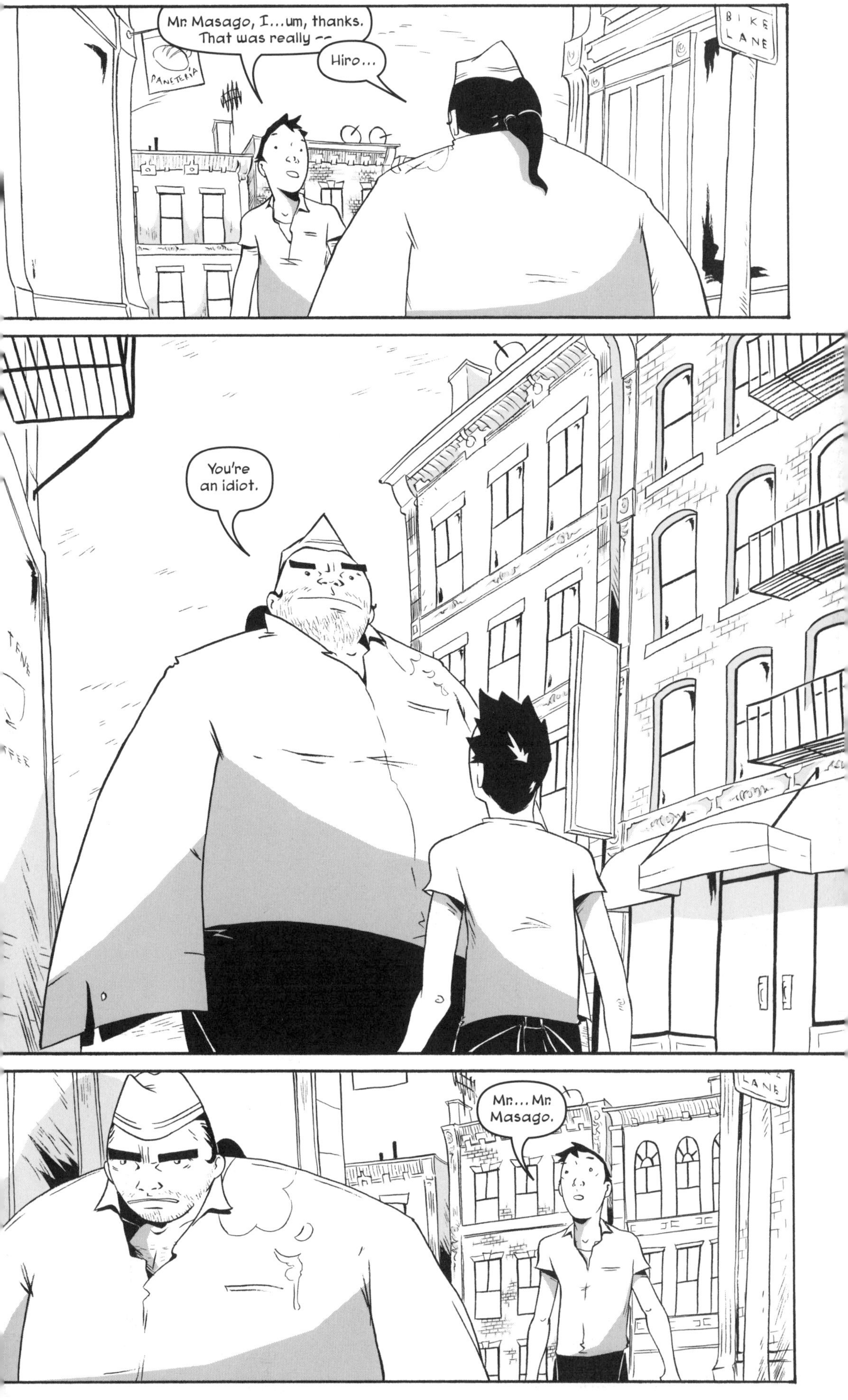
PANETERIA
BIKE LANE
Mr. Masago, I...um, thanks. That was really --
Hiro...
You're an idiot.
Mr.... Mr. Masago.

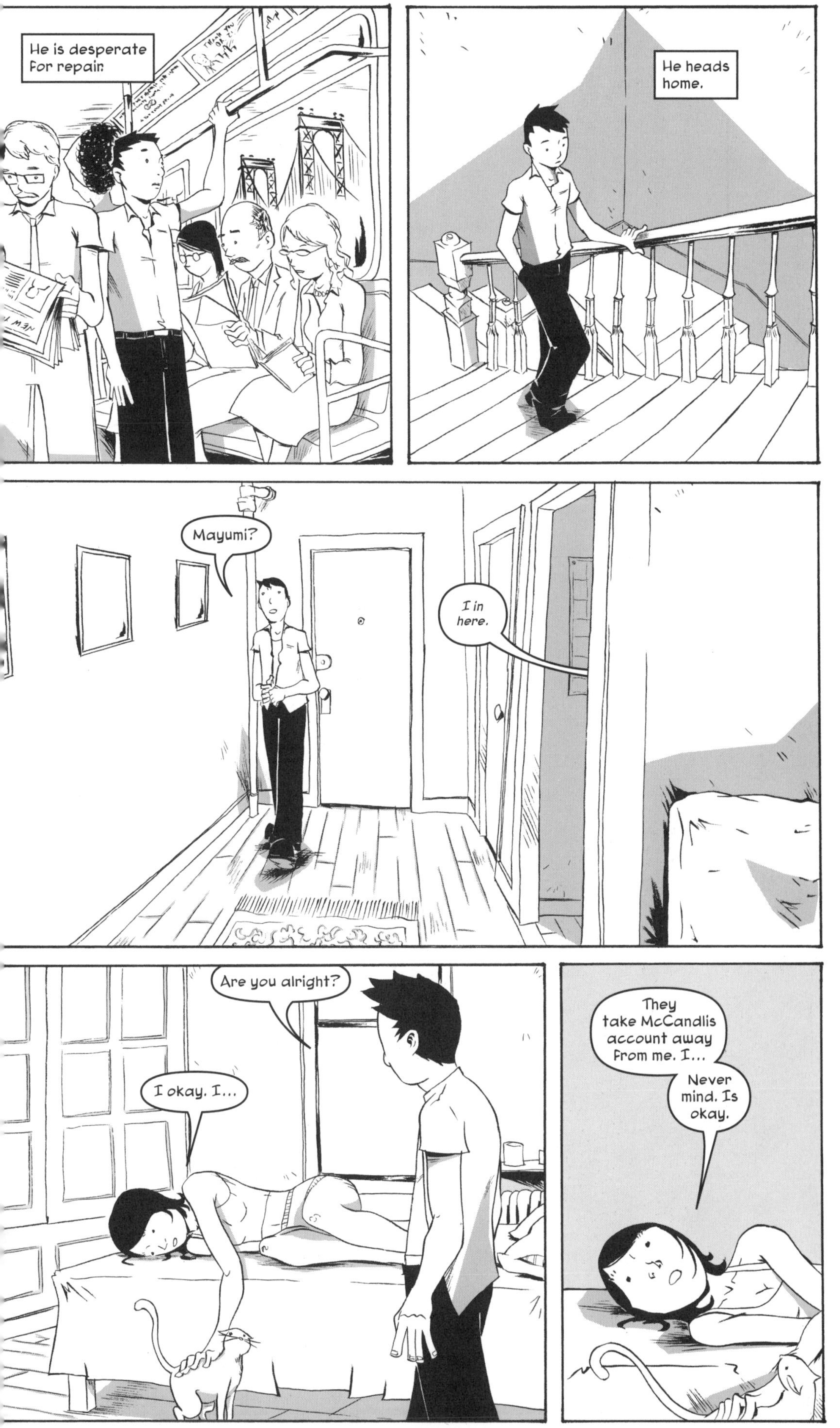
He is desperate for repair.
He heads home.
Mayumi?
I in here.
Are you alright?
I okay. I...
They take McCandlis account away from me. I...
Never mind. Is okay.

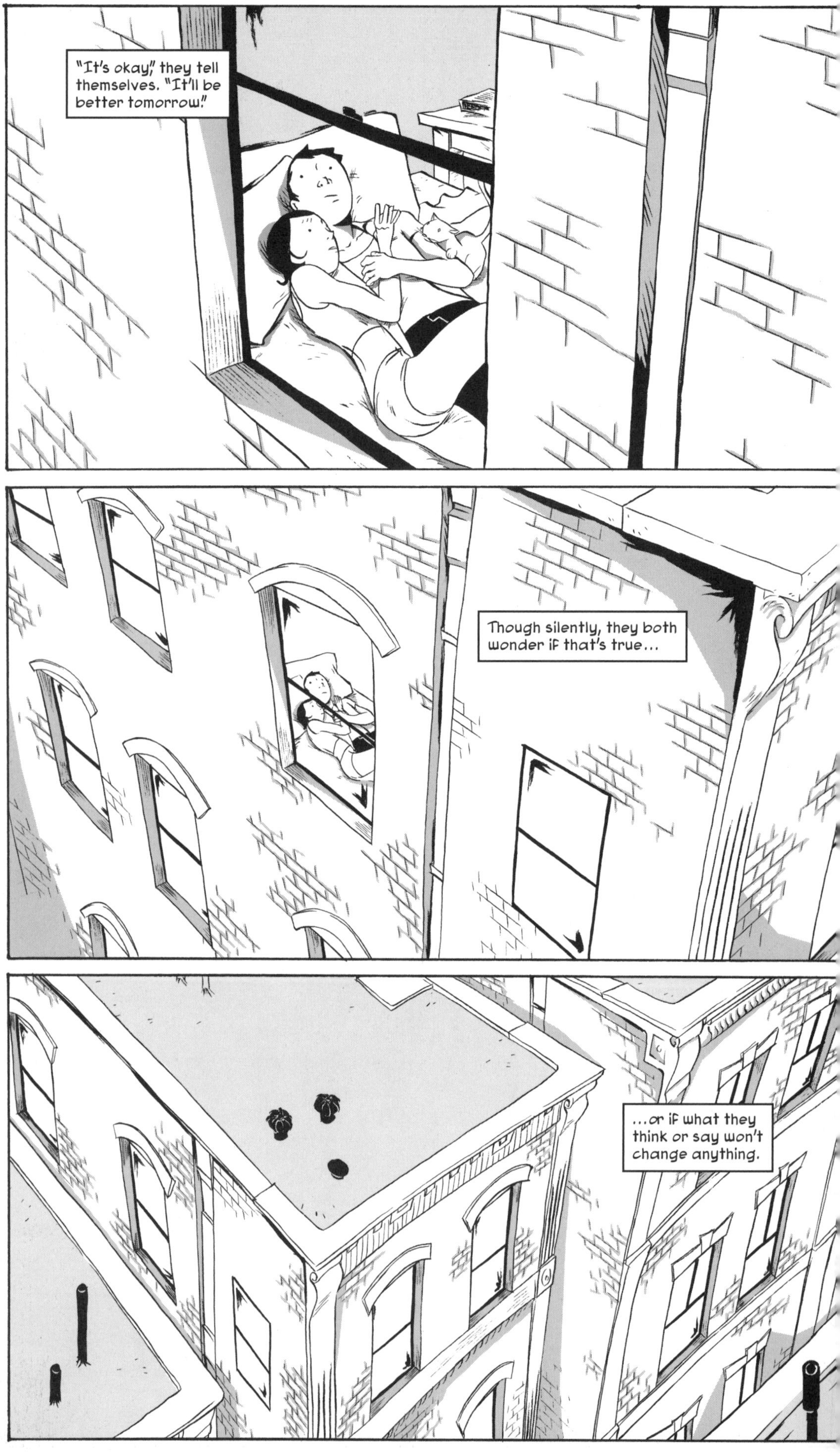
"It's okay," they tell themselves. "It'll be better tomorrow."
Though silently, they both wonder if that's true...
...or if what they think or say won't change anything.

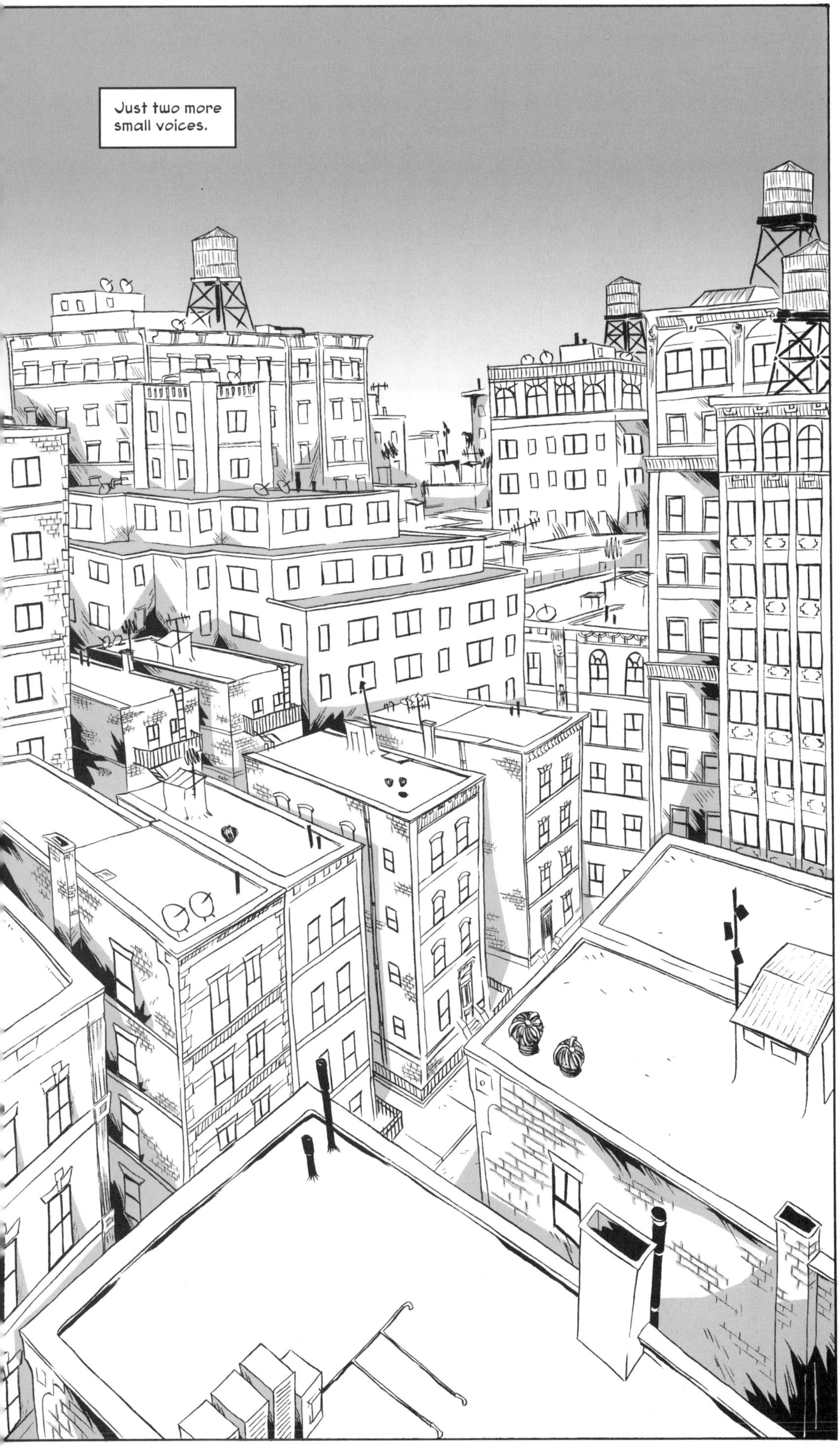
Just two more small voices.

カムバックは、

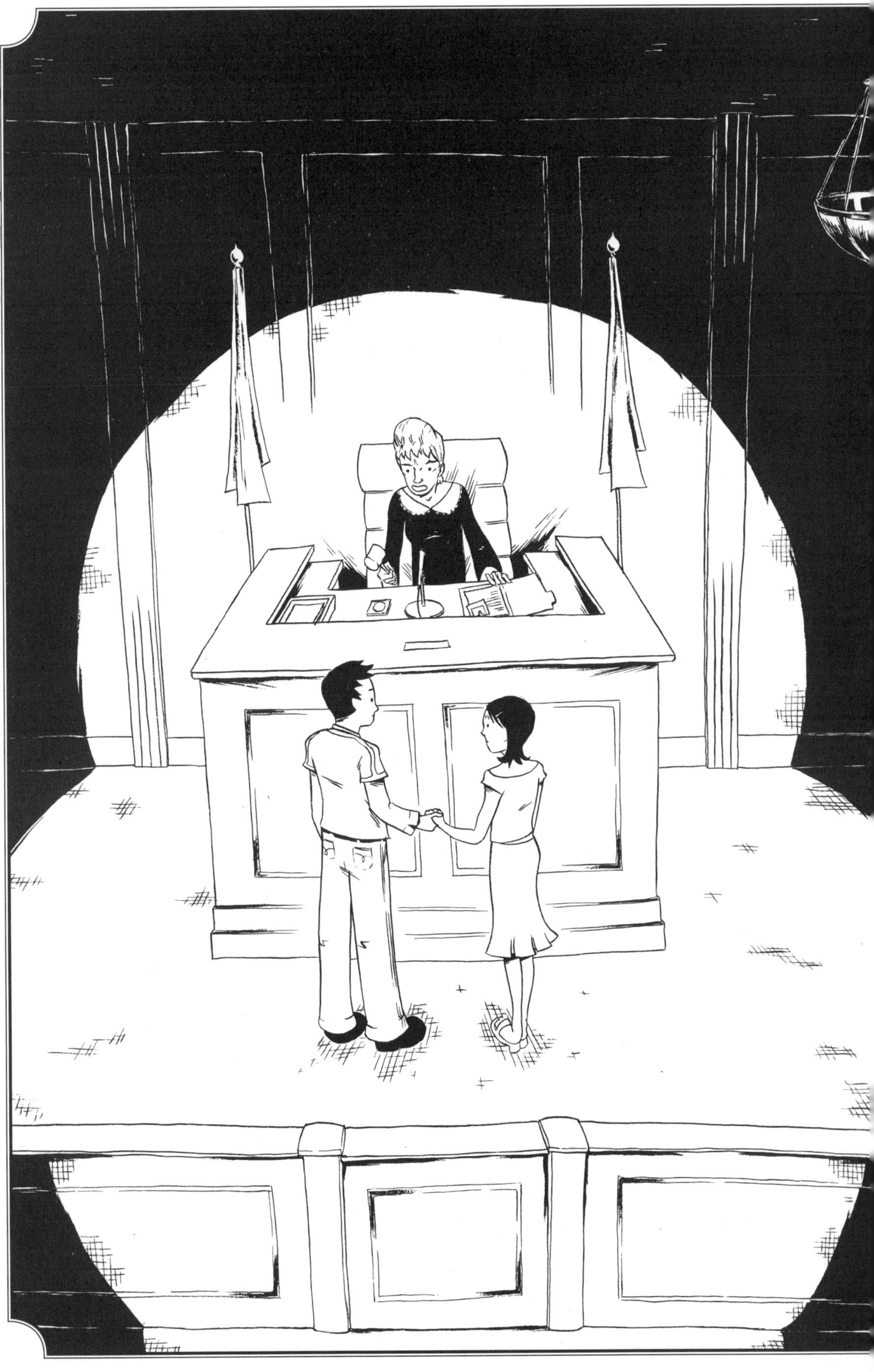

New York City -- the city of lights, where brightness shines on the lives of 8.3 million residents of the five boroughs.

Except when it's dark.

Which is more often than people like to admit.

So much time passes in solitude.

They drift aimlessly through those hours...

...convinced it's just them and the quiet.

THE TRUE ADMINISTRATION OF JUSTICE IS THE FIRMEST PILLAR OF GOOD GOVERNMENT

But those hours are powerful. They hold the most potential for *change.*

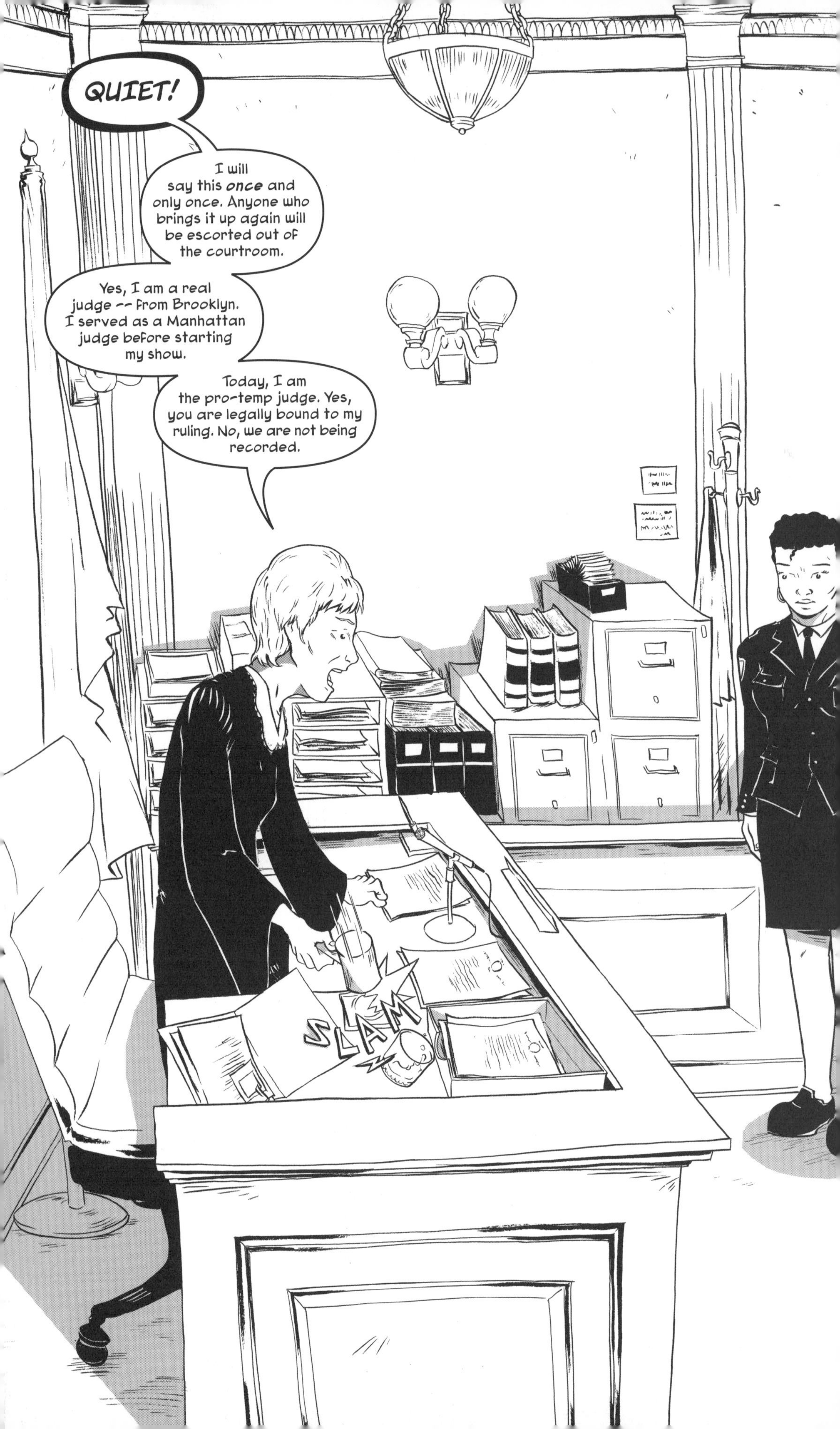
QUIET!
I will say this *once* and only once. Anyone who brings it up again will be escorted out of the courtroom.
Yes, I am a real judge -- from Brooklyn. I served as a Manhattan judge before starting my show.
Today, I am the pro-temp judge. Yes, you are legally bound to my ruling. No, we are not being recorded.
SLAM

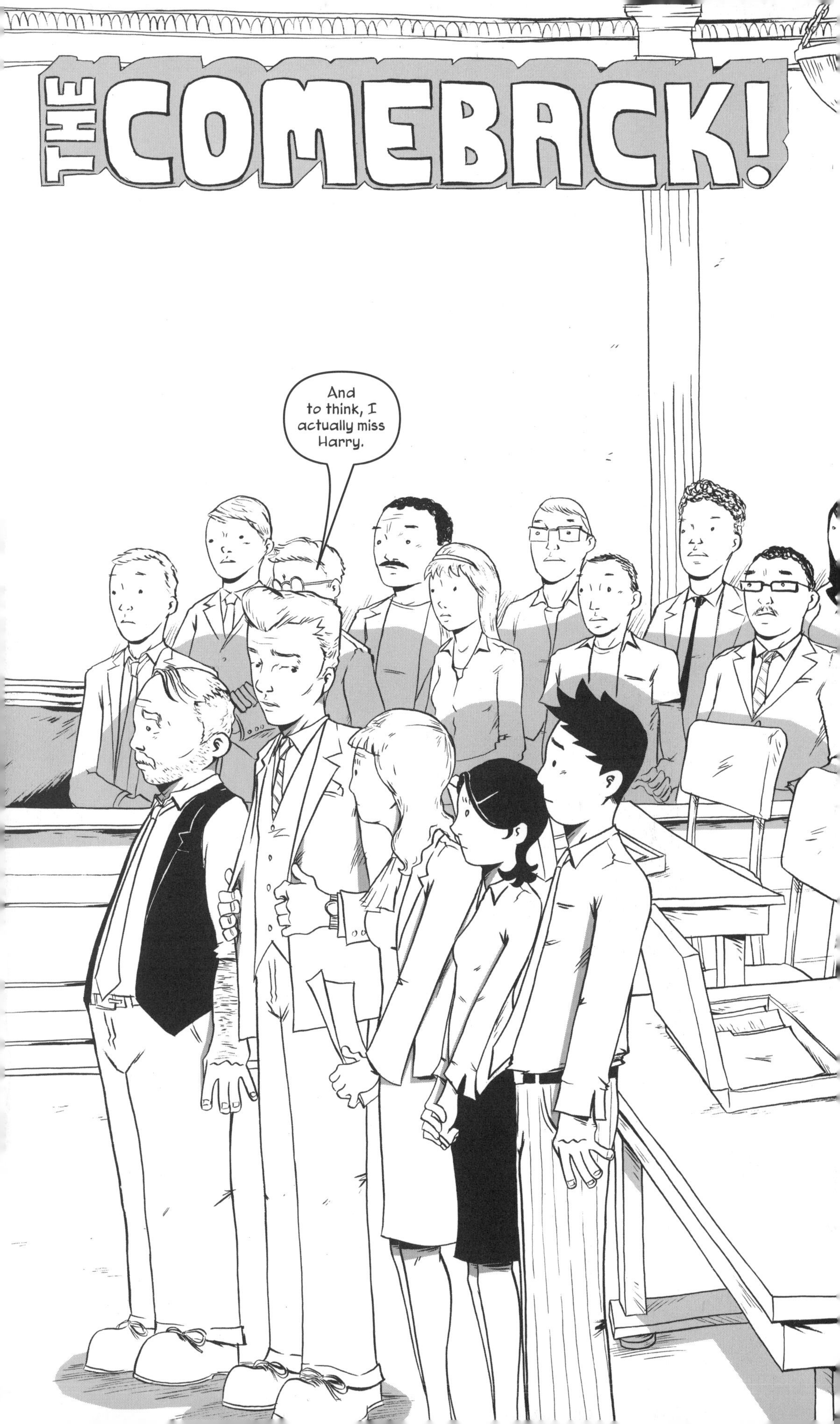
THE COMEBACK!
And to think, I actually miss Harry.

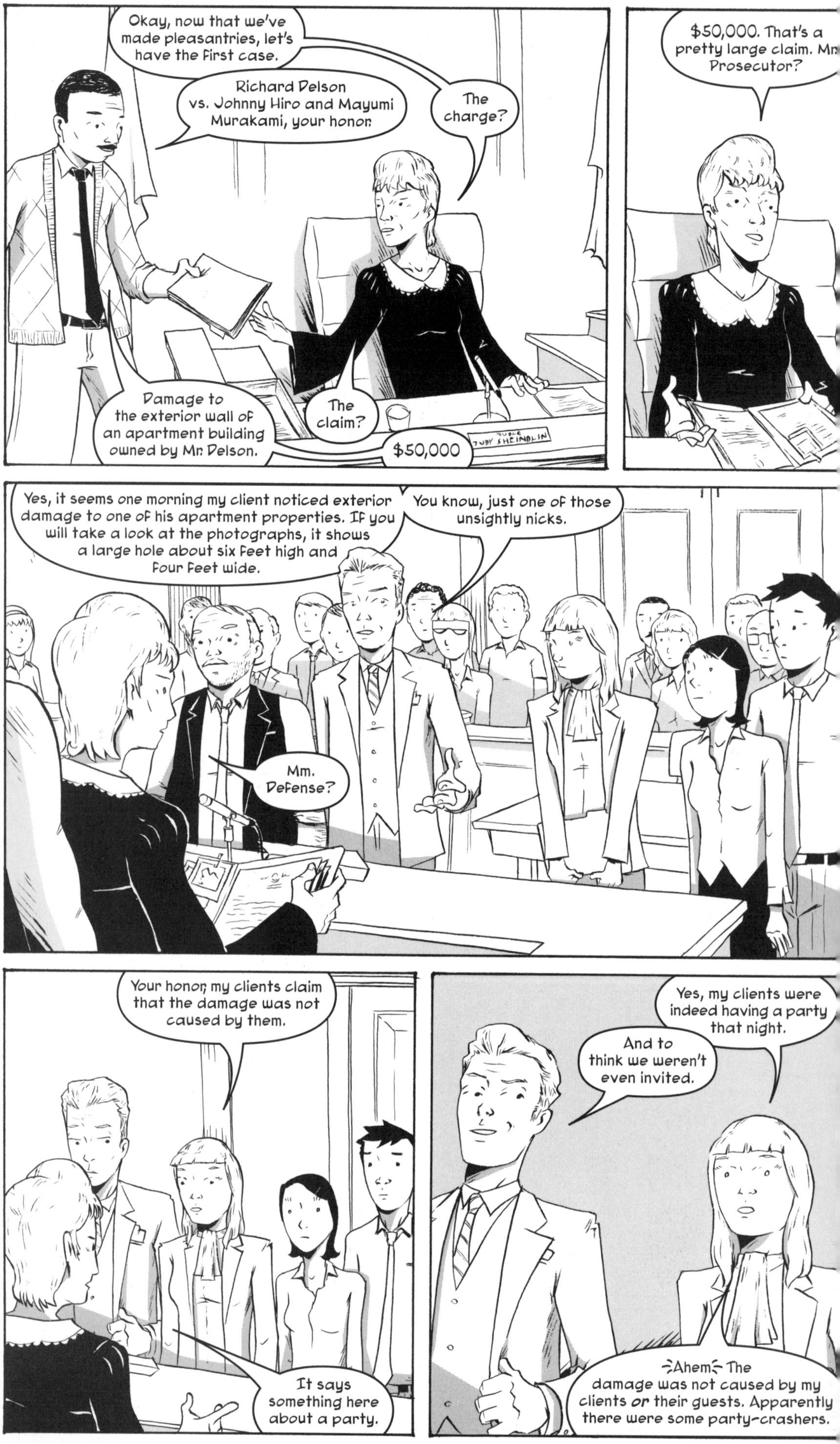

Okay, now that we've made pleasantries, let's have the first case.
Richard Delson vs. Johnny Hiro and Mayumi Murakami, your honor.
The charge?
Damage to the exterior wall of an apartment building owned by Mr. Delson.
The claim?
$50,000
JUDGE JUDY SHEINDLIN
$50,000. That's a pretty large claim. Mr. Prosecutor?
Yes, it seems one morning my client noticed exterior damage to one of his apartment properties. If you will take a look at the photographs, it shows a large hole about six feet high and four feet wide.
You know, just one of those unsightly nicks.
Mm. Defense?
Your honor, my clients claim that the damage was not caused by them.
It says something here about a party.
Yes, my clients were indeed having a party that night.
And to think we weren't even invited.
Ahem. The damage was not caused by my clients *or* their guests. Apparently there were some party-crashers.

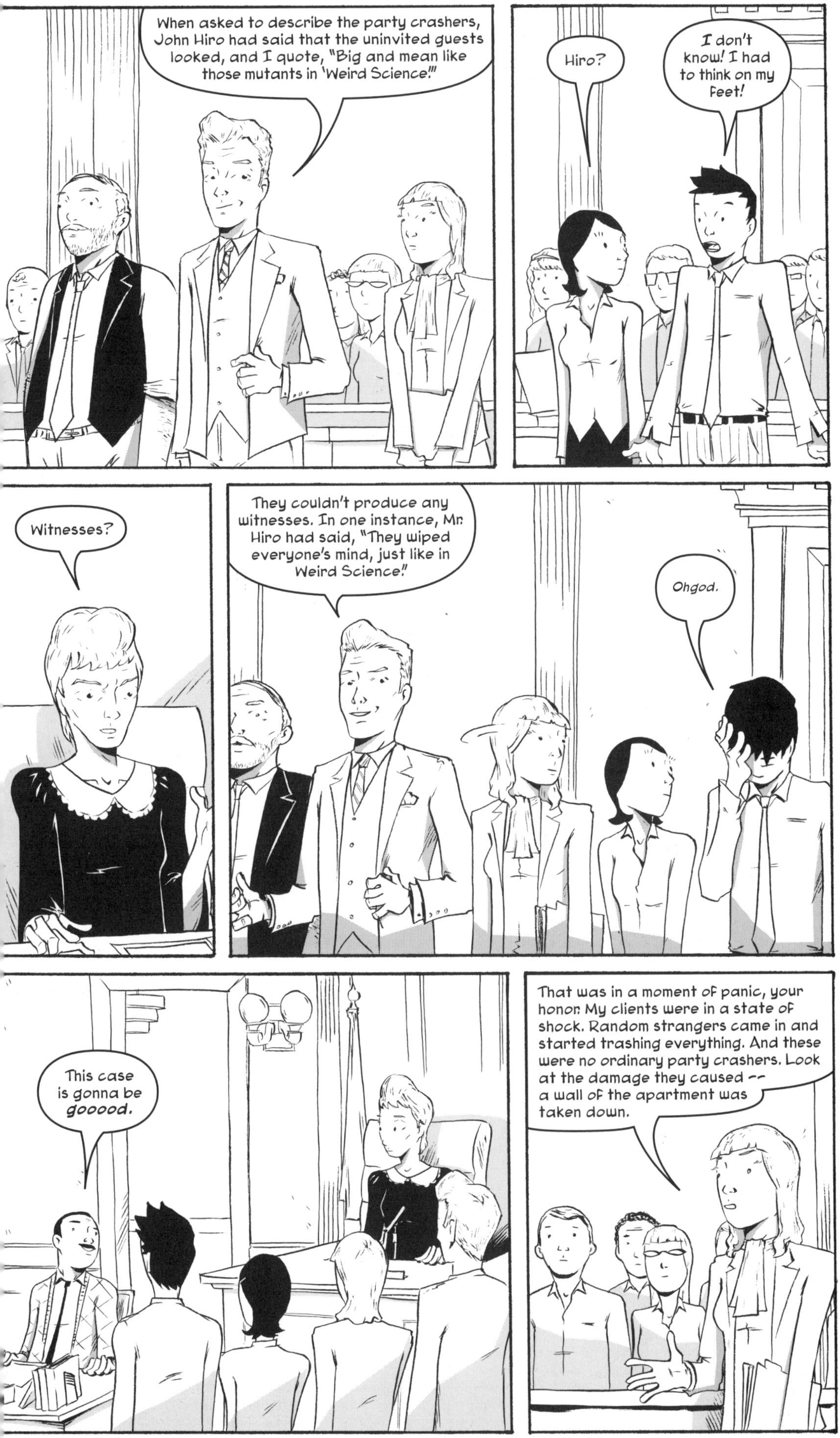
When asked to describe the party crashers, John Hiro had said that the uninvited guests looked, and I quote, "Big and mean like those mutants in 'Weird Science.'"
Hiro?
I don't know! I had to think on my feet!
Witnesses?
They couldn't produce any witnesses. In one instance, Mr. Hiro had said, "They wiped everyone's mind, just like in Weird Science."
Ohgod.
This case is gonna be *gooood.*
That was in a moment of panic, your honor. My clients were in a state of shock. Random strangers came in and started trashing everything. And these were no ordinary party crashers. Look at the damage they caused -- a wall of the apartment was taken down.

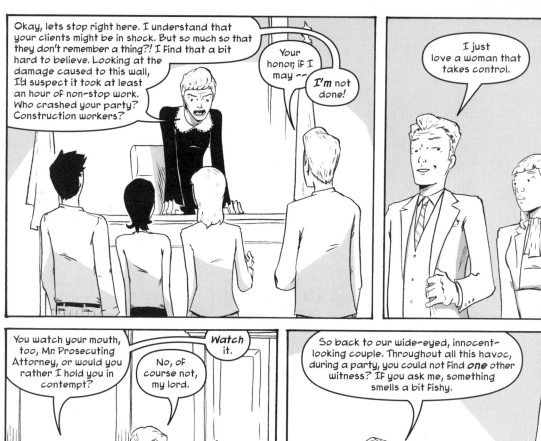

Okay, lets stop right here. I understand that your clients might be in shock. But so much so that they don't remember a thing?! I find that a bit hard to believe. Looking at the damage caused to this wall, I'd suspect it took at least an hour of non-stop work. Who crashed your party? Construction workers?

Your honor, if I may --

I'm not done!

I just love a woman that takes control.

You watch your mouth, too, Mr. Prosecuting Attorney, or would you rather I hold you in contempt?

Watch it.

No, of course not, my lord.

So back to our wide-eyed, innocent-looking couple. Throughout all this havoc, during a party, you could not find one other witness? If you ask me, something smells a bit fishy.

JUDGE JUDY SHEINDLIN

I think that's the smell of the defendant. He works in a sushi restaurant, you know.

--ahem-- Sorry, Judge. Won't happen again.

See that it doesn't, Mr. Prosecutor. Now, the defendant, Mr. John -- oh, you think that's pretty clever, huh? Johnny Hiro? You must be a laugh-a-minute.

Um, that's my name, ma'am. My dad chose it.

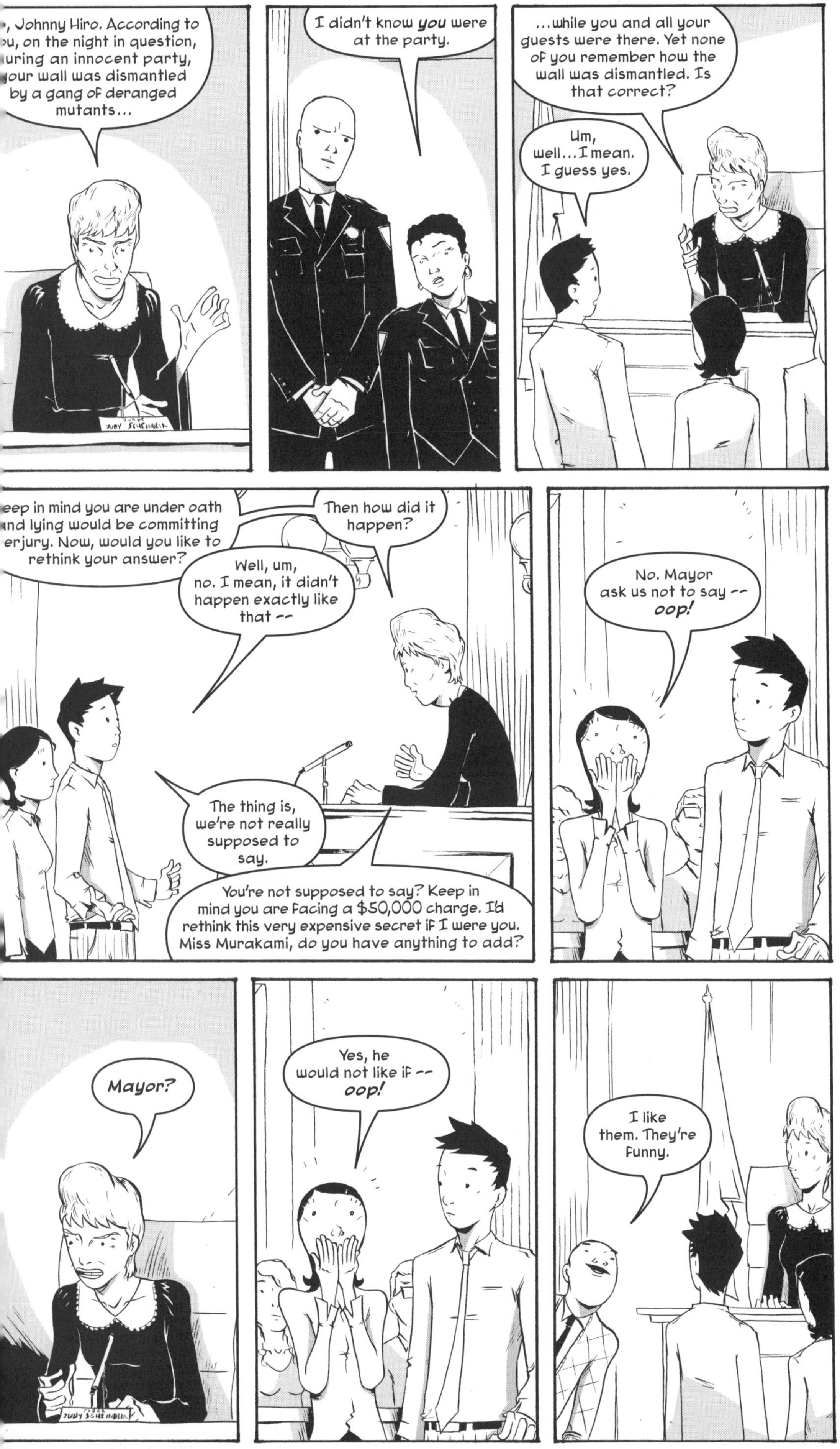
, Johnny Hiro. According to u, on the night in question, uring an innocent party, our wall was dismantled by a gang of deranged mutants...
I didn't know *you* were at the party.
...while you and all your guests were there. Yet none of you remember how the wall was dismantled. Is that correct?
Um, well...I mean. I guess yes.
eep in mind you are under oath nd lying would be committing erjury. Now, would you like to rethink your answer?
Then how did it happen?
Well, um, no. I mean, it didn't happen exactly like that --
The thing is, we're not really supposed to say.
You're not supposed to say? Keep in mind you are facing a $50,000 charge. I'd rethink this very expensive secret if I were you. Miss Murakami, do you have anything to add?
No. Mayor ask us not to say -- *oop!*
Mayor?
Yes, he would not like if -- *oop!*
I like them. They're funny.

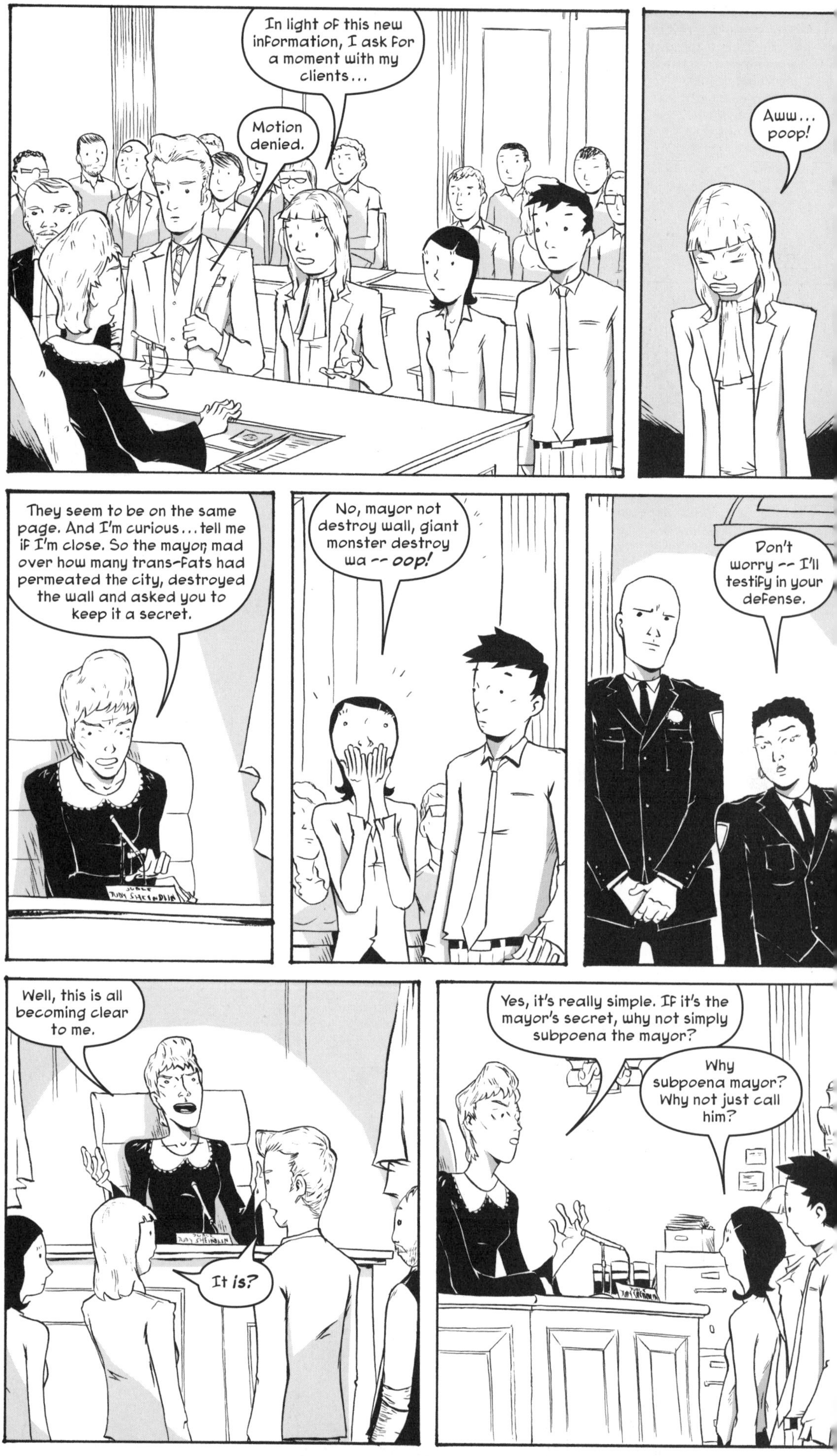
In light of this new information, I ask for a moment with my clients...
Motion denied.
Aww... poop!
They seem to be on the same page. And I'm curious... tell me if I'm close. So the mayor, mad over how many trans-fats had permeated the city, destroyed the wall and asked you to keep it a secret.
No, mayor not destroy wall, giant monster destroy wa -- oop!
Don't worry -- I'll testify in your defense.
Well, this is all becoming clear to me.
It is?
Yes, it's really simple. If it's the mayor's secret, why not simply subpoena the mayor?
Why subpoena mayor? Why not just call him?

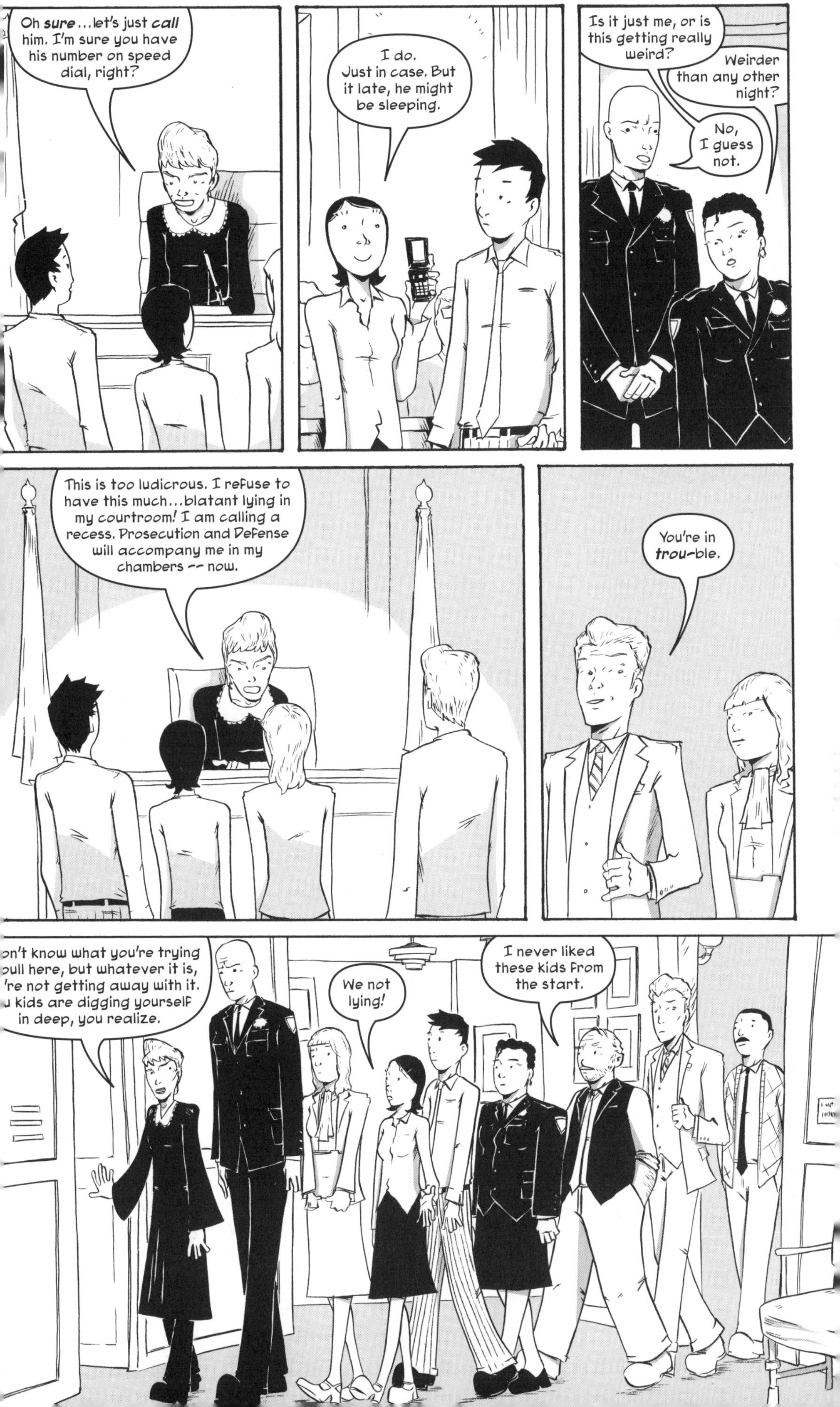
Oh sure…let's just call him. I'm sure you have his number on speed dial, right?
I do. Just in case. But it late, he might be sleeping.
Is it just me, or is this getting really weird?
Weirder than any other night?
No, I guess not.
This is too ludicrous. I refuse to have this much…blatant lying in my courtroom! I am calling a recess. Prosecution and Defense will accompany me in my chambers -- now.
You're in trou-ble.
on't know what you're trying pull here, but whatever it is, 're not getting away with it. kids are digging yourself in deep, you realize.
We not lying!
I never liked these kids from the start.

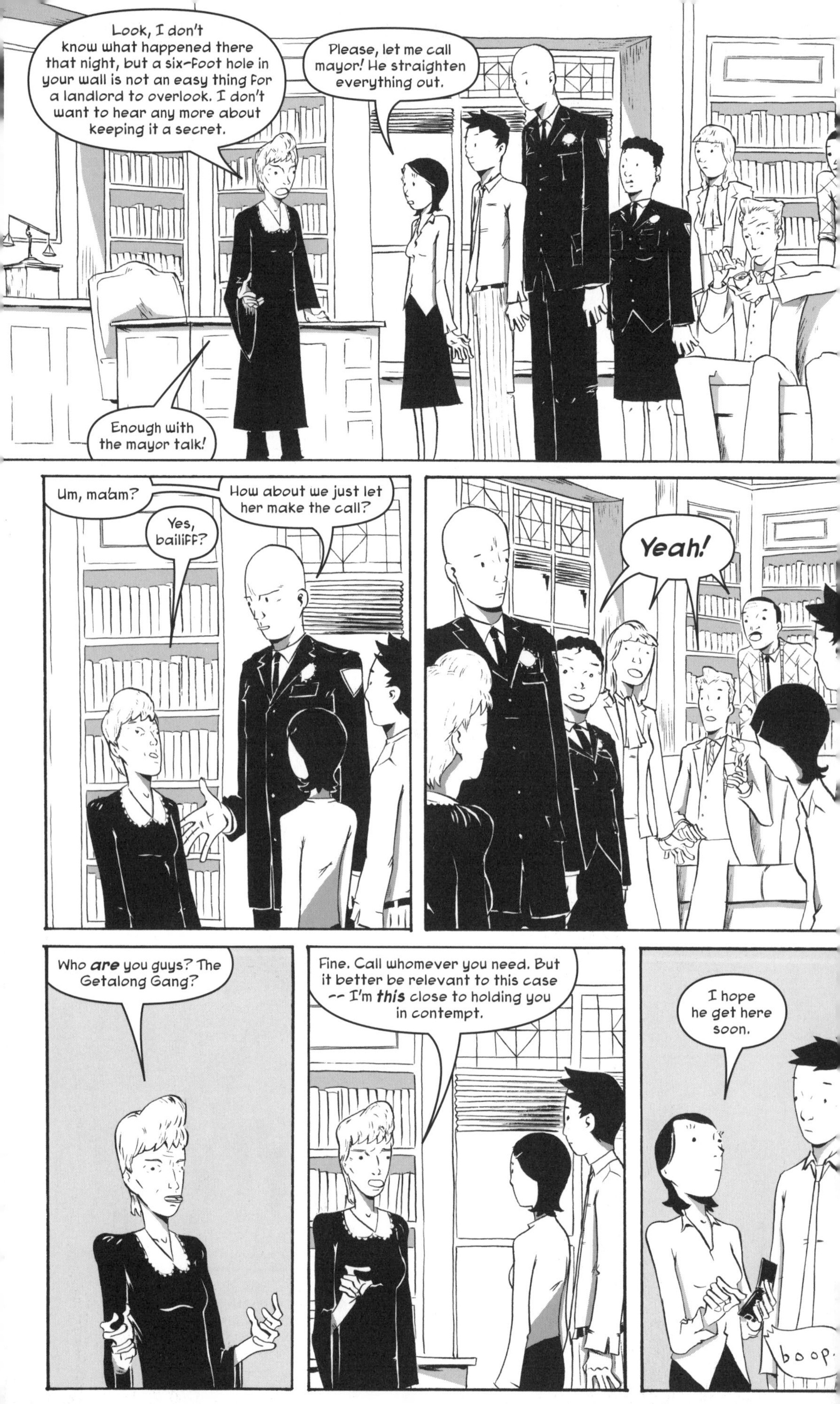
Look, I don't know what happened there that night, but a six-foot hole in your wall is not an easy thing for a landlord to overlook. I don't want to hear any more about keeping it a secret.
Please, let me call mayor! He straighten everything out.
Enough with the mayor talk!
Um, ma'am?
Yes, bailiff?
How about we just let her make the call?
Yeah!
Who are you guys? The Getalong Gang?
Fine. Call whomever you need. But it better be relevant to this case -- I'm this close to holding you in contempt.
I hope he get here soon.
boop.

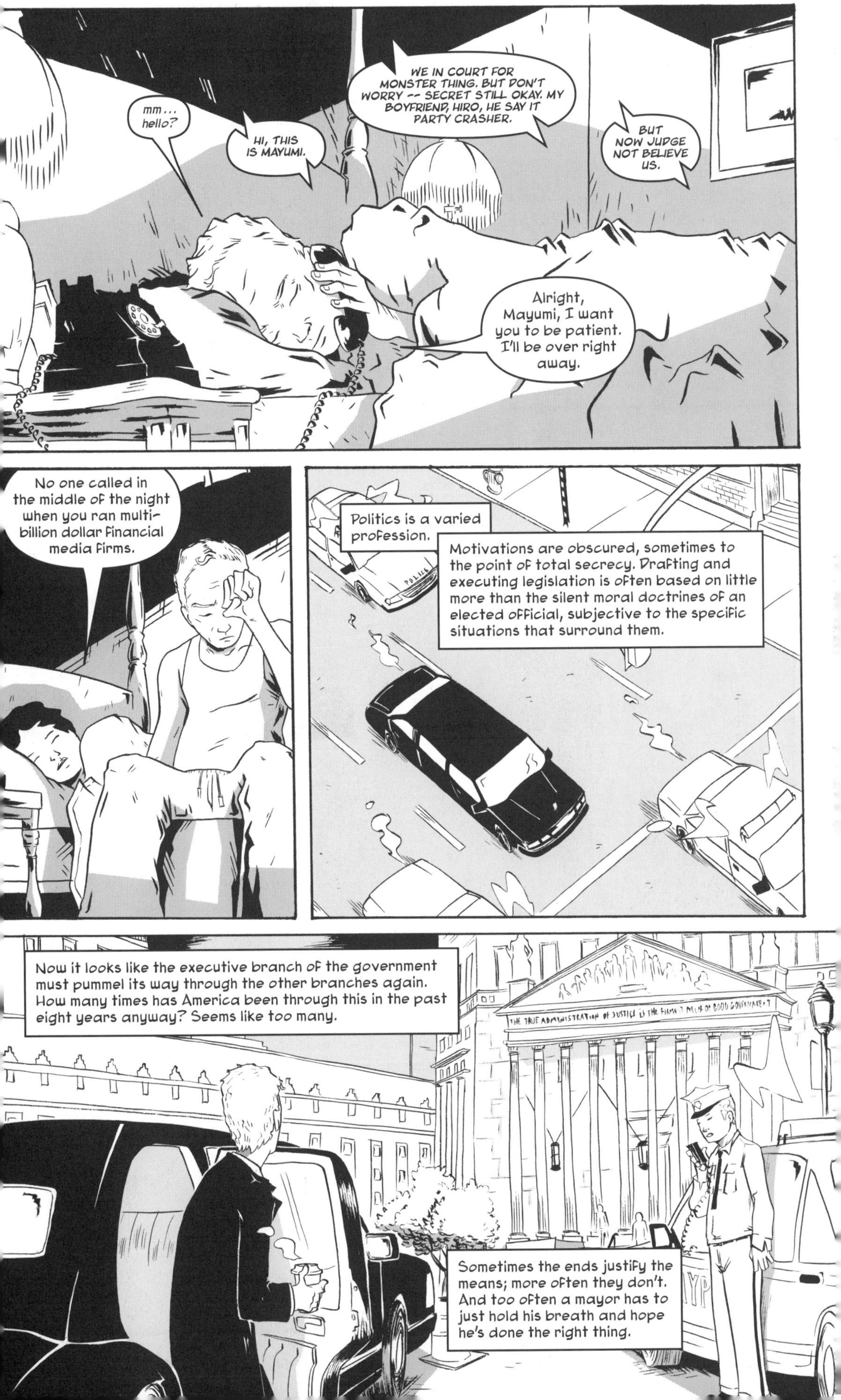
mm... hello?
HI, THIS IS MAYUMI.
WE IN COURT FOR MONSTER THING. BUT DON'T WORRY -- SECRET STILL OKAY. MY BOYFRIEND, HIRO, HE SAY IT PARTY CRASHER.
BUT NOW JUDGE NOT BELIEVE US.
Alright, Mayumi, I want you to be patient. I'll be over right away.
No one called in the middle of the night when you ran multi-billion dollar financial media firms.
Politics is a varied profession.
Motivations are obscured, sometimes to the point of total secrecy. Drafting and executing legislation is often based on little more than the silent moral doctrines of an elected official, subjective to the specific situations that surround them.
Now it looks like the executive branch of the government must pummel its way through the other branches again. How many times has America been through this in the past eight years anyway? Seems like too many.
THE TRUE ADMINISTRATION OF JUSTICE IS THE FIRMEST PILLAR OF GOOD GOVERNMENT
Sometimes the ends justify the means; more often they don't. And too often a mayor has to just hold his breath and hope he's done the right thing.

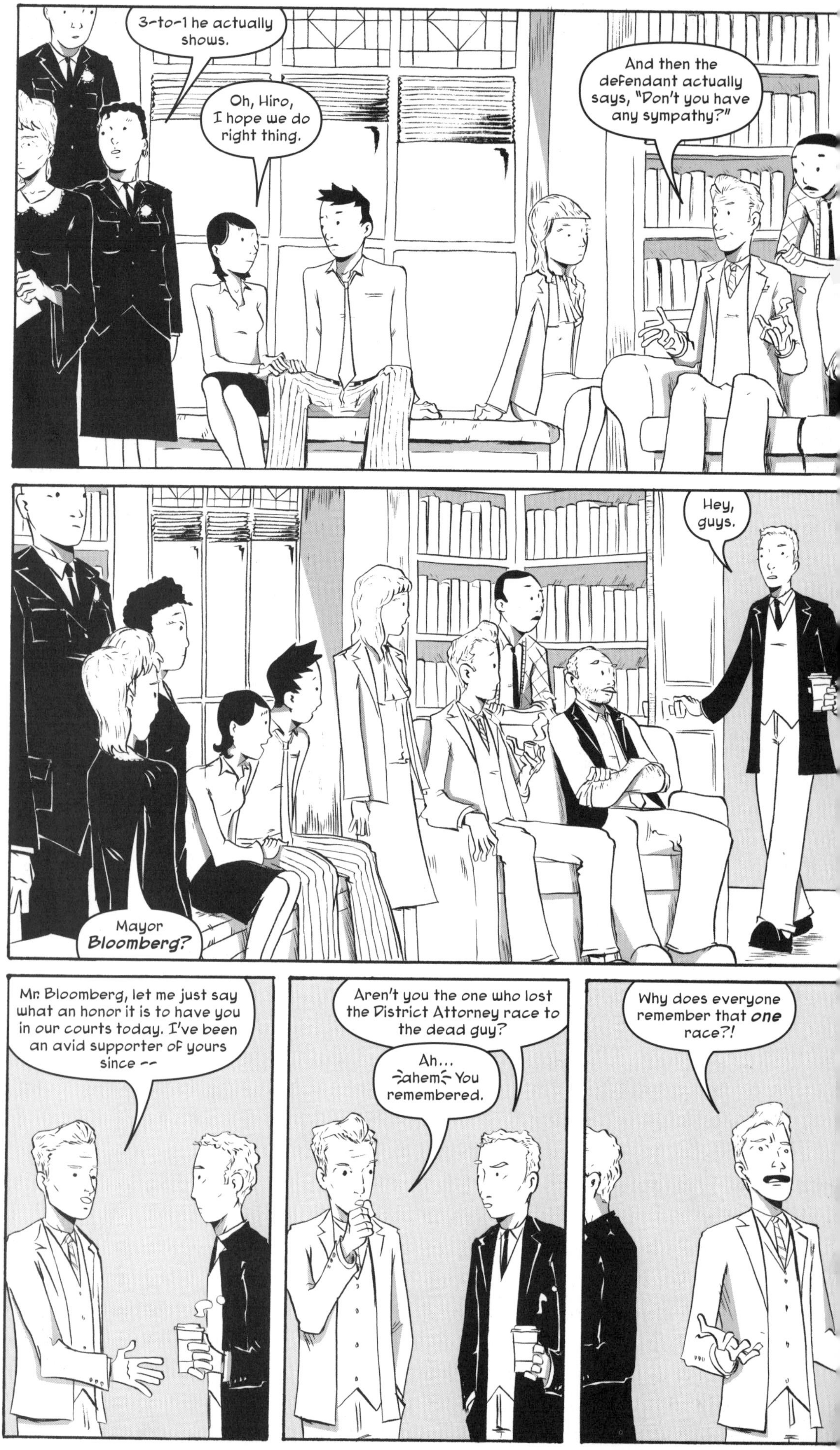
3-to-1 he actually shows.
Oh, Hiro, I hope we do right thing.
And then the defendant actually says, "Don't you have any sympathy?"
Hey, guys.
Mayor Bloomberg?
Mr. Bloomberg, let me just say what an honor it is to have you in our courts today. I've been an avid supporter of yours since --
Aren't you the one who lost the District Attorney race to the dead guy?
Ah... ahem You remembered.
Why does everyone remember that one race?!

There were no witnesses, your honor. No evidence of a party could be found. And two young adults surely aren't capable of causing that kind of damage.

It seems that an unstable infrastructure is the most likely scenario.

Should we have the building inspected?

It seems Mr. Delson has multiple properties. Maybe they should all be inspected. Perhaps we'll even find some health code violations.

Who's side are you on?

Quiet -- you're making me look bad in front of the mayor.

Health code violations, structural violations, tenant harassment. That might add up to a pretty sizable fine, Mr. Delson. This case may not be in your favor anymore. Maybe you should just drop the charges.

I--

Your honor, we don't even want to live there anymore. We're staying in a good place for now. I'd just as soon break the lease, but he won't let us out without a fine.

It seems like it would work out well for both parties, since he can charge the next tenant whatever he wants.

I'm sure someone will take it. It is New York, and property value is still 11.4% above the national average. *

So what do you say?

* S&P/Case-Shiller Home Price Index, Nov. 2008

I...

Charges dropped.

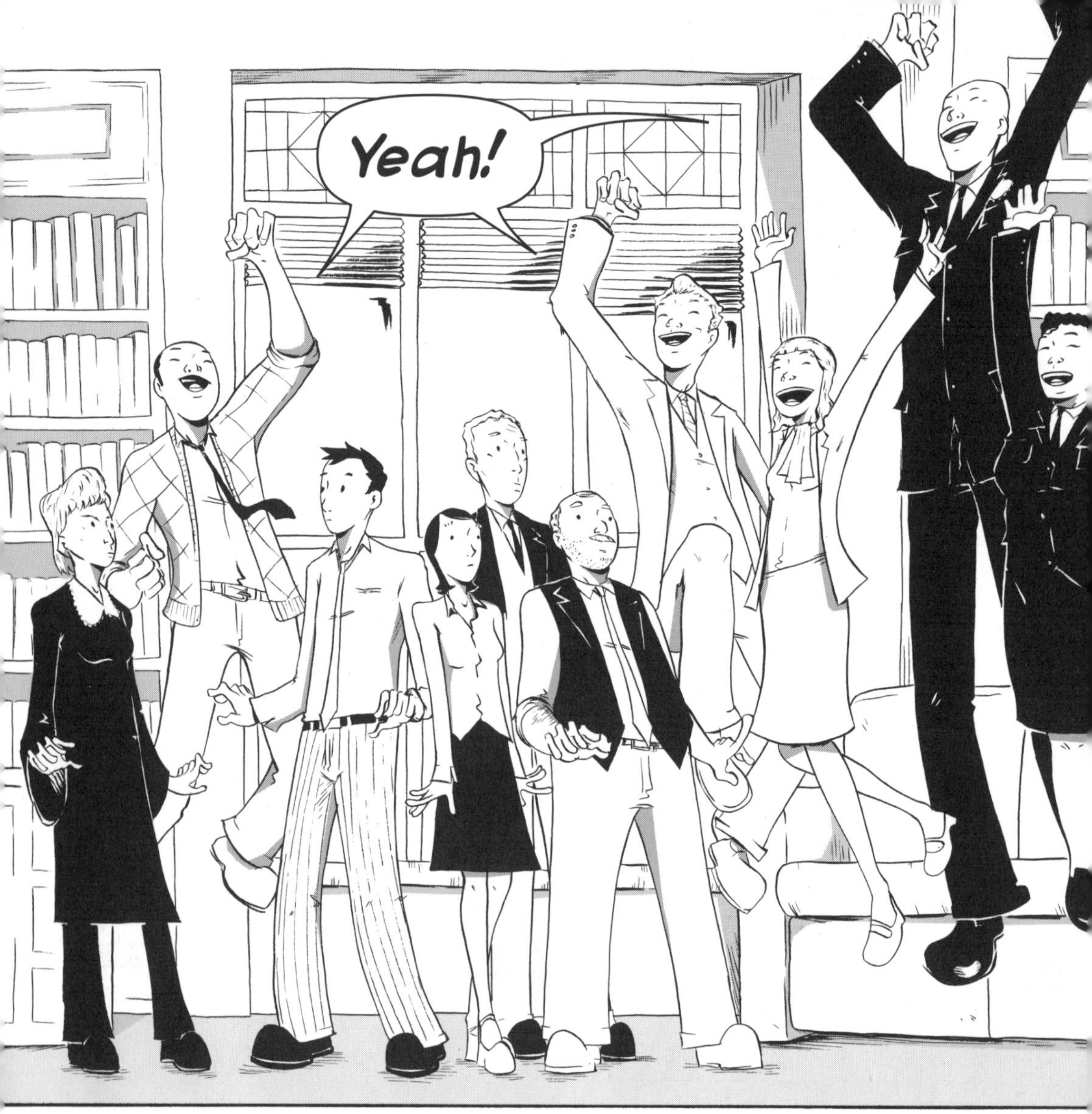
Yeah!

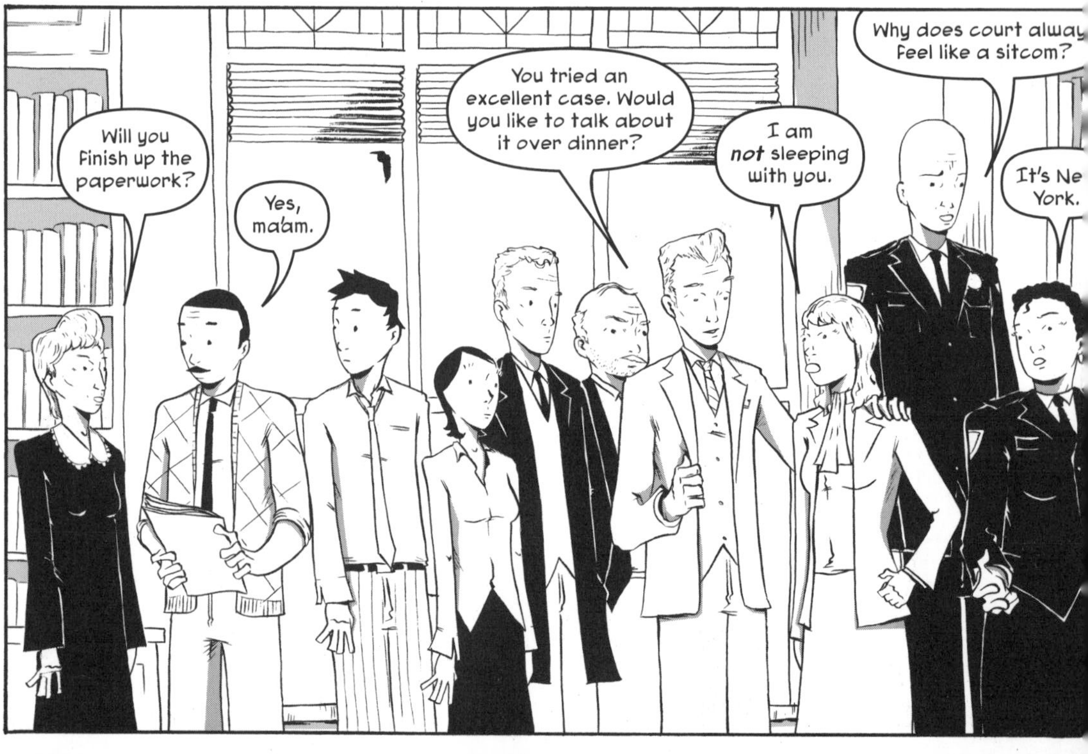
Will you finish up the paperwork?
Yes, ma'am.
You tried an excellent case. Would you like to talk about it over dinner?
I am *not* sleeping with you.
Why does court alway feel like a sitcom?
It's Ne York.

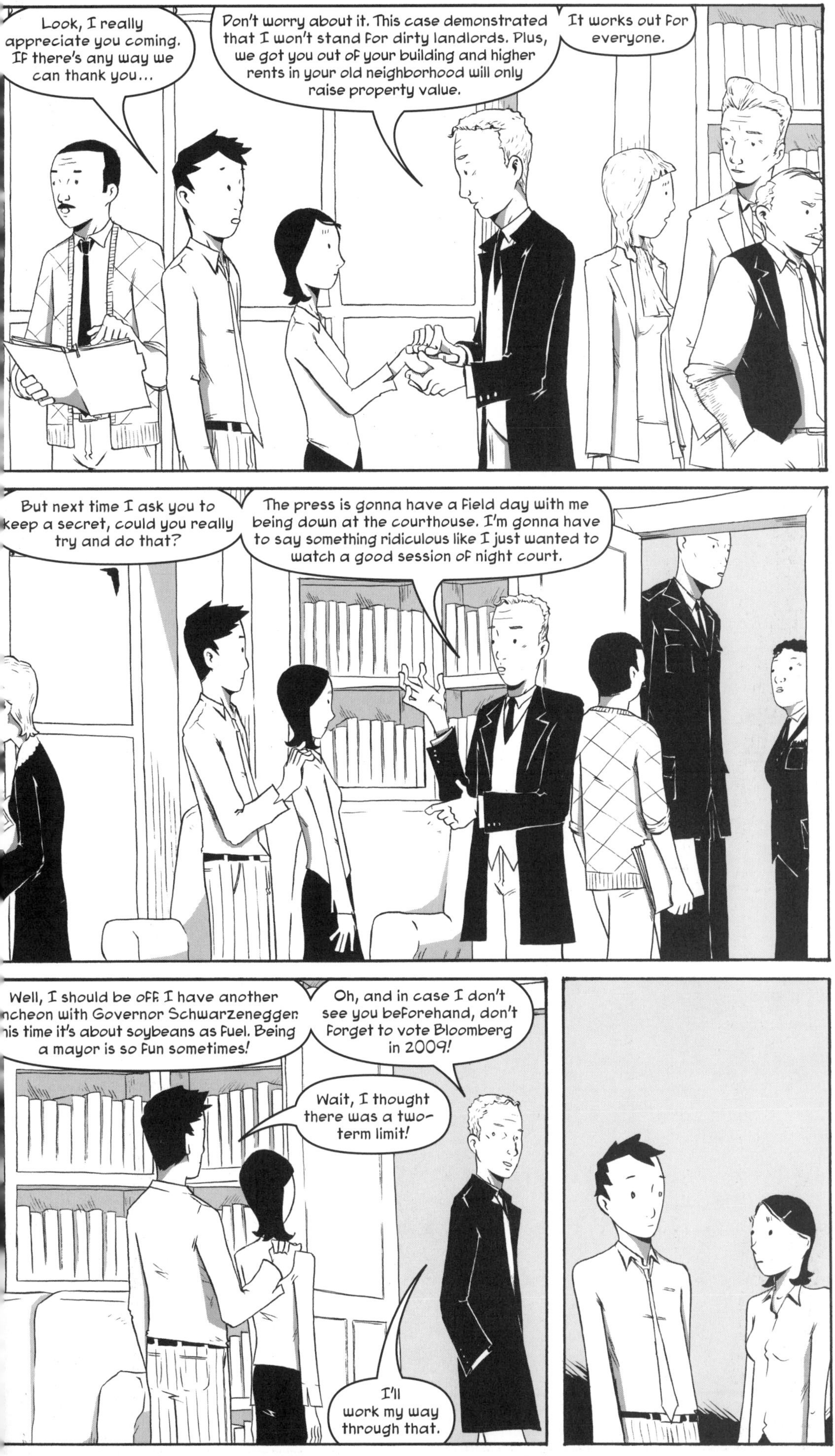

Look, I really appreciate you coming. If there's any way we can thank you...
Don't worry about it. This case demonstrated that I won't stand for dirty landlords. Plus, we got you out of your building and higher rents in your old neighborhood will only raise property value.
It works out for everyone.
But next time I ask you to keep a secret, could you really try and do that?
The press is gonna have a field day with me being down at the courthouse. I'm gonna have to say something ridiculous like I just wanted to watch a good session of night court.
Well, I should be off. I have another ncheon with Governor Schwarzenegger. his time it's about soybeans as fuel. Being a mayor is so fun sometimes!
Oh, and in case I don't see you beforehand, don't forget to vote Bloomberg in 2009!
Wait, I thought there was a two-term limit!
I'll work my way through that.

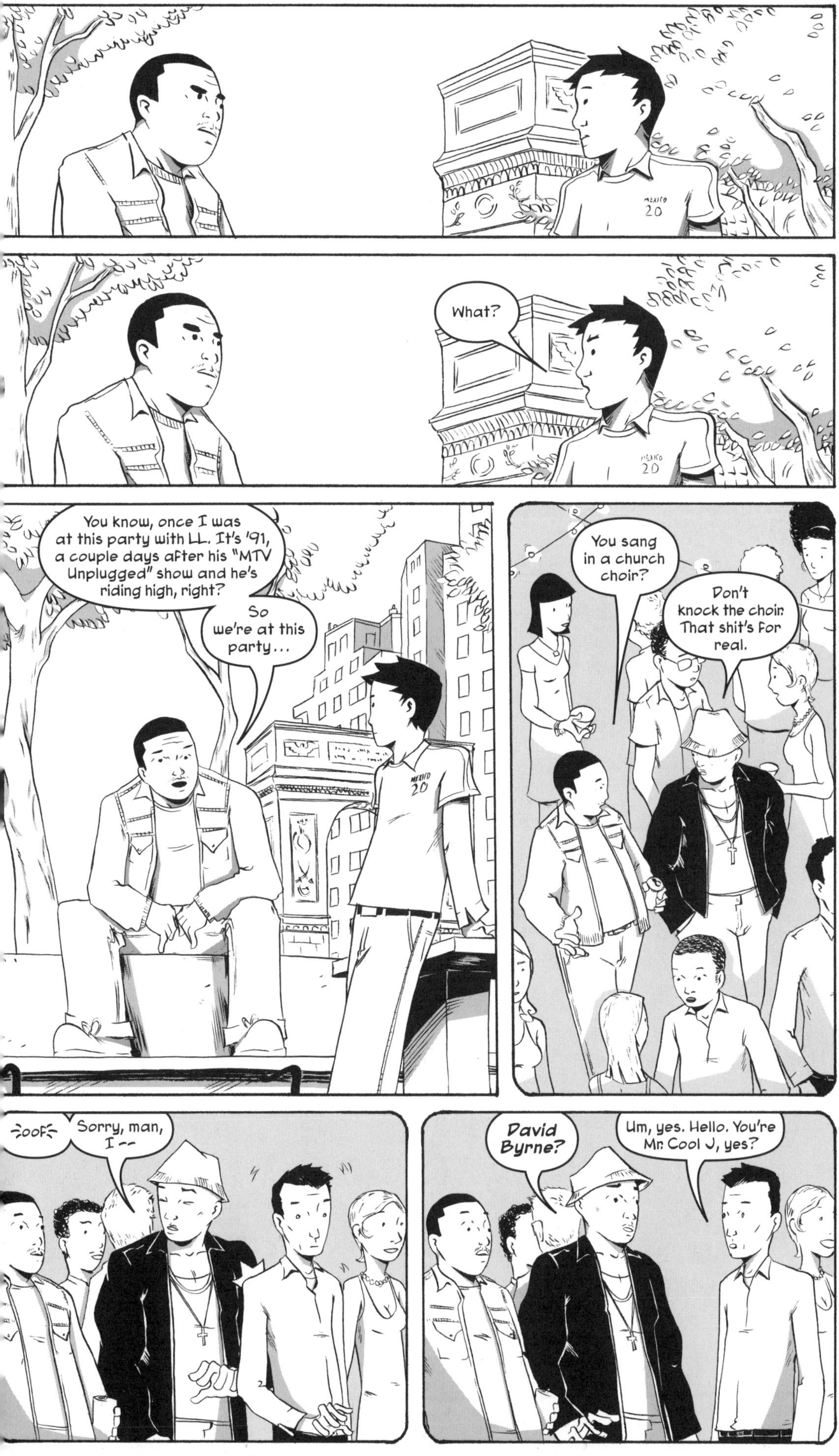
What?
You know, once I was at this party with LL. It's '91, a couple days after his "MTV Unplugged" show and he's riding high, right?
So we're at this party...
You sang in a church choir?
Don't knock the choir. That shit's for real.
OOF
Sorry, man, I --
David Byrne?
Um, yes. Hello. You're Mr. Cool J, yes?

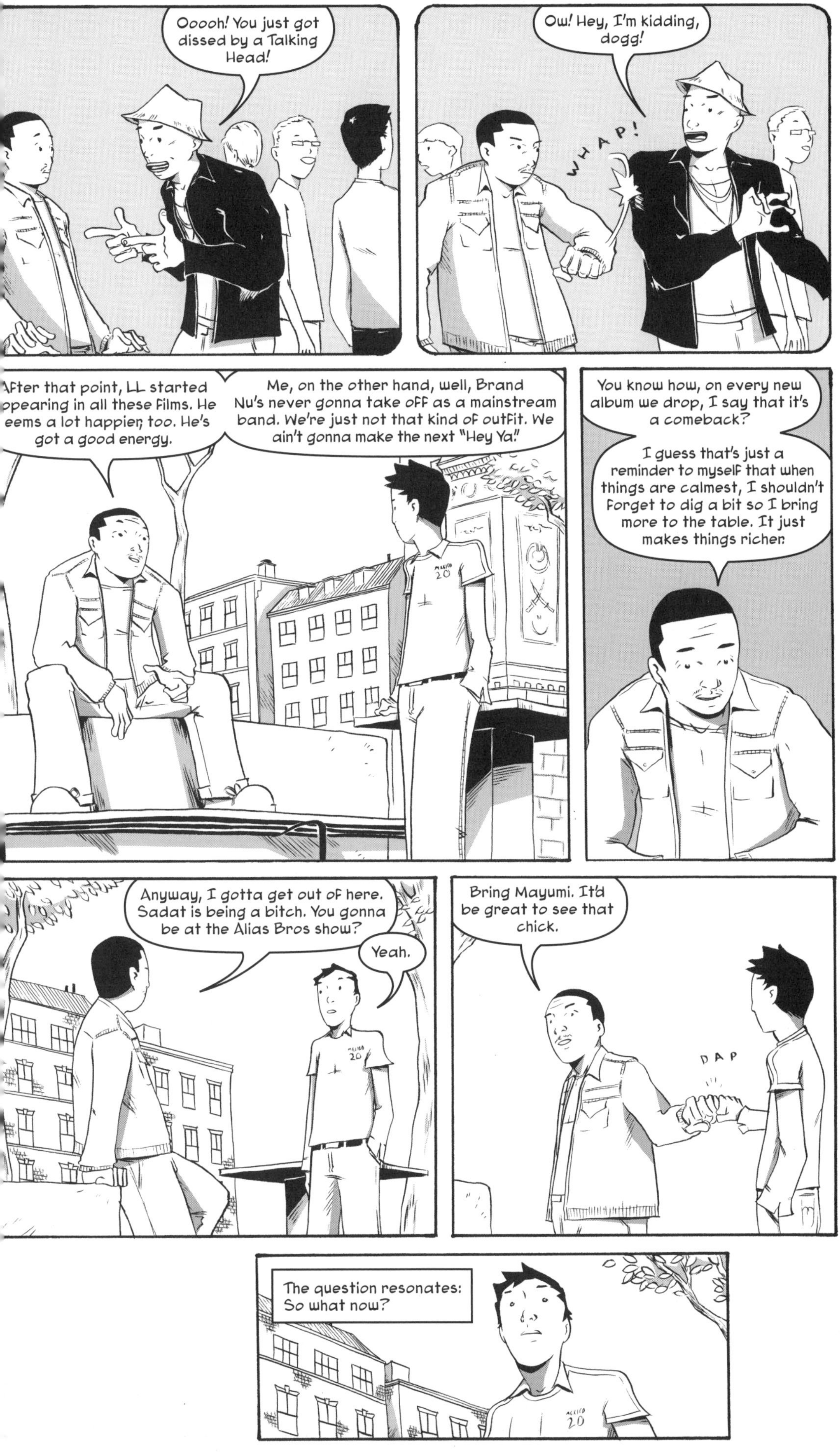
Ooooh! You just got dissed by a Talking Head!
Ow! Hey, I'm kidding, dogg!
WHAP!
After that point, LL started appearing in all these films. He seems a lot happier, too. He's got a good energy.
Me, on the other hand, well, Brand Nu's never gonna take off as a mainstream band. We're just not that kind of outfit. We ain't gonna make the next "Hey Ya."
You know how, on every new album we drop, I say that it's a comeback?
I guess that's just a reminder to myself that when things are calmest, I shouldn't forget to dig a bit so I bring more to the table. It just makes things richer.
Anyway, I gotta get out of here. Sadat is being a bitch. You gonna be at the Alias Bros show?
Yeah.
Bring Mayumi. It'd be great to see that chick.
DAP
The question resonates: So what now?

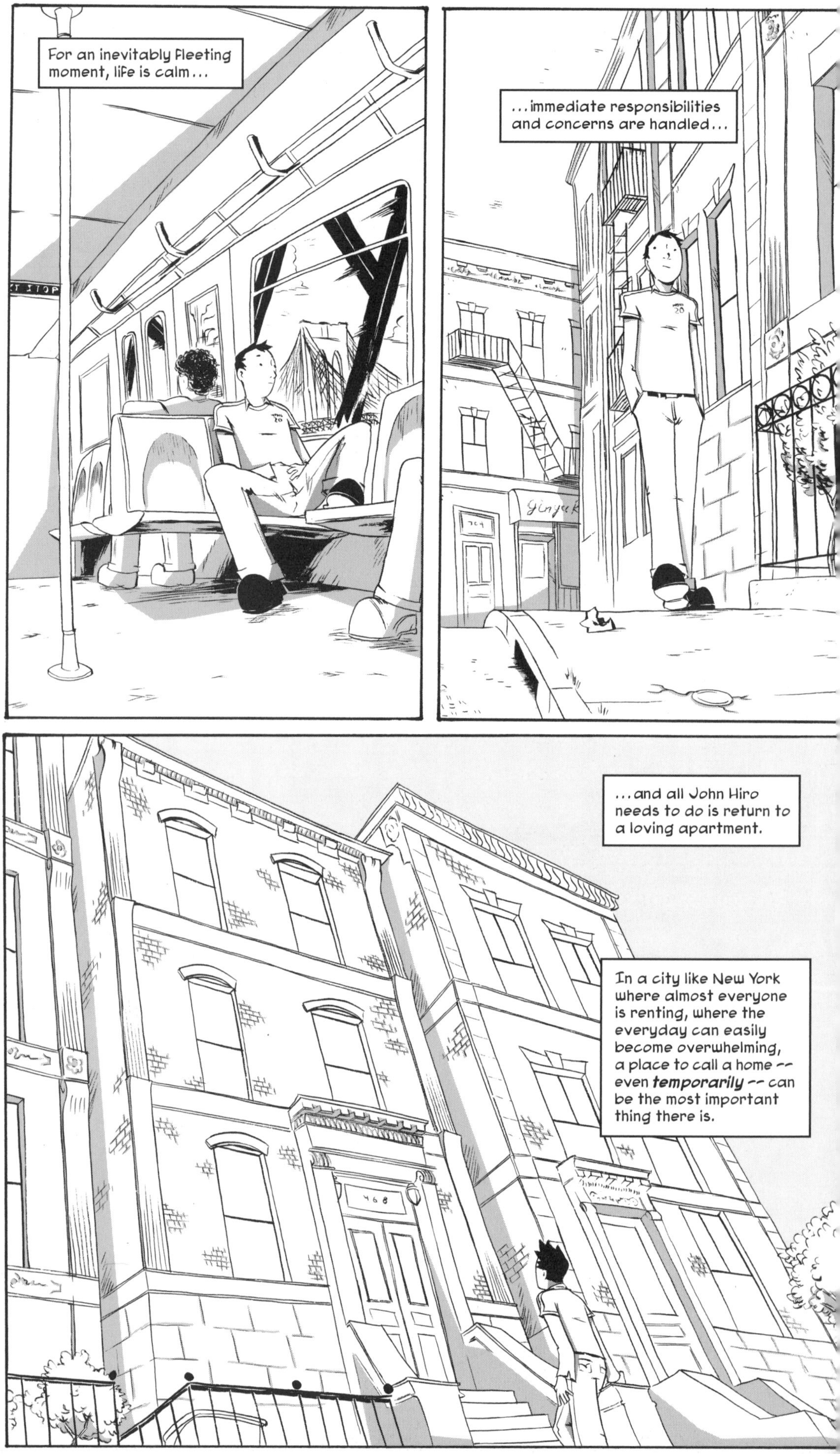
For an inevitably fleeting moment, life is calm...
...immediate responsibilities and concerns are handled...
...and all John Hiro needs to do is return to a loving apartment.
In a city like New York where almost everyone is renting, where the everyday can easily become overwhelming, a place to call a home -- even *temporarily* -- can be the most important thing there is.

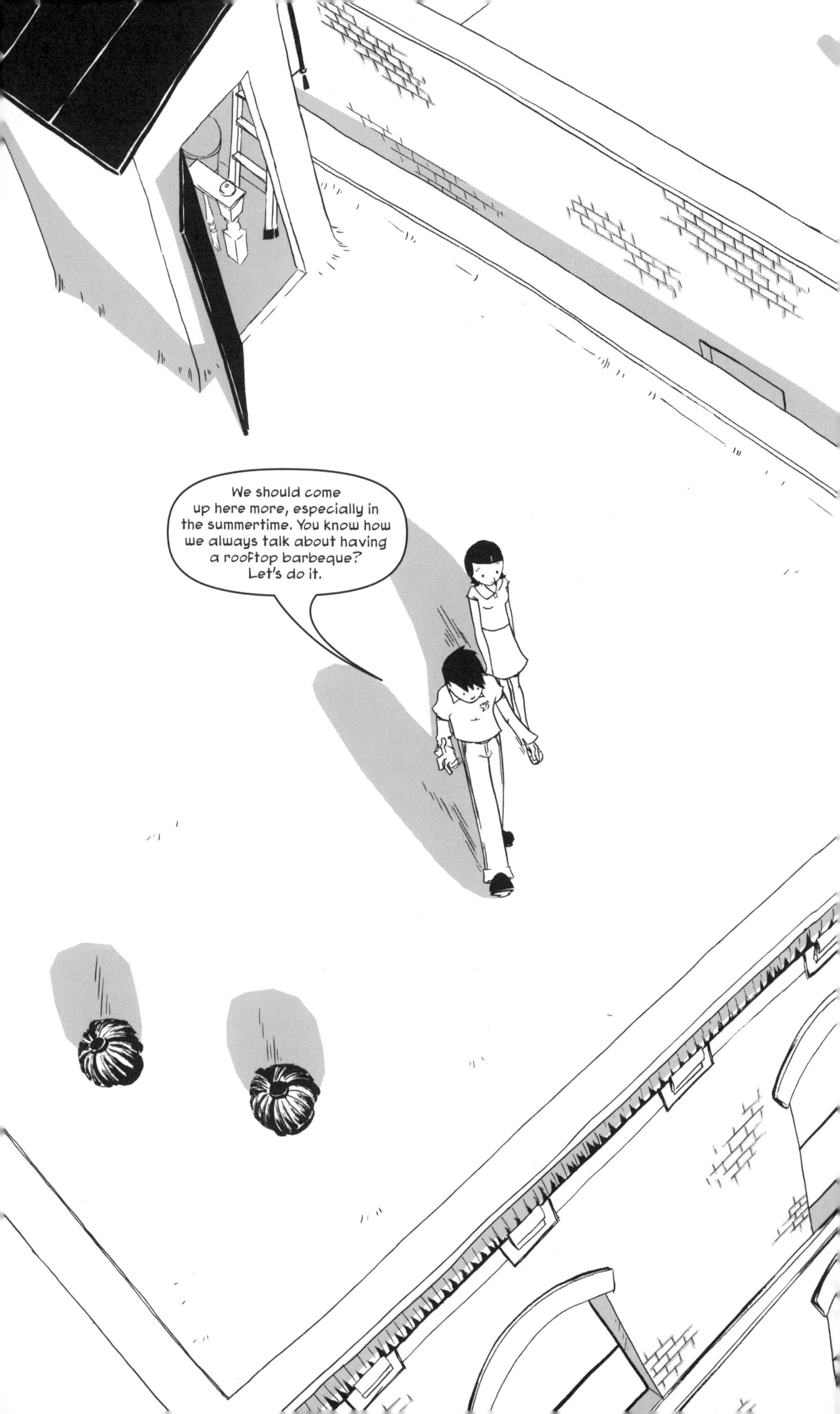
We should come up here more, especially in the summertime. You know how we always talk about having a rooftop barbeque? Let's do it.

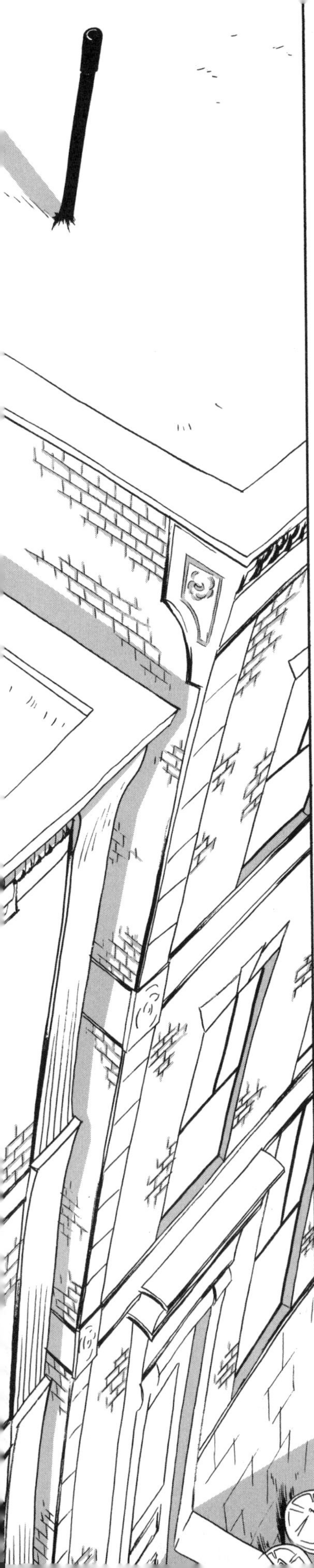

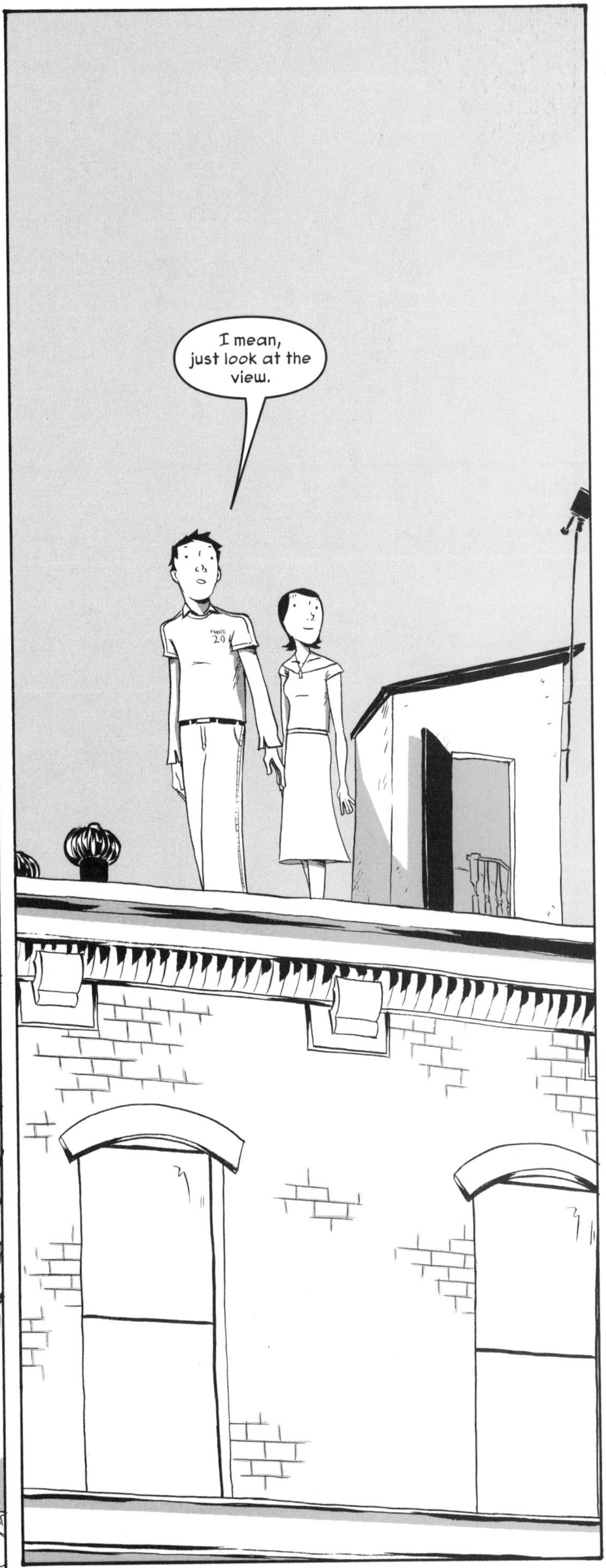
I mean, just look at the view.

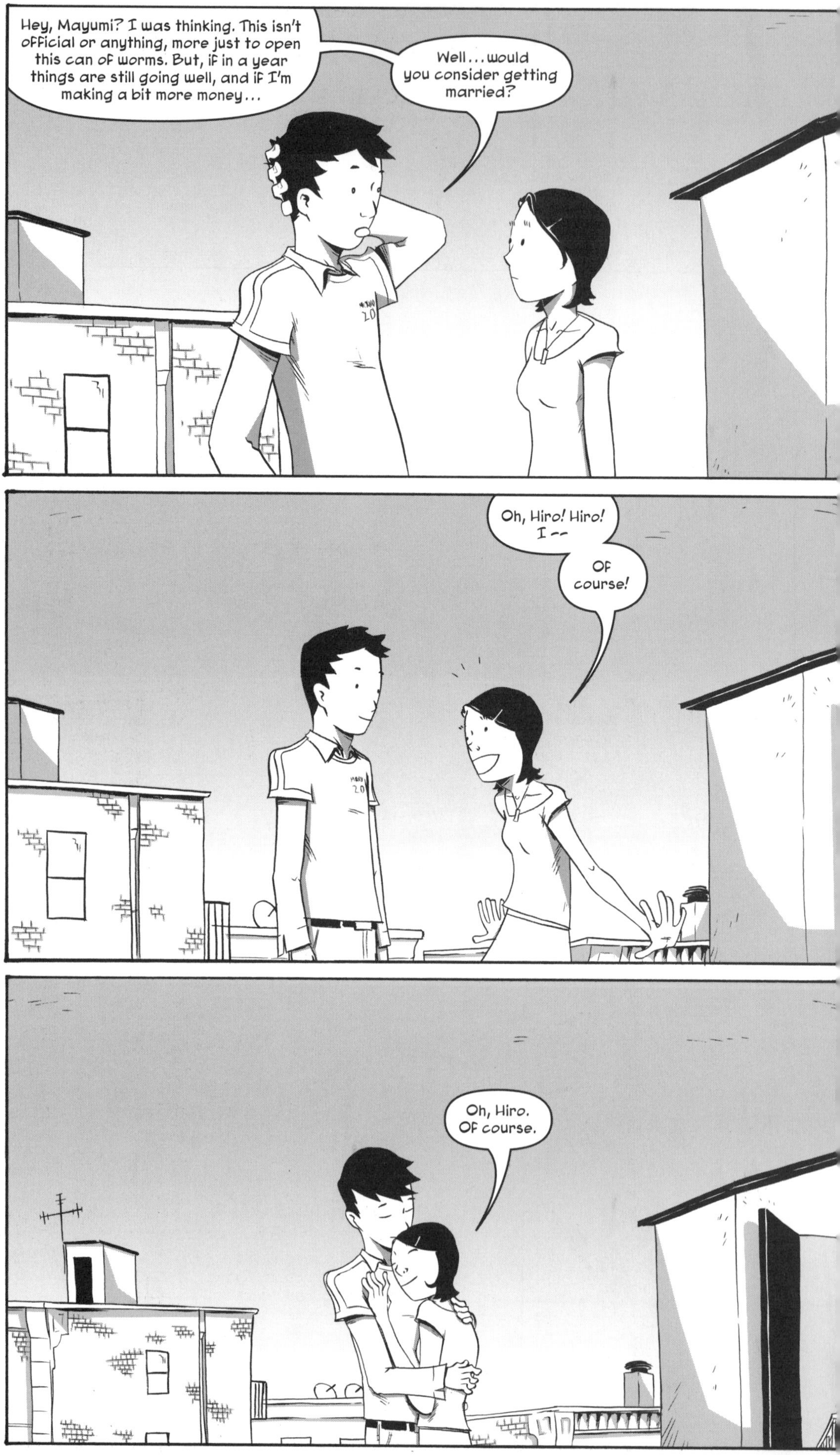
Hey, Mayumi? I was thinking. This isn't official or anything, more just to open this can of worms. But, if in a year things are still going well, and if I'm making a bit more money...
Well... would you consider getting married?
Oh, Hiro! Hiro! I --
Of course!
Oh, Hiro. Of course.

ボーナス材料

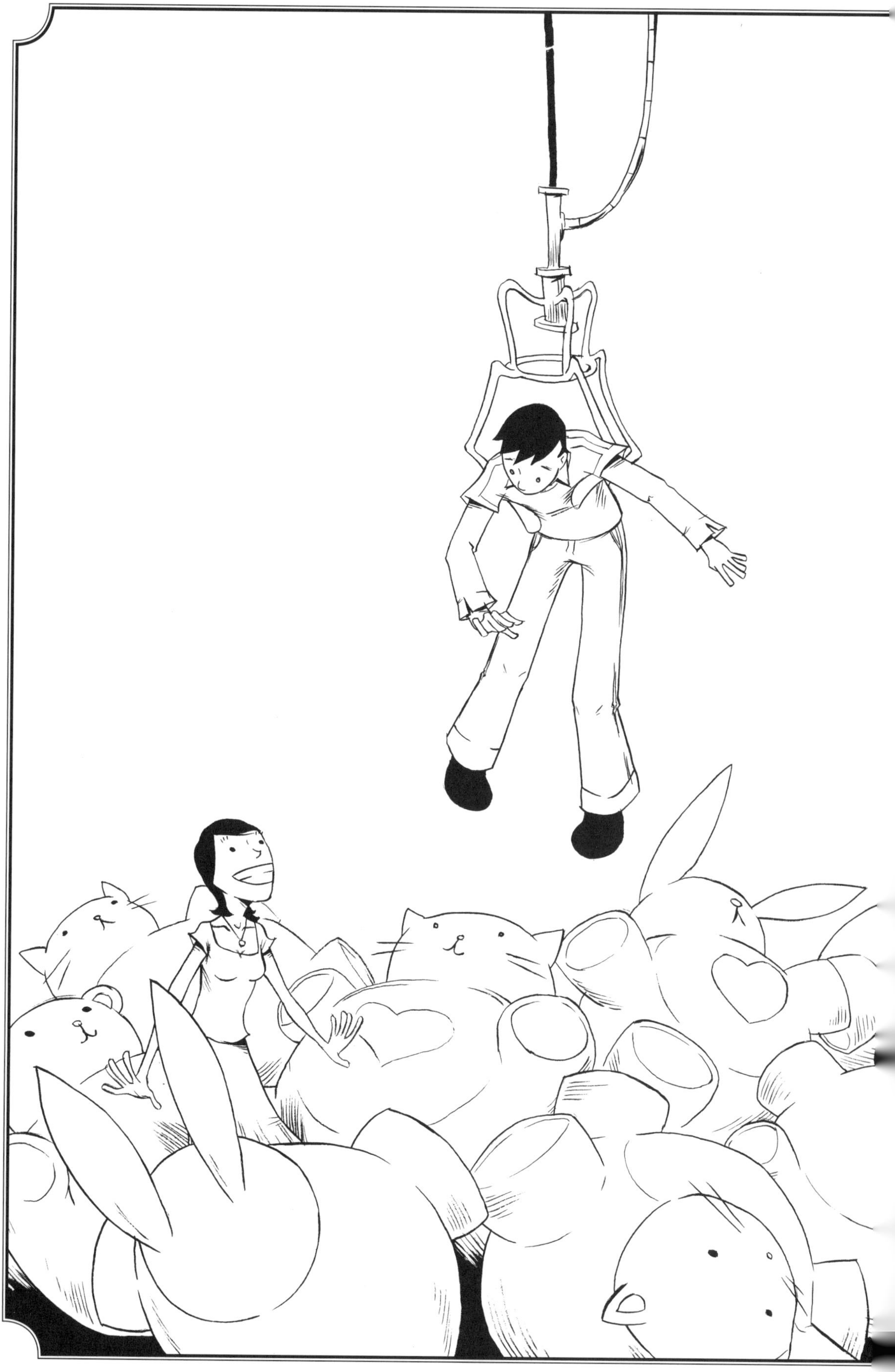

Fantastic Voyage

{ with Johnny Hiro and Coolio }

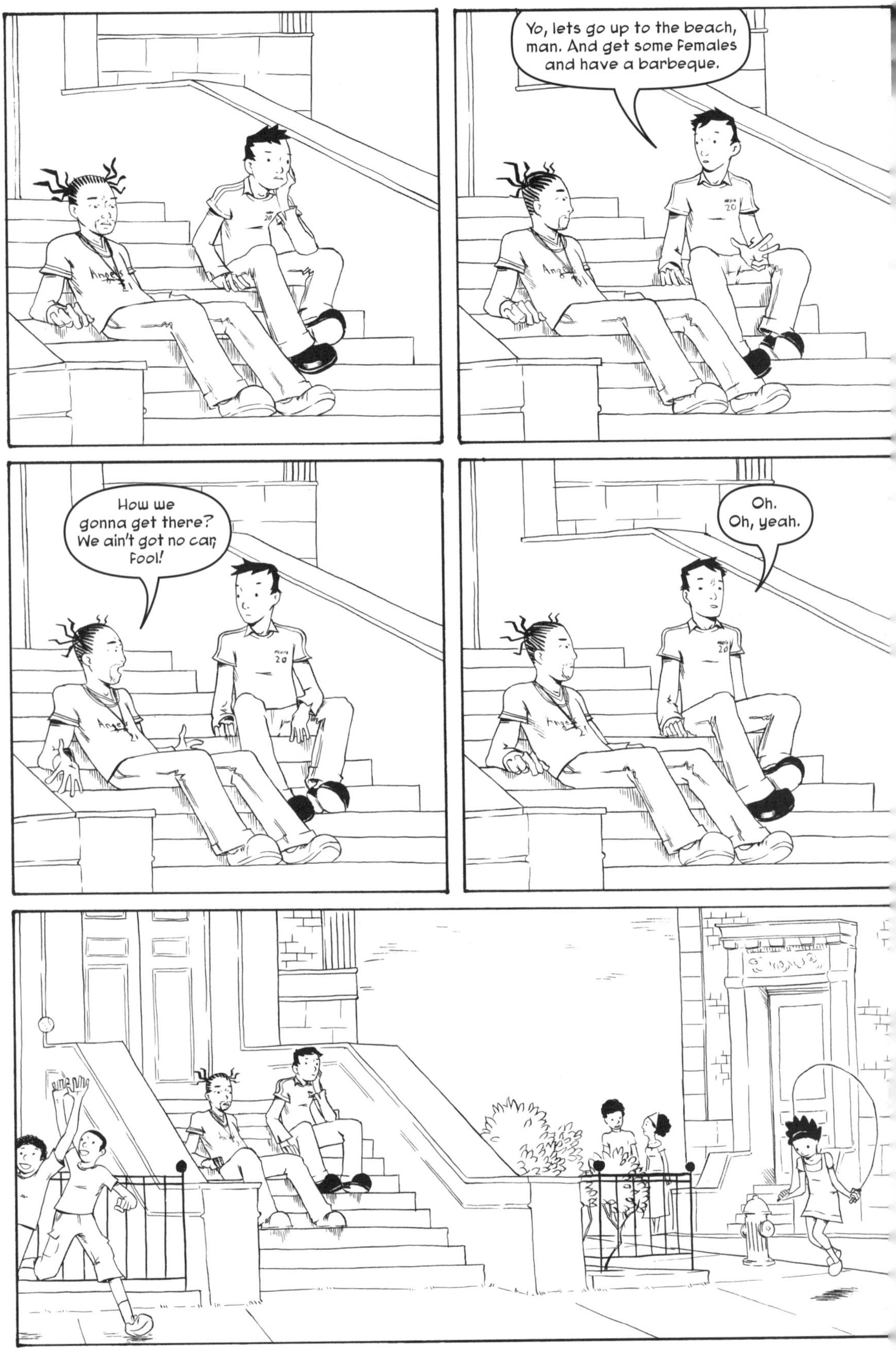

Yo, lets go up to the beach, man. And get some females and have a barbeque.
How we gonna get there? We ain't got no car, fool!
Oh. Oh, yeah.

Lets Go Shopping!

{ with Johnny Hiro and Mayumi Murakami }

Snacking Before Bedtime

{ with Johnny Hiro }

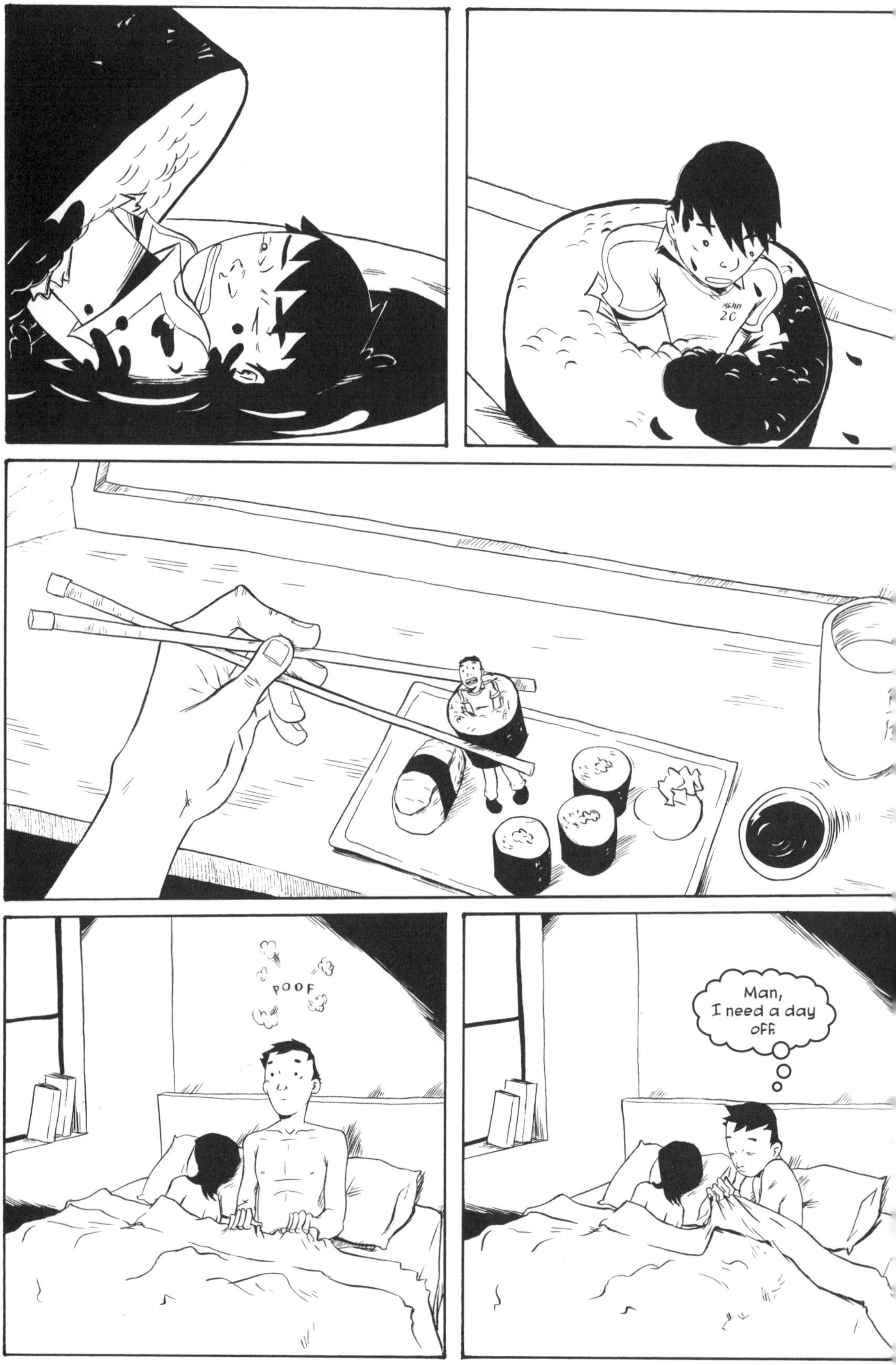
MCNN 20
POOF
Man, I need a day off.

Jeopardy

{ with Johnny Hiro and Alex Trebek }

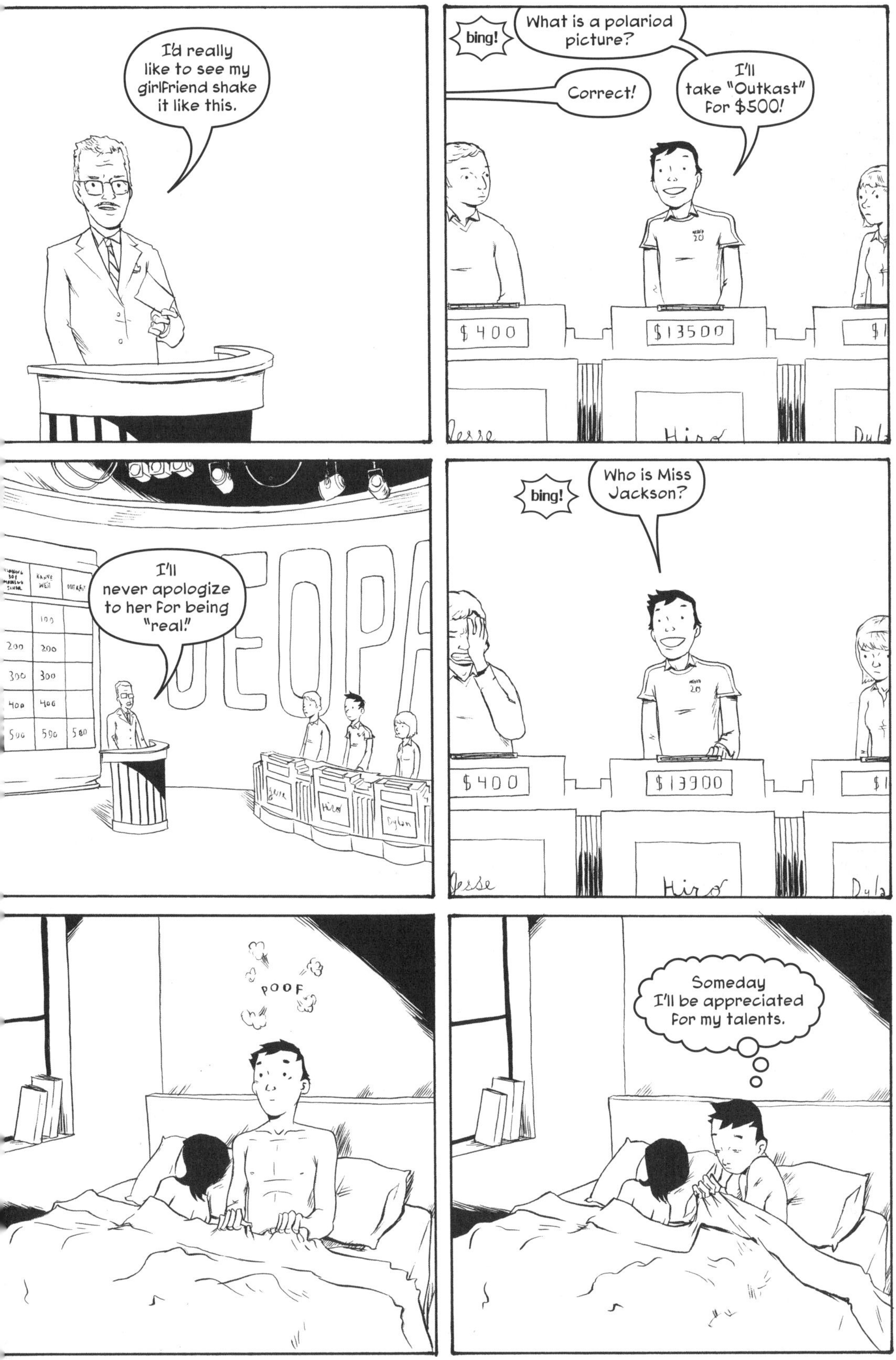
I'd really like to see my girlfriend shake it like this.
bing!
What is a polariod picture?
Correct!
I'll take "Outkast" for $500!
$400
$13500
I'll never apologize to her for being "real."
bing!
Who is Miss Jackson?
$400
$13900
POOF
Someday I'll be appreciated for my talents.

TOMO SAITO

{ all waiter, all hero }

Big Hug Time

{ with Hello Bunny and Ha-Ha Kitty }

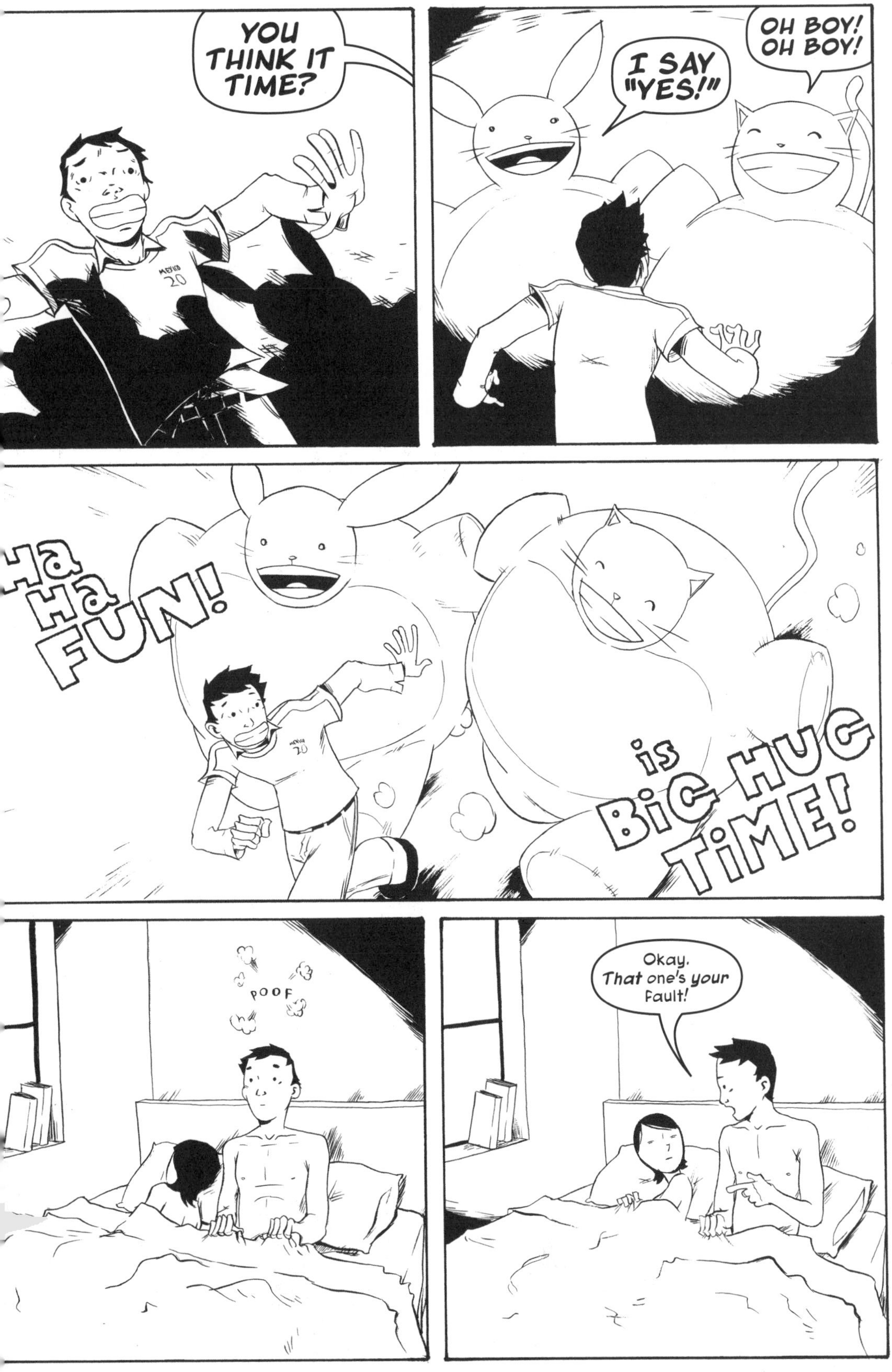

YOU THINK IT TIME?
I SAY "YES!"
OH BOY! OH BOY!
Ha Ha FUN!
is BIG HUG TIME!
POOF
Okay. That one's your Fault!

Nine to Five

{ with Johnny Hiro }

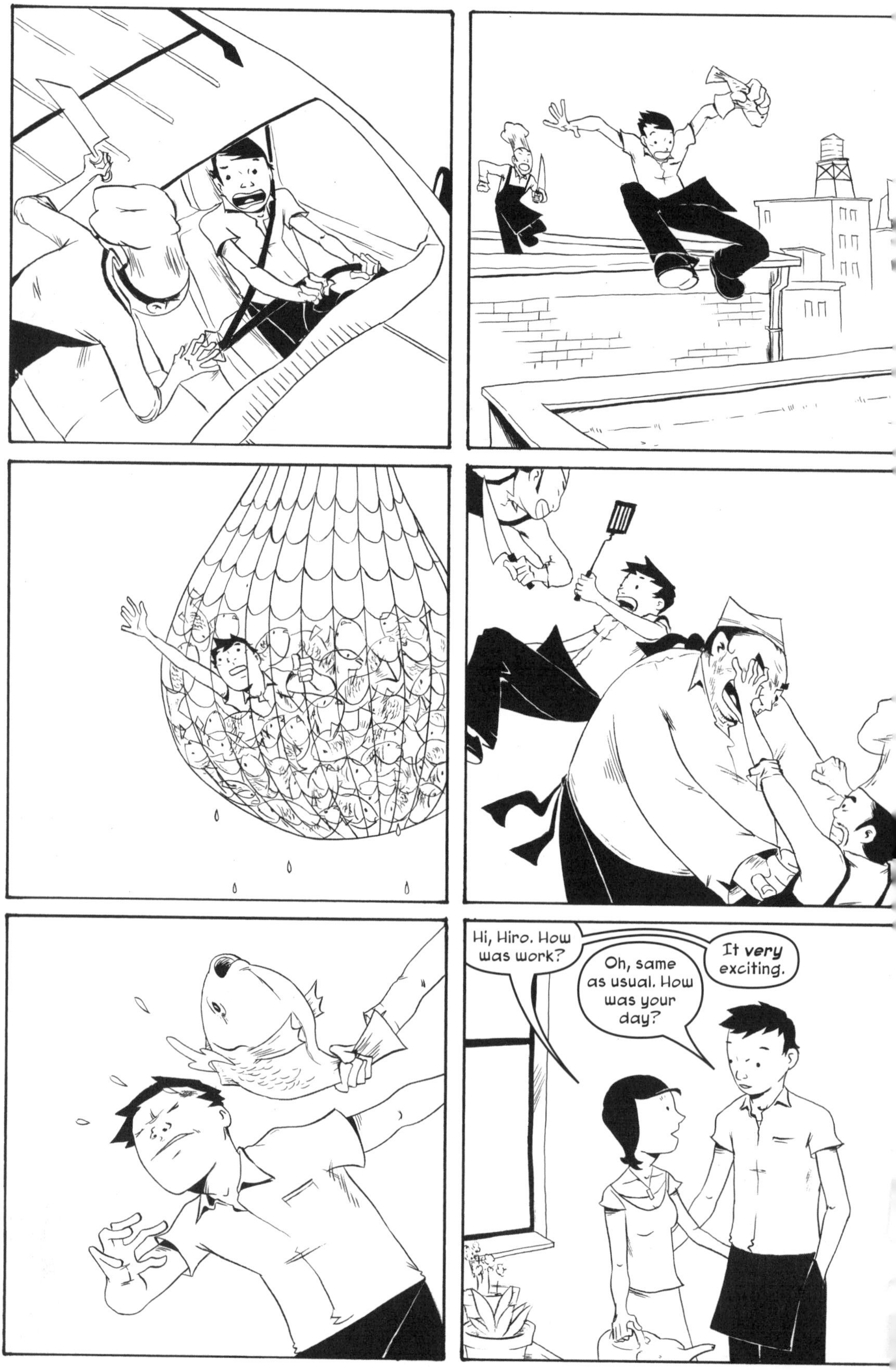
Hi, Hiro. How was work?
Oh, same as usual. How was your day?
It *very* exciting.

Bunny Slippers

{ with Johnny Hiro and Mayumi Murakami }

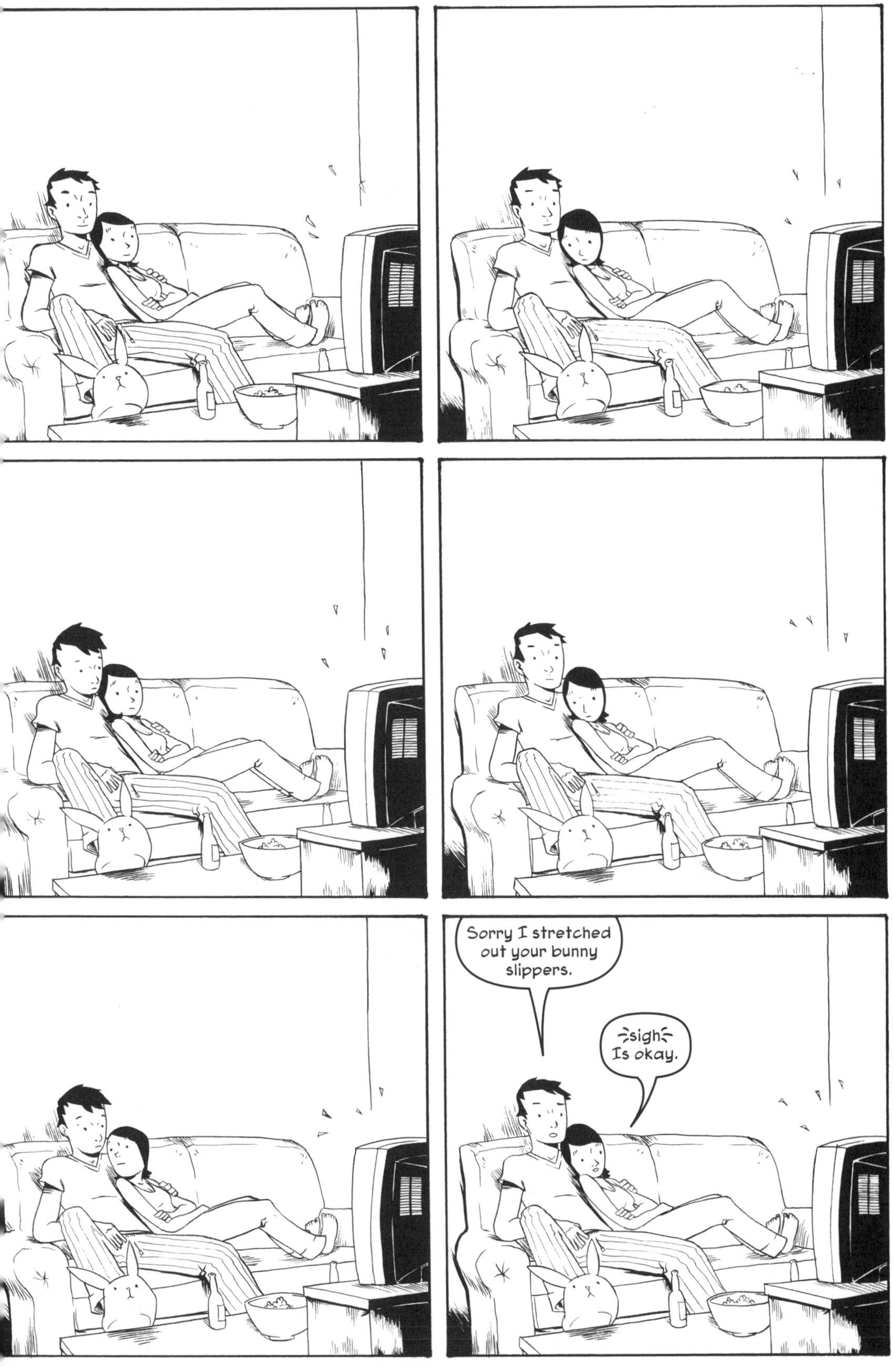

Sorry I stretched out your bunny slippers.
-sigh- Is okay.

FOOD FIGHT

{ with Fred Chao and Alton Brown }

ROADTRIP!

{ with Johnny Hiro and Mayumi Murakami }

Acknowledgments

None of this could have been done without my family — Mom, Dad, Shirley and Katherine — whose seemingly endless love and support has carried me further than they could possibly know.

As well as my extended family — San shu gong, Jiu jiu, Gu po, Gong gong, and everyone else in the Chao and Wang families. And Ye ye and Nai nai, who would have loved this.

For accompanying me through so many of the stupid/crazy experiences that eventually led to making comics, I am incredibly grateful for the friendships of Seth Brindis, Peter Chow, Scott Edmonds, Ethan Herr, Mike Plann, and Jeff Sammis.

Also to my doggs — Krista Asadorian, Beth Bayley, Nate Gibson, Tracey Long, Kathe McKenna, Opus Moreschi, Davy Rothbart, Michelle Sarrat, Lauren Ford, Peter Meulenbroek, Steve Shipps, and Thomas Turnbull.

More recently, I've met so many wonderful people in and around comics who have inspired me to keep at the desk writing and drawing — Josh Cotter, Robert Goodin, Charly LaGreca, Jamie Tanner, and GB Tran,

Also, Ryan Dunlavey, Fred Van Lente, Phil Jackson, Peter Rios, Monica Gallagher, Laura Hudson, Tim Leong, and Matthue Roth. Thank you so much for the bit of push in the end.

This comic would have taken so much longer without the support of John Sazaklis, Joe Merkel, Sean Boggs, Tom Forget, Rick Farley, and Tom Starace. Good part-time employment is hard to come across.

And many thanks to my editor and friend Jesse Post — whose efforts and dedication have made this comic far richer.

And of course, Chris Pitzer.